Foreword by Major General Patrick Cordingley, DSO, FRGS

EYEWITNESS TO WAR

THE FINEST WRITING ABOUT WAR
BY THOSE WHO WERE THERE

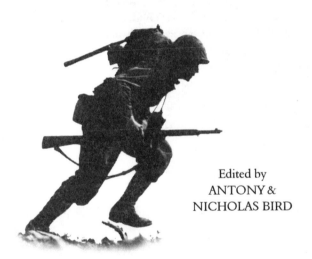

Edited by
ANTONY &
NICHOLAS BIRD

summersdale

EYEWITNESS TO WAR

Summersdale Publishers Ltd
46 West Street
Chichester
West Sussex
PO19 1RP
UK

www.summersdale.com

Printed and bound in Great Britain

ISBN: 1-84024-543-3
ISBN: 978-1-84024-543-1

Disclaimer
Every effort has been made to attribute the quotations in this collection to the correct source. Should there be any omissions or errors in this respect we apologise and shall be pleased to make the appropriate acknowledgements in any future edition.

EYEWITNESS TO WAR

Edited by
ANTONY &
NICHOLAS BIRD

In memory of
2nd Lieutenant Edward Arthur Bird
1st Battalion, the Rifle Brigade,
killed on 25 May 1940, aged 24, at the defence of Calais.

Courage and Fortitude are lovely words
And lovely are the virtues they define;
Yours was the Courage, laughing soldier, may
The Fortitude be mine.

[by Edward Bird's father, 'AWB' of *Punch* magazine]

Table of Contents

Foreword
Major General Patrick Cordingley, DSO, FRGS

Those whose writings and speeches have been chosen for this anthology encountered war at first hand. Whether through the spoken word, prose or poetry, they reported vividly, eloquently and truthfully what they experienced. The speeches by statesmen and military leaders show how language can be marshalled and harnessed to exhort troops to heroism in battle, or citizens to stoicism at home. The prose extracts and poems are chosen because of their powerful or evocative nature. It may not be necessary to be an orator or gifted writer to be a successful leader but here we can see that it is more than useful.

War is confusion and a mess; it is also different for each observer. To one it may be noble, triumphant. To another – a Sassoon or Owen in the First World War – it is futile. To Sherman, in the American Civil War, it was hell. It is all these things.

Gathered in this volume are some of the finest of military speeches and writing by those who were there. They saw that war brings out the best in men and women, and the worst: self-sacrifice and selfishness, humanity and viciousness. I have seen all these things. It is a trial and a test some fail. War is boring, thrilling, frightening, nasty, confusing – as each one of these well-chosen pieces attests.

Introduction

'... You should go to the past, looking not for messages or warnings, but simply to be humbled by the weight of human experience that has preceded the brief flicker of your own few days...'

Pat Barker, *Another World*, 1998

Eyewitness to War is a collection of military prose and verse in English at its best or most vivid.

Why does war provoke so much of our finest literature? Perhaps because in the tension and drama of battle, in the terror and pathos, all man's senses are engaged and heightened. Samuel Johnson wrote of the regret all men feel if they have never served in the colours. It is regret tinged with doubt: how would I have behaved under fire, would I have faltered or run away, am I a coward or the stuff of heroes? Those who have experienced the fear and elation of battle know the answer. Most passed this supreme test, and have the assurance of that memory. The rest of us are left to muse.

We have included great writing and crude but graphic writing. The songs of the Great War are not great poetry but these anonymous verses, witty and cynical, tell us much about Tommy's grumbles, his yearning for rum, women and Blighty, his contempt for chateau generals... and his total confusion.

Diaries, if written immediately after the events recorded, offer a window of truth where official histories sanitise or distort. Poetry can do the same. Sassoon, in his poem 'Counter-Attack', ends a vivid description of the reality and terror of battle with the laconic style of the military communiqué – 'The counter-attack had failed', an ironic parody of the sanitised words of officialdom.

For Shakespeare war and battle were often glorious. Henry V's great speech at Agincourt is a fictional example of what Lieutenant Colonel Collins was trying to do in his eloquent oration in the recent Iraq War: inspire. But Collins also added a warning – that conduct must be 'of the highest' (echoing Nelson's prayer), not something that Shakespeare thought Henry would have bothered about. In the event Henry butchered some of his prisoners. But if Shakespeare wrote for an audience still celebrating – after the Armada – nationhood, majesty and the nobility of battle, he also had a fine ear for the timeless truth that the poor bugger in the trench is dying while leaders dispute and dither:

GLOUCESTER: Is Paris lost? Is Rouen yielded up?…

EXETER: How were they lost? What treachery was used?

MESSENGER:
No treachery but want of men and money;
Among the soldiers, this is muttered –
That here you maintain several factions,
And whilst a field should be despatched and fought,
You are disputing of your generals:
One would have lingering wars, with little cost:
Another would fly swift, but wanteth wings:
A third man thinks, without expense at all,
By guileful fair words peace may be obtained.
Awake, awake, English nobility!
                                    (Henry VI Part I. Act I. Scene I)

There are echoes here of war and politics down the ages, and certainly of the confusion of politics and strategy that almost destroyed the Allies in the Kaiser's Battle of March 1918.

Lincoln's Gettysburg Address is an example of how to express 'the central idea of the occasion' in the briefest of speeches. The unusual proportion of words of one syllable – 200 out of 275 words – was deliberate, testimony to Lincoln's backwoods understanding of how simple words can convey complex ideas. Haig was notoriously inarticulate, but his 'Backs to the Wall' Order of the Day uses words carefully and effectively. So too does Montgomery in his clipped, staccato speech to his staff upon arriving in Egypt. 'We shall do no good work here' is to the point. MacArthur's grandiloquent speeches would have been scorned by Monty (or indeed Wellington) as florid and foreign but his farewell to West Point is oratory at its best.

Patton, similarly flamboyant, adopted a different tone in his pep-talk to his men – a man-to-man, foul-mouthed rant, and they loved it. Wellington would have abhorred such playing to the gallery. Churchill's speeches, harnessing the language of Macaulay, did what the greatest of speeches must do in time of war – inspire a belief in victory.

The broadcast by Richard Dimbleby from Belsen is a style of broadcast journalism that we have grown used to, but it was new then, and thus all the more devastating. Dispatches from the front line were mostly the stuff of newspapers, and any passion was in the prose. But here was a voice, describing horrors that some still struggled to believe, with the anger and pity all too real in its tone. It recalls the stark words of Ed Murrow, the distinguished American journalist, in his broadcast from Buchenwald: 'Murder had been done at Buchenwald... I have reported what I saw and heard, but only part of it. For most of it I have no words.' He added unapologetically: 'If I've offended you by this rather mild account of Buchenwald, I'm not in the least sorry.'

'War is hell', Sherman wrote. But it is not the complete picture, as Major General Cordingley points out in his Foreword. War is also thrilling, boring and ridiculous. And for every Sassoon or Owen traumatised by his ordeal, there is a Captain Greenwell of the Ox and Bucks Light Infantry, who wrote home during the Battle of the Somme: 'It is an extraordinary sort of battle and I wouldn't have missed it for anything.' Captain Sidney Rogerson of the West Yorks thought the Great War 'the happiest period' of his life, despite terror and discomfort, because 'though it may have let loose the worst it also brought out the finest qualities in men.' Rogerson's prose, like Graves' and Sassoon's, rises above the squalor of the trenches.

'The poetry of the Great War was the greatest flowering of verse since the Elizabethan age' (Sir Arthur Bryant). Its power and beauty reflects the shock and anger felt by citizen soldiers, mostly young officers, suddenly immersed in industrial war after their peaceful, often rural, pre-war idyll. Though it does not necessarily reflect the sullen determination to see the thing through of most rankers, evident from their letters home, the poetry is the true voice of a generation appalled at the suffering and carnage. Memoirs and fiction of the Great War began appearing ten years after the Armistice and, in the interim, attitudes had shifted. The futility and waste of the war years seemed palpable, particularly after the 'land fit for heroes' failed to materialise. The Second World War undoubtedly produced a lesser body of poetry because the shock of modern war had been partly expiated by the First. Nevertheless poets like Keith Douglas used freer verse forms to memorable effect. Douglas himself felt the legacy of Great War poetry on his battlefield: 'the behaviour of the living and the appearance of the dead were so accurately described by the poets of the Great War that every day on the battlefields of the western desert... their poems are illustrated.'

We have included some grim and sardonic poems, like Johnstone's 'High Wood'; and A. P. Herbert's witty, lavatorial 'Shute', which was gleefully sung across the Western Front, and whose humour masks quiet anger.

Rudyard Kipling, devastated by the loss of his only son Jack at Loos in 1915 (for whose remains he searched in vain – they were found long after Kipling died), produced some bitter lines about the war's conduct, yet he honoured the dead by suggesting the biblical inscription (inspired by Ecclesiasticus ch. 44, v. 14) on the altar-like Stone of Remembrance in hundreds of war cemeteries across the world – 'Their Names Liveth Forever More'. And is there anything in the English language more affecting than the simple words Kipling chose to mark the headstone beneath which an unidentified soldier lies?

A Soldier of the Great War
KNOWN UNTO GOD

For visitors to the Western Front, monuments and memorials offer many such examples of apt and moving lines and quotations. On the Menin Gate at Ypres, commemorating the Missing of the Salient, are written these words from I Peter 5:4 –

THEY SHALL RECEIVE A CROWN OF GLORY THAT
FADETH NOT AWAY

And elsewhere on the Menin Gate are inscribed these words which never fail to move, as one listens to the nightly ceremony of the Last Post –

IN MAIOREM DEI GLORIAM

HERE ARE RECORDED NAMES
OF OFFICERS AND MEN WHO FELL
IN YPRES SALIENT BUT TO WHOM
THE FORTUNE OF WAR DENIED
THE KNOWN AND HONOURED BURIAL
GIVEN TO THEIR COMRADES IN DEATH

Look in the Introduction to the Cemetery Register at Thiepval, where Lutyens great Monument to the Missing of the Somme stands, and you will find this paragraph, written by an anonymous hand, that does justice to the dead:

INTRODUCTION

'A few will be found and identified as the woods are cleared, or when the remaining tracts of devastated land are brought under the plough. Many more are already buried in the larger British cemeteries of the Somme, but as yet unidentified. To the great majority this memorial stands for grave and headstone, and this register for as proud a record as that for any grave.'

This anthology presents eloquent, evocative prose and poetry in English about war – mostly on land, at the sharpest end of battle – set out chronologically, written or recorded by those who were there, eyewitnesses to war. Or, in the cases of war leaders anthologised, like Lincoln, Churchill and Roosevelt, eyewitnesses to events, and as involved and moved by war's tragedies as any soldier. It is a personal choice that does not strive for balance. It is far from comprehensive. Some great military writing has been left out because it is too familiar. Not all the pieces are examples of fine, literary writing – certainly not Patton's barrack-room speech or A. P. Herbert's filthy poem. A few extracts are included because – in their vivid use of language – they paint a picture, catch a mood. The introductions describe the author and historical context in, we hope, an informative way, highlighting quirks of personality or history not generally known. We start with Elizabeth I's Armada speech as a Prologue. Elizabeth's tone and purpose nicely contrasts with Tim Collins' famous Iraq speech 400 years later, which appears at the end as a postscript. War is still with us, despite centuries of enlightenment, rationalism and idealism for 'only the dead have seen the end of war' (not Plato's words, as MacArthur thought, but the American philosopher George Santayana).

Our anthology proper is from Trafalgar to Vietnam, because more recent examples have yet to stand the test of time and earlier writing, while fascinating to specialists, too often suffers from a self-conscious literariness that can seem indigestible to lay readers, to whom this anthology is addressed. Before the Napoleonic era literacy among rankers was rare. The simple, direct prose of self-educated private soldiers like Bugler Green or Frank Richards, was yet to be.

We make no apologies for anthologising so much British writing on war. As Barbara Tuchman wrote in *Sand against the Wind* (1981), no nation other than the British 'has ever produced a military history of such verbal nobility... win or lose, blunder or bravery, murderous folly or unyielding resolution, all emerge alike clothed in dignity and touched with glory.'

Much about war is timeless ('War is not an aberration; it is what men do' – Martin Windrow, *The Last Valley*, London, 2005). Technology may have altered the face of battle, and the scale of combat, but soldiers still have to engage closely with the enemy and eliminate him from the battlefield. General Cordingley, commanding 7th Armoured Brigade in the Gulf War of 1991, had far greater firepower than Montgomery and his Desert Rats of 1942, and Cordingley's tanks outgunned and outranged anything Saddam Hussein had; Cordingley had nothing to fear from the air. But in that final few yards when they crossed the berms, his men still could not know what the enemy would do, whether they would fight or flee or surrender. Their ancestors on the Somme, if they got through the wire, faced the same unnerving test. Whether in puttees or flak jackets, footsoldiers, the 'poor bloody infantry', do most of the fighting and dying; and when they confront the enemy as they must, in jungle, desert or mud, it is the same old things that prevail: training, morale and loyalty – to your unit and regiment, and to your mate in the next foxhole.

Sassoon wrote in 'Aftermath': 'the past is just the same – and War's a bloody game...' Fear and violence are timeless too. Sassoon recognised the amnesia that brings war around and pleaded for remembrance, a theme of this anthology: 'Remembering, we forget/ Much that was monstrous... We forget our fear...' ('To One Who Was With Me in the War').

INTRODUCTION

Do you remember that hour of din before the attack –
And the anger, the blind compassion that seized and
shook you then
As you peered at the doomed and haggard faces of your
men?
Do you remember the stretcher-cases lurching back
With dying eyes and lolling heads – those ashen-grey
Masks of the lads who once were keen and kind and gay?
Have you forgotten yet?...
Look up, and swear by the green of the spring that you'll
never forget.

Aftermath, Siegfried Sassoon, March 1919

ABOUT THE EDITORS

Antony Bird was educated at Winchester College and Exeter University, where he graduated in Sociology. After post graduate studies, he became a town planner in Chichester, where he still lives, but changed careers and began publishing military titles in 1979.

Nicholas Bird was also educated at Winchester, read art history at Sussex University and joined the auctioneers Christie's, before moving to the Victoria and Albert Museum, where he became the publisher. He is a member of the Royal United Services Institute and writes on military history for several journals, including *International Affairs*, the Chatham House journal. He has been elected to Council of the Society for Army Historical Research.

Both Antony and Nicholas Bird were interested in military history and the literature of war at an early age (their father is a much-decorated Desert Rat). They began visiting battlefields while staying with French families in the mid-60s and learning about the effects of war and occupation from their hosts. They run Bird Battlefield Tours, which takes small groups to battlefields from Gallipoli to Gettysburg, from Falaise to Verdun.

Prologue

'I have the heart and stomach of a king': Armada Speech at West Tilbury

Queen Elizabeth 1, 9 August 1588

Threat of invasion by Spain was ever present for much of Elizabeth I's reign (1558–1603), culminating in the Armada of 1588. Its failure boosted the Queen's popularity, gave the English a firm sense of nationhood, centred on its insularity and Protestantism, and irretrievably damaged the standing of Philip II of Spain (1527–1598), the Catholic widower of England's Mary I (1553–58).

In the Catholic world, the overthrow of the new Protestant regime in England was considered by some a sacred duty. Philip was also motivated by his (dubious) claim to the English throne, by outrage at English piracy in his American empire, and above all by fury at Elizabeth's military intervention in the Netherlands in 1585, where the Dutch were in revolt against Spanish rule.

The Armada, commanded by the Duke of Medina Sidonia, took over two years to prepare, a delay only partly caused by Drake's raid on Cadiz in April, 1587. The Duke of Parma commanded an invasion army of 30,000 in the Spanish Netherlands, which included 4000 horse and 700 English rebels under the Earl of Westmoreland. The Spanish plan involved Parma's army rendezvousing with the Armada fleet and being escorted to a beachhead in Kent, which the Armada was supposed to secure. Like Napoleon and Hitler after him, Philip knew that he had to command the Channel for at least the time needed to ferry troops across. But he never did command the straits, and without the seas being safe, Parma was confined to port. He could not sail unescorted because – 'These craft are so light and small that four warships could sink every boat we have' (letter to Philip II, Jan. 31, 1588). An Anglo-Dutch force of 40 ships further frustrated Parma by blockading his sea exits.

The Armada's 122 ships (8,500 sailors, 16,000 troops), sailing in a defensive, crescent shape, arrived off Land's End on 29 July 1588. A force of 22 huge fighting galleons was positioned in the middle, protected by smaller ships. It was a vast undertaking – below decks were 14,000 barrels of wine, 11 million lbs. of biscuits, 40,000 gallons of olive oil and 180 priests. The main defensive force, 66 ships of the English fleet under Lord Howard of Effingham, was caught by surprise re-supplying in Plymouth. But they broke out of Plymouth Sound that evening and chased the Armada up the Channel. Two Spanish ships were lost, both by accidents. Lumbering galleons would be no match for nimble English ships or ship-handling, and some Spanish ships were further handicapped by carrying the wrong size of shot for their cannon.

Medina Sidonia then decided to anchor off Calais on 6 August. An English fireship attack dispersed the Armada fleet piecemeal and gales blew it into the North Sea. Four Spanish ships were lost, but the rest escaped northwards, forced to sail home via Scotland and Ireland. They were not harried, for Howard's ordnance was expended and exposure and typhus had broken his crews' health (surviving English crews were neglected after the battle, starving in the Channel ports). An estimated 34 Spanish ships foundered. Perhaps 11,000 Spanish seamen and troops died.

On 8 August 1588, Queen Elizabeth travelled by royal barge from Lambeth to her blockhouse fort (built by Henry VIII) at West Tilbury, on the first narrowing of the Thames Estuary on the Essex coast, where the distance between the two shores allowed a lethal crossfire from the forts on either side. An Armada Camp of 12,000 foot soldiers and 1,000 cavalry was stationed at West Tilbury, commanded by the 'Lord General' of the land army, the Earl of Leicester (who died of cancer a month later). After discussing the military situation with Leicester, she stayed the night at the house of a prominent local JP, returning next day to review the troops. Before doing so, Leicester put on a 'show' – a great mock-battle. Then she reviewed her troops and delivered her famous speech. It is possible that her words were addressed to officers only, who passed them on to the men.

After the speech she rode to Leicester's pavilion ('yor pore Lyvetenants cabyn', as he described it) and an early dinner. While dining the news arrived that Parma had set forth with '50,000 infantry and 6,000 horse' – in fact they had only made ready to embark. The pavilion stood on the highest spot of what is now called Gun Hill (then Tilbury Hill), half a mile north-west of West Tilbury church. In her speech, delivered in sight of the windmill that stood by a crossroads, she emphasised the importance and primacy of monarchy over masculinity. Printed versions, differing considerably, were quickly distributed around the country. After dining, a storm gathered and she departed by barge. She may have resolved to 'die amongst' her men and 'lay down' her 'blood even in the dust' but this was Tudor rhetoric.

MY LOVING PEOPLE, we have been persuaded by some that we are careful of our safety, to take heed how we commit ourselves to armed multitudes for fear of treachery; but, I do assure you, I do not desire to live to distrust my faithful and loving people.

Let tyrants fear, I have always so behaved myself, that under God I have placed my chiefest strength and safeguard in the loyal hearts and goodwill of my subjects; and, therefore, I am come amongst you as you see at this time, not for my recreation and disport, but being resolved, in the midst and heat of battle, to live or die amongst you all – to lay down for my God, and for my kingdoms, and for my people, my honour and my blood even in the dust.

I know I have the body of a weak, feeble woman; but I have the heart and stomach of a king – and of a king of England too, and think foul scorn that Parma or Spain, or any prince of Europe, should dare to invade the borders of my realm; to which, rather than any dishonour should grow by me, I myself will take up arms – I myself will be your general, judge, and rewarder of every one of your virtues in the field.

I know already, for your forwardness, you have deserved rewards and crowns, and, we do assure you, on the word of a prince, they shall be duly paid you. For the meantime, my Lieutenant-General Leicester shall be in my stead, than whom never prince commanded a more noble or worthy subject; not doubting but by your obedience to my General, by your concord in the camp, and your valour in the field, we shall shortly have a famous victory over these enemies of my God, of my kingdom and of my people.

Lord Nelson's prayer

Before the Battle of Trafalgar, 21 October 1805

Napoleon had assembled an army to invade Britain (L'Armée de L'Angleterre) at Boulogne but needed a naval victory to give at least a few days maritime supremacy in the Straits of Dover to transport the army safely across. Most French naval ships had been blockaded for long years and the enforced idleness had sapped efficiency and morale. Their sailors and ships were no match for the British fleet, or Nelson; yet Napoleon insisted that his Franco-Spanish navy fight – even when it became strategically nonsensical after Napoleon sent the Boulogne army to confront Russia and Austria, who had massed against him in a new coalition. The French naval commander, Admiral Villeneuve, heard rumours that Napoleon was to sack him (an envoy was on the way to Villeneuve in Cadiz, dismissal in pocket, even as he put to sea), so a victory, however unlikely, was his only chance of vindication and retaining command.

Nelson's original battle plan was for the fleet to be divided into three lines: the first, to the windward of the battle, awaiting the decisive moment to join; the other two would split the combined fleet from the side. In the event he used only two columns, because his fleet was smaller than anticipated and because he lacked a competent admiral to command a third column. Nelson's plan was not completely new. What was new was Nelson's determination that every captain should know the plan, and that it anticipated the fog of battle and allowed individual captains freedom of action – 'No captain can do very wrong if he places his ship alongside that of an enemy,' he instructed in case signals could not be seen.

Nelson's attack in two divisions, a mile apart, cut off the enemy's rearguard and van as intended. It was a move predicted by Villeneuve but which he was powerless to resist. Nelson's ships engaged 'pell mell' at the closest of quarters – the enemy centre and rear were overwhelmed, not least by superior gunnery and ship handling. The Franco-Spanish fleet lost some 2,000 killed and many more in the week-long gales that followed. Only 11 of their ships survived, 9 of which escaped to Cadiz, only to be blockaded once again. Trafalgar made Britain safe from invasion. She controlled the sea, her sea trade and colonies were secure, and she could continue to blockade continental ports unhindered.

The British lost about 500 men. And in the hour of victory they lost Nelson, who, amidst the crash of big guns all around him, was killed by a single musket shot. He had done his duty. His body was preserved in a barrel of French brandy for the long journey home. The story of sailors taking nips out of the barrel while Nelson was in it is untrue; the libel arose because a small amount evaporated. Although not averse to flogging (particularly to preserve discipline during the strain of blockading) Nelson was held in enormous affection below decks, and greatly admired by his captains. He entertained lavishly and expansively and was a 'merry' host. He explained tactics with the utmost lucidity. But he was not always loved by his peers.

Eighteen Admirals declined to attend his funeral at St. Paul's on 8 January 1806 perhaps influenced by distaste for his affair with Emma Hamilton, the wife of the British consul in Naples, which George III also deplored; but also perhaps by jealousy, and disdain for Nelson's craving for honours, decorations and baubles. Earl St Vincent, whose 'violent inflammation of eyes' made it 'impossible' for him to attend, somehow managed to go riding for three hours the next day. Three other Admirals pleaded colds, three had gout, one merely said that he couldn't come to town. Nelson's prayer is written in his last diary entry with his left hand (he lost his right arm at the Battle of Tenerife in 1797). As the fleets closed he amended his will, pleading that England look after Emma. England did not. She died in poverty.

May the great God, whom I worship, grant to my Country and for the benefit of Europe in general, a great and glorious Victory: and may no misconduct, in any one, tarnish it and may humanity after victory be the predominant feature in the British Fleet.

For myself individually, I commit my life to Him who made me and may His blessing light upon my endeavours for serving my Country faithfully. To Him I resign myself and the just cause which is entrusted to me to defend. AMEN AMEN AMEN

'The ever to be lamented death of Vice-Admiral Lord Viscount Nelson'

Admiral Collingwood's Dispatch,
HMS *Euryalas*, 22 October 1805

Vice-Admiral Collingwood (1750–1810) was Second-in-Command to Nelson at Trafalgar (off Cadiz) and commanded the fleet on his death, succeeding Nelson as Commander-in-Chief, Mediterranean. The Dispatch, addressed to the British Admiralty, captures the extent of Nelson's achievement, the spirit of the fleet and the grievous loss of England's finest naval commander. It was published in the *London Gazette* on 6 November 1805. Collingwood was more stoical and balanced than his great friend Nelson, and equal in courage. He was raised to the peerage but died soon afterwards at sea, worn out with the strain of the constant activity and vigilance required in blockading the enemy. He is buried close to Nelson in St. Paul's.

The dispatch, with others, was entrusted to Lieutenant John Richards Lapenotiere of the fast schooner *Pickle*. Collingwood urged him to use 'every exertion, that a moment's time may not be lost in their delivery'. But he nearly didn't make it. The *Pickle* was buffeted by a ferocious storm in the Bay of Biscay and only saved by jettisoning her cannon. Lapenotiere took 11 days to deliver the news from the Atlantic to the Admiralty in Whitehall, where he arrived at 1.00 a.m. on 6 November 1805. The final stage of the journey was non-stop by post chaise from

Falmouth, a distance of 271 miles, which he completed in only 37 hours. Lapenotiere claimed travel expenses of £46 19s 1d.

———————◆◆◆◆◆———————

Euryalas, off Cape Trafalgar, 22 October 1805.

SIR –

The ever to be lamented death of Vice-Admiral Lord Viscount Nelson who, in the late conflict with the enemy, fell in the hour of victory, leaves to me the duty of informing my Lords Commissioners of the Admiralty, that on the 19th instant [October], it was communicated to the Commander in Chief from the ships watching the motions of the enemy in Cadiz, that the Combined Fleet had put to sea; as they sailed with light winds westerly, his Lordship concluded their destination was the Mediterranean, and immediately made all sail for the Streights' [straits'] entrance, with the British squadron, consisting of twenty-seven ships, three of them sixty-fours, where his Lordship was informed that they had not yet passed the Streights.

On Monday the 21st instant, at day-light, when Cape Trafalgar bore E. by S. about seven leagues, the enemy was discovered six or seven miles to the Eastwards, the wind about West, and very light; the Commander in Chief immediately made the signal for the fleet to bear up in two columns, as they are formed in order of sailing; a mode of attack his Lordship had previously directed, to avoid the inconvenience and delay in forming a line of battle in the usual manner.

The enemy's line consisted of 33 ships, Commanded in Chief by Admiral Villeneuve. The Spaniards under the direction of Gravina, wore with their heads to the northwards, and formed their line of battle with great coolness and correctness; but as the mode of attack was unusual, so the structure of their line was new.

As the mode of our attack had been previously determined on, and communicated to the Flag Officers, and Captains, few signals were necessary, and none were made, except to direct close order as the lines bore down.

The Commander in Chief, in the Victory, led the weather column, and the Royal Sovereign, which bore my flag, the lee. The action began at twelve o'clock, by the leading ships of the column breaking through the enemy's line, the Commander in Chief about the tenth ship from the van, the Second in Command about the twelfth from the rear, leaving the van of the enemy unoccupied; the succeeding ships breaking through, in all parts, astern of their leaders, and engaging the enemy at the muzzles of their guns; the conflict was severe; the enemy's ships were fought with a gallantry highly honourable to their Officers; but the attack on them was irresistible, and it pleased the Almighty Disposer of all events to grant his Majesty's arms a complete and glorious victory…

A Circumstance occurred during the action, which so strongly marks the invincible spirit of British seamen, when engaging the enemies of their country, that I cannot resist the pleasure I have in making it known to their Lordships; the Temeraire was boarded by accident, or design, by a French ship on one side, and a Spaniard on the other; the contest was vigorous, but, in the end, the Combined Ensigns were torn from the poop, and the British hoisted in their places. Such a battle could not be fought without sustaining a great loss of men.

I have not only to lament, in common with the British Navy, and the British Nation, the Fall of the Commander in Chief, the loss of a Hero, whose name will be immortal, and his memory ever dear to his country: but my heart is rent with the most poignant grief for the death of a friend, to whom, by many years intimacy, and a perfect knowledge of the virtues of his mind, which inspired ideas superior to the common race of men, I was bound by the strongest ties of affection; a grief to which even the most glorious occasion in which he fell, does not bring the consolation which, perhaps, it ought: his Lordship received a musket ball in his left breast, about the middle of the action, and sent an Officer to me immediately with his last farewell; and soon after expired.

The whole fleet were now in a very perilous situation, many dismasted, all shattered, in thirteen fathoms of water, off the shoals of Trafalgar; and when I made the signal to prepare to anchor, few of the ships had an anchor to let go, their cables being shot; but the same good Providence which aided us through such a day preserved us in the night.

Having thus detailed the proceedings of the fleet on this occasion, I beg to congratulate their Lordships on a victory which, I hope, will add a ray to the glory of his Majesty's crown, and be attended with public benefit to our country. I am, &c.

(Signed) C. Collingwood

The Retreat to Corunna, 1808–09

Bugler Green, 95th Rifles

In 1807, the Emperor Napoleon joined with Spain in occupying the defenceless kingdom of Portugal, the Portuguese royal family escaping to Brazil. Napoleon then betrayed his ally, swelling his garrisons in Spain until they were strong enough (February 1808) to grab vital towns and forts from the unsuspecting Spanish. Napoleon promptly installed his brother Joseph on the Spanish throne. But on 2 May Madrid rose against the French – in support of their captive King Ferdinand, their Catholic faith and their fatherland.

The rising was put down ferociously, and news of the barbarity spread. Despite qualms by conservative Spaniards, the uprising rampaged across the country, and to Portugal. Britain saw an opportunity of establishing a presence in the Iberian peninsula, and landed a force in Portugal, which beat the French at Vimeiro on 21 August. The British now controlled Portugal. Napoleon suffered more humiliation when Spanish regulars captured 20,000 French troops at Bailén the same year, the first defeat of a French army since the French Revolution had begun some 20 years earlier.

Napoleon was incensed. He led fresh troops from Germany across the Pyrenees and by the end of 1808 had re-conquered the heart of Spain and would have taken Portugal had not a deep north-easterly advance into Spain by Sir John Moore diverted Napoleon's march on Lisbon. The Emperor was forced by Austria's renewal of war to return to Germany – so it was left to Marshal Soult to encircle and destroy Moore's army, but Moore managed the difficult art of retreat skilfully (23 December 1808–17 January 1809). Although he was killed himself, his forces were evacuated at Corunna on the north-west tip of Spain by the Royal Navy. The defensive Battle of Corunna (16 January 1808), where 14,000 British prevented 60,000 French from breaking through, allowed evacuation the next day ('We fought more desperate, as the enemy had deprived us of our daily allowance of wine' – Green). Men were cannonaded with grape shot even as they raced for the boats ('The grape shot… came plentifully through the rigging… as well as amongst the soldiers of the boat'). As at Dunkirk in 1940, a British army was expelled from continental Europe at the beginning of a long war, only to return with Allies to ultimate victory.

William Green was born in 1784 in Leicestershire and 'having a disposition to ramble' enlisted in the Leicester Militia aged 19. In 1805 he volunteered to join the newly formed 2nd Battalion, 95th Rifles (later the Rifle Brigade), transferring to the 1st Battalion the same year. He sailed for Portugal in 1808, arriving on 28 August, a week after the Battle of Vimiero ('we had to march over the battlefield; a great number lay unburied…').

<hr/>

It fell to our lot, the Light Division, to cover the retreat of the whole British army. Marshal Soult lost no time, with a very strong force of cavalry, infantry and artillery, in driving us. Their cavalry had a rifleman mounted behind each dragoon; and when any good position, or bushes by the road side, gave them any advantage to give our men a few shots, those riflemen would dismount and get under cover of the bushes, so that we were obliged to do the same; their dragoons at the same time dismounting and laying their carbines on their saddles, with their horse standing in front of them for a sort of defence, would give us a few shots as well. In this way we were obliged to make a stand and drive them back. We used to laugh to see the riflemen run to the road, put their feet into the stirrups, and mount behind the dragons and gallop back. We served many of these fellows off; and then we had to run to get up to the regiment. This was the sport for many days; and we could not avoid it.

A long march, about 250 English miles, before we could arrive at Corunna. We had no tents; a blanket had to be served out to each man; we marched from daylight to dark; the bullocks were driven before us and slaughtered as they were needed; they had little or no fat on them. But if we had time to boil our mess well, we counted more of the soup than the meat, as it was so tough. But it was not often that we could do this, as we had no shelter but the canopy of heaven and we seldom halted more than two hours; and having wood and water to seek to cook our victuals, before we could do so, the order would be given to get under arms and get on the march.

We had some artillery with us, six pounders; and we had to muffle the gun-wheels with grass, or anything we could find, to prevent the enemy from hearing us move; and we made up large fires, and moved on the road as still as possible. This was the game we had to play many nights; as the French advanced guard would seldom be more than half a mile from us, when we halted. Our captains were all mounted, but the lieutenants had to walk, and I have seen some of them move on fast asleep until they had been jostled on some of the men, and been thus awakened. They were long nights in the months of December and January. At daylight the enemy would be close on our rear, they had seen our fires burn out; and then the day proved as the day before – a continual harassing. Many days we had no commissary with our bread; our spirits so low with hunger and fatigue, that we often said we would as soon die as live.

We had several rivers to cross, and a large stone bridge across each; and when we came to these bridges, an engineer officer with three or four of his men, who had put a bag or barrel of powder under the main arch, and laid a long trail of loose powder some 40 or 50 yards, would ask 'if all was over?' If the answer was 'yes' they would put the slow match to the powder, and when it reached the cask or bag, the large arch would be blown into the air with a report as loud as thunder. Then he would say, 'Now Mr Frenchman, you will be kind enough to halt, until we get on a mile or two'.

The roads being very bad, the British army could not move on very fast, I think not more than two miles an hour. Our colonel had orders for us to throw away our knapsacks, but to keep either the great coat, or blanket, which we chose. We did not much mind parting with our kits, our orders must be obeyed, so we left them by the road side. But we then had enough to carry; fifty rounds of ball cartridge; thirty loose balls in our waist belt; and a flask, and a horn of powder; and rifle, and sword [bayonet]: the two weighing 14 pounds. These were plenty for us to carry; with empty bellies, and the enemy close at our heels, thirsting for blood!

Many of our men sat down by the road-side, and gave up the ghost, fairly worn down! Those who could use tobacco held out the best. I was one of this number. We had seven or eight women belonging to the regiment. There were no baggage wagons on which they could ride; and some of them fell into the hands of the enemy; and after using them as they pleased, they gave them some food, and sent them to us!

When we had marched two or three hours on a night, our colonel would give the word to halt, for the purpose that the men might do what they wanted; and I have seen many who did not want to drop out of the ranks for that purpose, drop down nine or ten on each other, some with big coats on, some with blankets; and they would be fast asleep on the snow, huddled together, in the space of a minute; and when the word was given to 'fall in', the sergeants would have to kick them very hard to awaken them.

Waterloo: wounded and plundered

Colonel Fredrick Ponsonby of the 12th Light Dragoons
[from *The Ponsonby Family* by Major-General Sir John
Ponsonby KCB, London, 1929]

The Battle of Waterloo (18 June 1815) ended the scourge of
Bonapartism. Wellington and the Prussian Field Marshal Prince
Blücher, commanding the two wings of the Allied army, defeated
Napoleon at the end of a day of 'hard pounding'. Blücher
'understood nothing whatever of the conduct of a war... [but]
acted as an example of the bravest in battle and the most
indefatigable in exertion' wrote General Müffling, the Prussian
liaison officer in Brussels. After being rolled on by his horse at
Ligny (16 June 1815), the 72 year old Field Marshal was missing
for two hours but, when he emerged, reversed an order to
retreat eastwards, away from Wellington, which would have
handed Bonaparte victory. Blücher's Chief-of-Staff, Gneisenau,
provided sound staff work and method to Blücher's headstrong
bravery, but Blücher's loyalty to his ally determined his strategy,
and countered Gneisenau's anglophobia.

Napoleon unwisely handed tactical command at Waterloo to
the courageous but impulsive Ney, whose cavalry, unsupported by
field artillery, fruitlessly charged unbroken British squares. When
– late in the afternoon – an opportunity occurred to break through
the British centre, Napoleon refused Ney reinforcements.

Ponsonby (1783–1837), later Major-General the Hon. Sir Fred Ponsonby KCB, GCMG, had 6 children by Lady Emily Bathurst, the daughter of Earl Bathurst (Secretary of State for War, to whom Wellington's Waterloo Dispatch was addressed). He was a brother of Lady Caroline Lamb, Byron's lover, and a cousin of Major-General the Hon. Sir William Ponsonby, who was killed leading the Union Brigade in a cavalry attack on d'Erlon's infantry at Waterloo.

On June 15th I was going to the Duchess of Richmond's Ball at Brussels. An Officer however came up to my quarters and told me that a sharp skirmish had taken place on our front and that the enemy were advancing; I determined not to go and about 3 in the Mg we received an order to assemble at Enghein.

We were on the ground at 6 o'clock in the morning, the rest of the Cavalry having further to come, did not arrive till nine or ten. We moved towards Nivelles, halting in the middle of the day to feed.

We now heard the constant roar of Artillery very distinctly and as we passed Nivelles at a Trot we met a great many wounded. Dawson, A.D.C. to Lord Anglesea, came to us; he told us of the death of the Duke of Brunswick. We arrived on the Ground of Quatre Bras, but the action was over, and there was only a skirmish going on, with a cannon shot or a shell now and then.

The Ground was covered with the French Cuirassiers and a good many of our men and also Brunswickers. Night came on; we bivouacked on the ground. Early in the morning the Duke [of Wellington], having ascertained the retreat and the defeat of Blucher, gave orders for all the Infantry to retire to Waterloo. The Cavalry with two Battalions of the 95th remained as a rear guard to mask the retreat of our Infantry. The whole of the

Cavalry were drawn up on some rising ground and remained there till after two. It was a most interesting time for the Duke who had every reason to expect that the whole of Bonaparte's army would immediately fall upon him, before he could collect his army on the position of Waterloo.

I was with him, the Duke, just in front of this line of Cavalry when we were all observing the preparations and movements of the immense mass of Troops before us. He was occupied in reading the newspapers, looking through his glass when anything was observed, and then making observations and laughing at the fashionable news from London.

The French Cavalry were now mounted, it was past two and the whole of their army were seen getting under arms. We commenced our retreat in three columns. I was with the left column. We had nothing however but a skirmish. The centre column had a sharp affair, but we all arrived at Waterloo without suffering any material loss. The rain fell in torrents, it was so heavy that my large thick cloak was wet thro' in a few minutes. The whole country became almost a swamp.

We bivouacked just in rear of the position, the rain continued all night. I dined with General Pack in the Village, and slept on the road.

In the Morning (the 18th) my Servant, who had not gone off to the rear like almost all the Servants of the Army, had a good breakfast for me, and a change of things. It is a very curious thing that very few of us expected a battle. Why, I cannot tell, but so it was. About 10 however the Artillery began and soon after we saw large bodies of the Enemy in motion. The first attack was very formidable; it was repulsed and my cousin General Ponsonby charged and had a great success.

We were on the left and seeing a large mass of Infantry in retreat and in confusion, my Regt charged. It entered the mass and at the same time a Body of French Lancers charged us on our flank. Nothing could equal the confusion of this melée, as we had succeeded in destroying and putting to flight the Infantry. I was anxious to withdraw my Reg^t but almost at the same moment I was wounded in both arms, my Horse sprung forward and carried me to the rising ground on the right of the French Position, where I was knocked off my Horse by a blow in the head.

I was stunned with the blow and when I recovered, finding I was only wounded in my arms and seeing some of my Reg^t at the foot of the Hill, I attempted to get up, but a Lancer who saw me immediately plunged his Lance into my back and said 'Coquin, tu n'es pas mort.' [Rascal, you are not dead.] My mouth filled with blood and my breathing became very difficult as the Lance had penetrated my Lungs but I did not lose my senses. The French *Tirailleurs* who had joined that Battalion when the charge took place took up their ground again at the crest of the rising Ground where I was; the first man who came along plundered me. An officer then came up and gave me some brandy; I begged him to have me removed but this he could not do. He put a knapsack under my head and said I should be taken care of after the battle. He told me the Duke of Wellington was killed and that several of our Battalions in the night had surrendered. There was a constant fire kept up by those about me; a young *Tirailleur* who fired over me talked the whole time, always observing that he had killed a man every shot he fired. Towards the Evening the fire became much sharper. He told me our Troops were moving on to attack and with his last shot he said 'Adieu Mon Ami nous allons nous retirer.' [Goodbye, my friend, we're retreating] A squadron of Prussian Cavalry passed over me. I was a good deal hurt by the Horses – in general Horses will avoid treading upon men but the Field was so covered, that they had no spare space for their feet.

Night now came on. I knew the Battle was won. I had felt little anxiety about myself during the day as I considered my case desperate, but now the night air relieved my breathing, and I had a hope of seeing somebody I knew. I was plundered again by the Prussians. Soon after an English Soldier examined me. I persuaded him to stay with me. I suffered but little pain from my wounds, but I had a most dreadful thirst and there were no means of getting a drop of water, I thought the night never would end. At last Morning came, the Soldier saw a Dragoon, he was fortunately of the 11th in the same Brigade with me. He came and they tried to get me on his Horse, but not being able to do so, he rode in to Head Quarters, and a waggon was sent for me. Young Vandeleur of my Reg^t came with it, he brought a Canteen of Water. It is impossible to describe the gratification I felt in drinking it. I was of course very much exhausted having lost a great deal of blood from five wounds. I had been on the ground for near 18 hours. I was taken to the Inn in Waterloo, it had been the Duke's Quarters. Hume dressed my wounds. I remained about a week in this Village and was then carried into Brussels.

Waterloo: The Finale, 18 June 1815

Lieutenant John Kincaid, 95th Rifle

[from *Adventures in the Rifle Brigade*, 1830]

Lieutenant Kincaid (1787–1862) served with the 1st Battalion, the 95th Rifles (later known as the Rifle Brigade) in the Peninsular War (1808–14), where he fought in nearly all the major battles, and at Waterloo. Kincaid had joined the 2nd Battalion in 1809 and went to Walcheren. Invalided home with malaria (which, many years later, killed him) he transferred to the 1st Battalion in 1810. His diaries are an invaluable historical source. His eye for detail is telling and informative – viz. this little insight into the miserable British sabre: '... our small regulation half-moon sabre [is] better calculated to shave a lady's maid than a Frenchman's head...' French cavalry sabres were, in contrast, long and lethal and allowed them 'to stab wounded allied troops as they rode over them. It made me mad to see the cuirassiers in their retreat stooping and stabbing at our wounded men.' This gallant and able soldier was 39 when he was promoted Captain in 1826, slow going, because he could not afford to buy his commission, being born of quite humble parents in Falkirk. But he was knighted in 1852 after his elevation to Senior Exon of the Royal Body Guard of the Yeoman of the Guard. In 1850 he was H.M. Inspector of both prisons and factories in Scotland. He became a member of the Athenaeum.

At Waterloo Kincaid was Adjutant of the 1st Battalion. Several companies of the 95th fought with such distinction at Waterloo, at the sandpit by La Haye Sainte and holding the crucial central crossroads while being cannonaded mercilessly, that they were honoured by being named the Rifle Brigade and taken out of the Line. The extract below tells of the climax of 18 June 1815. It reminds us that in the era of black powder, battle was enveloped in dense smoke, as well as din and death.

———◆━◆✕◆━◆———

I shall never forget the scene which the field of battle presented about seven in the evening. I felt weary and worn out, less from fatigue than anxiety.

Our division, which had stood upwards of 5,000 men at the commencement of the battle, had gradually dwindled down into a solitary line of skirmishers. The 27th regiment were lying literally dead, in square, a few yards behind us. My horse had received another shot through the leg, and one through the flap of the saddle, which lodged in his body, sending him a step beyond the pension list. The smoke still hung so thick about us that we could see nothing. I walked a little way to each flank to endeavour to get a glimpse of what was going on; but nothing met my eye except the mangled remains of men and horses, and I was obliged to return to my post as wise as I went.

I had never yet heard of a battle in which everybody was killed; but this seemed likely to be an exception, as all were going by turns...

Presently a cheer which we knew to be British commenced far to the right, and made everyone prick up his ears; it was Lord Wellington's long-wished-for orders to advance. It gradually approached, growing louder as it grew near. We took it up by instinct, charged through the hedge down upon the old knoll, sending our adversaries flying at the point of the bayonet. Lord Wellington galloped up to us at the instant, and our men began to cheer him; but he called out, 'No cheering, my lads, but forward, and complete our victory!'

This movement had carried us clear of the smoke; and to people who had been so many hours enveloped in darkness, in the midst of destruction, and naturally anxious about the result of the day, the scene, which now met the eye conveyed a feeling of more exquisite gratification than can be conceived. It was a fine summer evening just before sunset. The French were flying in one confused mass. British lines were seen in close pursuit, and in admirable order, as far as the eye could reach to the right, while the plain to the left was filled with Prussians. The enemy made one last attempt at a stand on the rising ground to our right of [an inn called] La Belle Alliance; but a charge from General Adam's Brigade again threw them into a state of confusion, which was now inextricable, and their ruin was complete. Artillery, baggage, and everything belonging to them, fell into our hands. After pursuing them until dark, we halted about two miles beyond the field of battle, leaving the Prussians to follow up the victory.

Letter from the Crimea after the Battle of Alma, 1853

Captain the Hon. Henry Clifford VC

The Crimean War (1853–56) could have been averted with skilful diplomacy and compromise. Instead a squabble over jurisdiction within Turkish-ruled Jerusalem's holy places split France (protector of Catholics) and Russia (protector of Orthodox Christians) and squeezed Turkey. Russia used the Turkish sultan's failure to resolve the issue as a pretext to annex Ottoman Rumanian principalities, a move that Britain and France saw as expansionist and the precursor to a Russian attempt to secure entrance into the Mediterranean through the Turkish Straits, with serious consequences for the balance of power in the Near East. British and French fleets were dispatched to encourage Turkish resistance. The Turks attacked the Russian army but the Tsar retaliated by destroying the entire Turkish navy at Sinop harbour on the Black Sea (30 November 1853). An Anglo-French ultimatum to withdraw was ignored by Russia and war was declared.

Like the Somme in the Great War, the Crimean War has become a byword for muddle and incompetence. In fact the number of British war dead – 22,182 out of a total force of 97,864 engaged – was only slightly more than the British army suffered on the first day of the Somme alone. In the Crimea most died from disease, and only

4,602 British soldiers were killed in action or died of wounds (20 per cent from 'friendly fire').

Henry Clifford of the Rifle Brigade was Aide de Camp to Brigadier George Buller, commanding one of two brigades of the Light Division. Although officially a staff officer, not a fighting soldier, he was invariably in the thick of the fighting, particularly when he saw that a crisis called for immediate and decisive leadership. He was an appalled witness of the Charge of the Light Brigade, and the horrors of the Crimea. Buller succumbed to depression and was invalided home. Clifford was not impressed; he complained of Buller's 'grumbling', unbefitting a Rifleman of any rank.

Clifford begins his account of the Alma by commenting on the dense fog that covered the battlefield as the action began. He then continues.

———◆▸✕◂◆———

I saw the enemy in great numbers in our front about 15 yards from us; it was a moment or two before I could make General Buller believe that they were Russians. 'In God's name,' I said, 'fix bayonets and charge.' He gave the order and in another moment we were hand to hand with them… 'Come on,' I said, 'my lads,' and the brave fellows dashed in amongst the astonished Russians, bayoneting them in every direction. One of the bullets in my revolver had partly come out and prevented it revolving, and I could not get it off. The Russians fired their pieces off within a few yards of my head, but none touched me. I drew my sword and cut off one man's arm who was in the act of bayoneting me, and a second, seeing it turned round and was in the act of running out of my way when I hit him over the back of the neck and laid him dead at my feet…. Out of the small party with me – twelve – six men were killed and three wounded, so my escape was wonderful… The Russians, who kept up a tremendous fire upon us with heavy guns from 6 in the morning till 5 in the evening, kept sending up fresh columns of infantry to try and take our position, but they were always repulsed with very great slaughter... I rode over the field of battle after it was over and the sight was truly heart-rending. The Russians lay in such heaps it was quite impossible to form any idea of their numbers... But they never drove us one inch from our position – not a Russian with arms in his hands saw over the hill on which we first took up our stand and on which, had we taken common precautions by throwing up works, many a brave officer and man would not have fallen on our side.

[Next day] This morning, as I passed the Russian prisoners and wounded, a man amongst them ran up and called out to me and pointed to his shoulder bound up. It was the poor fellow whose arm I had cut off yesterday; he laughed and said, 'Bono Johnny'. I took his hand and shook it heartily and the tears came in my eyes. I had not a shilling in my pocket; had I a bag of gold he should have had it. I enquired if he had been cared for, and the doctor told me he had and was doing well.

The Charge of the Light Brigade

William Howard Russell, Crimea, 1854
[from *The Times*, 14 November 1854]

The Battle of Balaclava (25 October 1854), although now remembered for the Charge of the Light Brigade, in which 157 out of 673 who rode were killed, was actually a successful allied engagement by Britain, Turkey, France, and Piedmont against the Russians during the Crimean War. It saved the British anchorage from capture and thus secured the army's supply lines. The 93rd Highlanders standing only two-deep – known ever after as the 'Thin Red Line' – checked a Russian cavalry attempt to break through. The forgotten charge of the Heavy Brigade, as gallant as that of the Light Brigade, repulsed a second Russian cavalry attack.

At Balaclava, the British commander Field Marshal Lord Raglan on the commanding Sapoune Heights – where all was visible and clear – had issued an imprecise order at 10.00 a.m. on 25 October to the cavalry commander, Lord Lucan, on the plain 650 feet below to –

'... *advance and take any opportunity to recover the Heights. [Cavalry] will be supported by infantry...*'

Allied redoubts on the Causeway Heights, which ran between two valleys, had just been captured. But Raglan did not use the word 'immediately' and Lucan assumed he was to wait for infantry support. The two infantry divisions commanded by the Duke of Cambridge and Sir George Cathcart had not arrived despite being summoned at 8.00 a.m. from their camp some 4 miles away. Sir George, for one, insisted on finishing his breakfast.

Raglan was furious at the delay, and when a staff officer shouted that the Russians were dragging away captured British cannon (an insignificant material loss, but a psychological blow), he sent the brilliant but impetuous ADC Captain Nolan with a hastily-written supplementary order:

'Cavalry to advance rapidly to the front… try to prevent the Enemy carrying away the guns… Immediate.'

It was meant to be taken in conjunction with the previous instruction, to do immediately what he had previously ordered. But Lucan saw it as an unconnected, fresh instruction: crucially there was no mention of 'Heights', only 'front', and from Lucan's position he could not see 'the Enemy carrying away the guns'. Nolan perceived Lucan dithering and added in an insolent voice, 'Lord Raglan's orders are that the cavalry should attack immediately.' Lucan replied 'Attack what?' This was too much for Nolan who despised the ineffectual Lucan (who he nicknamed 'Lord Look-on'). 'There, my Lord!' he shouted. 'There is your enemy! There are your guns!' And he pointed, whether by accident or frustration, to the guns visible at the end of the valley, with cannon to left and right – not at the intended point of attack, the invisible guns on the Causeway Heights to the right.

Lucan felt constrained to obey Raglan's seemingly suicidal order and instructed his despised brother-in-law Lord Cardigan, commanding the Light Brigade, to advance. Nolan joined the attack. After riding barely 200 yards he suddenly galloped across the leading lancers, wheeling his sword as if to change the direction of the advance, when he was hit and killed by shrapnel bursting above him. Cardigan was unimpressed – he described Nolan as 'screaming like a woman'.

Cardigan was involved in a skirmish with Cossacks behind the Russian guns. There, he later claimed, he was 'slightly wounded' and 'with difficulty got away from them'. But in fact he was saved by a Russian officer, Prince Radziwell, who had met him socially in London before the war and ordered that he be captured unharmed. Cossack lancers could have killed him easily. Cardigan believed that he had done his duty by leading his men to their target and that he could then hand over to the regimental commanders. Having reached the guns, he rode around pointlessly, with no attempt to lead groups of survivors or pursue the Russian cavalry. He retired before the majority of his troops – hardly the actions of an inspiring or even adequate senior officer. In defence of Cardigan, he had previously used some initiative, which had only invited rebuke. He was undoubtedly brave, stoical in the face of what seemed inevitable death. As he formed up for the Charge he was heard to say, 'Well, here goes the last of the Brudenells' (his family name).

This vivid description of the 'blunder' by Irishman William Howard Russell (1820–1907), *The Times'* war correspondent, caught the public imagination. Russell had been sent to the Crimea in February 1854 by his editor, John Thadeus Delane. He dispatched his letter on 26 October; it took almost 20 days to reach London and was published on 14 November. It inspired Alfred Lord Tennyson to write his poem *Charge of the Light Brigade* in 1855.

Russell's reports from the Crimea on the deficiencies of the army supply system and the lack of nursing care shocked a hitherto ignorant public and helped bring down Lord Aberdeen's government. This was brave reporting, uncowed by officialdom. Writing for an English audience he was however less than generous to the French allies whose heroic exploits led to the fall of Sevastopol, and who saved the retreating remnants of the Light Brigade from destruction. The French constituted by far the largest Allied army – 309,268 to

Britain's 97,864 – losing 95,615 war dead, of which 20,240 died as a result of enemy action. The British public did not know this.

Russell was friendly with the bumbling, one-armed Lord Raglan (he lost the limb at Waterloo); thus his report on the Charge fails to investigate properly the chain of command, and who precisely was responsible for the debacle. Instead he starts with an inspiring 'spin' and has a gratuitous swipe at 'a savage and barbarian enemy' – for having the cheek to cannonade our gallant lads. If Russell's dispatch distorts the reality of war by glorying in its spectacle, it is graphic reporting at its finest.

HEIGHTS BEFORE SEBASTOPOL, 25 OCTOBER

If the exhibition of the most brilliant valour, of the excess of courage, and of a daring which would have reflected lustre on the best days of chivalry can afford full consolation for the disaster of today, we can have no reason to regret the melancholy loss which we sustained in a contest with a savage and barbarian enemy…

It appeared that the Quartermaster-General, Brigadier Airey, thinking that the Light Cavalry had not gone far enough in front… when the enemy's horse had fled, gave an order in writing to Captain Nolan, 15th Hussars, to take to Lord Lucan, directing his Lordship 'to advance' his cavalry nearer the enemy. A braver soldier than Captain Nolan the army did not possess. He was known to all his arm of the service for his entire devotion to his profession, and his name must be familiar to all who take interest in our cavalry for his excellent work on our drill and system of remount and breaking horses. I had the pleasure of his acquaintance, and I know he entertained the most exalted opinions respecting the capabilities of the English horse soldier. Properly led, the British Hussar and Dragoon could in his mind break squares, take batteries, ride over columns of infantry, and pierce any other cavalry in the world as if they were made of straw. He thought they had not had the opportunity of doing all that was in their power, and that they had missed even such chances as had been offered to them – that, in fact, they were in some measure disgraced… He is now dead and gone. God forbid I should cast a shade on the brightness of his honour, but I am bound to state what I am told occurred… When Lord Lucan received the order from Captain Nolan, and had read it, he asked, we are told, 'Where are we to advance to?' Captain Nolan pointed with his finger to the line of the Russians, and said, 'There are the enemy, and there are the guns', or words to that effect, according to statements made after his death…

At ten minutes past eleven, our Light Cavalry Brigade advanced. As they rushed towards the front, the Russians opened on them from guns in the redoubt on the right, with volleys of musketry and rifles. They swept proudly past, glittering in the morning sun in all the pride and splendour of war. We could scarcely believe the evidence of our senses! Surely that handful of men are not going to charge an army in position? Alas! it was but too true, their desperate valour knew no bounds, as far indeed was it removed from its so-called better part of discretion. They advanced in two lines, quickening their pace as they closed towards the enemy. A more fearful spectacle was never witnessed than by those who, without the power to aid, beheld their heroic countrymen rushing to the arms of death. At the distance of 1200 yards the whole line of the enemy belched forth, from thirty iron mouths, a flood of smoke and flame, through which hissed the deadly balls. Their flight was marked by instant gaps in our ranks, by dead men and horses, by steeds flying wounded or riderless across the plain. The first line is broken, it is joined by the second, they never halt or check their speed an instant; with diminished ranks, thinned by those thirty guns, which the Russians had laid with the most deadly accuracy, with a halo of flashing steel above their heads, and with a cheer that was many a noble fellow's death-cry, they flew into the smoke of the batteries, but ere they were lost from view the plain was strewed with their bodies and with the carcasses of horses.

They were exposed to an oblique fire from the batteries on the hills on both sides, as well as a direct fire of musketry. Through the clouds of smoke we could see their sabres flashing as they rode up to the guns and dashed between them, cutting down the gunners as they stood. The blaze of their steel, like an officer standing near me said, 'was like the turn of a shoal of mackerel.' We saw them riding through the guns, as I have said; to our delight we saw them returning, after breaking through a column of Russian infantry and scattering them like chaff, when the flank fire of the battery on the hill swept them down, scattered and broken as they were. Wounded men and dismounted troopers flying towards us told the sad tale – demi-gods could not have done what we had failed to do.

At the very moment when they were about to retreat, a regiment of lancers was hurled upon their flank. Colonel Shewell, of the 8th Hussars, saw the danger and rode his men straight at them, cutting his way through with fearful loss. The other regiments turned and engaged in a desperate encounter. With courage too great almost for credence, they were breaking their way through the columns which enveloped them, when there took place an act of atrocity without parallel in modern warfare of civilized nations. The Russian gunners, when the storm of cavalry passed, returned to their guns. They saw their own cavalry mingled with the troopers who had just ridden over them, and to the eternal disgrace of the Russian name, the miscreants poured a murderous volley of grape and canister on the mass of struggling men and horses, mingling friend and foe in one common ruin. It was as much as our Heavy Cavalry Brigade could do to cover the retreat of the miserable remnants of that band of heroes as they returned to the place they had so lately quitted in all the pride of life.

At thirty-five minutes past eleven not a British soldier, except the dead and dying, was left in front of those bloody Muscovite guns.

'Dead lying with their eyes wide open, the wounded begging piteously for help': Shiloh, 1862

Private Sam R. Watkins

[from *Co. Aytch: Maury Grays, First Tennessee Regiment or, A Side Show of the Big Show*, 1882]

The election in 1860 of the Republican and pro-Union Abraham Lincoln (1809–1865), set off the train of events that led to the American Civil War (1861–1865). The war was fought primarily because the Northern states with a growing, free labour force to man its expanding industry sought to outlaw slavery, the core of the South's economy with its settled plantation system. The Southern states thought such matters were for individual states to decide, not the Union. In 1861, 11 southern states seceded from the Union to set up their own government, which they called the Confederate States of America. They were within their rights to do so. The war began with a dispute over who should own property belonging to the Union government which lay in the Confederate states. The first shots were fired on 10 April 1861, when local Confederate forces bombarded Fort Sumter, a Union garrison in Charleston Harbour, South Carolina. No-one was hurt during the bombardment but two Union soldiers died when their cannon exploded while firing a salute during evacuation. War spread across the country, the rights and wrongs of secession becoming a central issue.

Those fighting for the northern states were known as Federals, Unionists or Yankees, those fighting for the southern states were Confederates or rebels. Some 360,000 Yankees and 260,000 rebels (roughly 25 per cent of white males of military age) lost their lives in the war, about 65 per cent of them from disease.

Sam R. Watkins (1839–1901), who lived and died in Columbia, Tennessee, served in Company H of the Confederate (thus southern) 1st Tennessee Infantry Regiment throughout the American Civil War and, although wounded, survived – despite fighting in some of the war's bloodiest engagements. His memoir is that of a brave and patriotic private soldier, disdainful of authority and appalled at the bungles that doom his friends:

> 'The average staff officer and courier were always called "yaller dogs," and were regarded as non-combatants and a nuisance, and the average private never let one pass without whistling and calling dogs. In fact, the general had to issue an army order threatening punishment for the ridicule hurled at staff officers and couriers. They were looked upon as simply "hangers on," or in other words, as yellow sheep-killing dogs, that if you would say "booh" at, would yelp and get under their master's heels...'

He and his comrades were openly contemptuous of officers who failed. At the Battle Of Chickamauga (18–20 September 1863) he saw –

> '... a cowardly colonel... come dashing back looking the very picture of terror and fear, exclaiming, "O, men, men, for God's sake go forward and help my men! they are being cut all to pieces! we can't hold our position. O, for God's sake, please go and help my command!" To hear some of

our boys ask, "What regiment is that? What regiment is that?" He replies, such and such regiment. And then to hear some fellow ask, "Why ain't you with them, then, you cowardly puppy? Take off that coat and those chicken guts; coo, sheep; baa, baa, black sheep; flicker, flicker; ain't you ashamed of yourself? flicker, flicker; I've got a notion to take my gun and kill him," etc.'

But he recognised the limits of his horizon: 'a private soldier is but an automaton, and knows nothing of what is going on among the generals, and I am only giving the chronicles of little things...'. Although, he would add, 'The generals risked their reputation, the private soldier his life.' This was unfair – 112 Civil War generals were killed in battle or died of wounds, often leading from the front. His regiment had numbered some 1,000 officers and men at the outset of the war; at the Surrender only 65 of those mustered. In his own company, of the original 120, seven remained.

Watkins' first battle, Shiloh (6–7 April 1862), was named after a church near the battlefield, though it was known to many Confederates as Pittsburg Landing. The Confederate General Albert S. Johnston ordered an attack on Union troops led by General Ulysses S. Grant at 0300 on 5 April, but storms, bad roads and poor staff work caused fatal delays and, after two days of fighting, Union forces – despite initially being caught off guard – drove the now demoralised and disorganised rebels back. Confederate troops evacuated much of Tennessee and their forces were split along the lines formed by the Mississippi River. Minnie balls (named after co-inventor Captain Minié of the French army), which Watkins refers to, were conical, soft lead bullets whose grooves made it spin as it expanded in a rifled musket barrel – the result was a lethal range of 600 yards and a maximum range of 1,500.

This was the first big battle in which our regiment had ever been engaged. I do not pretend to tell of what command distinguished itself; of heroes; of blood and wounds; of shrieks and groans; of brilliant charges; of cannon captured, etc. I was but a private soldier, and if I happened to look to see if I could find out anything, 'Eyes right, guide center,' was the order. 'Close up, guide right, halt, forward, right oblique, left oblique, halt, forward, guide center, eyes right, dress up promptly in the rear, steady, double quick, charge bayonets, fire at will,' is about all that a private soldier ever knows of a battle. He can see the smoke rise and the flash of the enemy's guns, and he can hear the whistle of the minnie and cannon balls, but he has got to load and shoot as hard as he can tear and ram cartridge, or he will soon find out, like the Irishman who had been shooting blank cartridges, when a ball happened to strike him, and he hallooed out, 'Faith, Pat, and be jabbers, them fellows are shooting bullets.' But I nevertheless remember many things that came under my observation in this battle. I remember a man by the name of Smith stepping deliberately out of the ranks and shooting his finger off to keep out of the fight; of another poor fellow who was accidentally shot and killed by the discharge of another person's gun, and of others suddenly taken sick with colic...

On Sunday morning, a clear, beautiful, and still day, the order was given for the whole army to advance, and to attack immediately. We were supporting an Alabama brigade. The fire opened – bang, bang, bang, a rattle de bang, bang, bang, a boom, de bang, bang, bang, boom, bang, boom, bang, boom, bang, boom, bang, boom, whirr-siz-siz-siz-a ripping, roaring boom, bang! The air was full of balls and deadly missiles. The litter corps was carrying off the dying and wounded. We could hear the shout of the charge and the incessant roar of the guns, the rattle of the musketry, and knew that the contending forces were engaged in a breast to breast struggle. But cheering news continued to come back. Every one who passed would be hailed with, 'Well, what news from the front?' 'Well, boys, we are driving 'em. We have captured all their encampments, everything that they had, and all their provisions and army stores, and everything.'

As we were advancing to the attack and to support the Alabama brigade in our front, and which had given way and were stricken with fear, some of the boys of our regiment would laugh at them, and ask what they were running for, and would commence to say 'Flicker! flicker! flicker!' like the bird called the yellowhammer, 'Flicker! flicker! flicker!'

As we advanced, on the edge of the battlefield, we saw a big fat colonel of the 23rd Tennessee regiment badly wounded, whose name, if I remember correctly, was Matt. Martin. He said to us, 'Give 'em goss, boys. That's right, my brave First Tennessee. Give 'em Hail Columbia!' We halted but a moment, and said I, 'Colonel, where are you wounded?' He answered in a deep bass voice, 'My son, I am wounded in the arm, in the leg, in the head, in the body, and in another place which I have a delicacy in mentioning.' That is what the gallant old Colonel said.

Advancing a little further on, we saw General Albert Sidney Johnson surrounded by his staff and Governor Harris, of Tennessee. We saw some little commotion among those who surrounded him, but we did not know at the time that he was dead. The fact was kept from the troops.

About noon a courier dashed up and ordered us to go forward and support General Bragg's center. We had to pass over the ground where troops had been fighting all day.

I had heard and read of battlefields, seen pictures of battlefields, of horses and men, of cannon and wagons, all jumbled together, while the ground was strewn with dead and dying and wounded, but I must confess that I never realized the 'pomp and circumstance' of the thing called glorious war until I saw this. Men were lying in every conceivable position; the dead lying with their eyes wide open, the wounded begging piteously for help, and some waving their hats and shouting to us to go forward.

It all seemed to me a dream; I seemed to be in a sort of haze, when siz, siz, siz, the minnie balls from the Yankee line began to whistle around our ears, and I thought of the Irishman when he said, 'Sure enough, those fellows are shooting bullets!'

Down would drop first one fellow and then another, either killed or wounded, when we were ordered to charge bayonets. I had been feeling mean all the morning as if I had stolen a sheep, but when the order to charge was given, I got happy. I felt happier than a fellow does when he professes religion at a big Methodist camp-meeting. I shouted. It was fun then. Everybody looked happy. We were crowding them. One more charge, then their lines waver and break. They retreat in wild confusion. We were jubilant; we were triumphant. Officers could not curb the men to keep in line. Discharge after discharge was poured into the retreating line. The Federal dead and wounded covered the ground.

When in the very midst of our victory, here comes an order to halt. What! halt after today's victory? Sidney Johnson killed, General Gladden killed, and a host of generals and other brave men killed, and the whole Yankee army in full retreat.

These four letters, h-a-l-t, O, how harsh they did break upon our ears. The victory was complete, but the word 'halt' turned victory into defeat.

The soldiers had passed through the Yankee camps and saw all the good things that they had to eat in their sutlers' stores and officers' marquees, and it was but a short time before every soldier was rummaging to see what he could find.

The harvest was great and the laborers were not few.

The negro boys, who were with their young masters as servants, got rich. Greenbacks were plentiful, good clothes were plentiful, rations were not in demand. The boys were in clover.

This was Sunday.

On Monday the tide was reversed.

Now, those Yankees were whipped, fairly whipped, and according to all the rules of war they ought to have retreated. But they didn't. Flushed with their victories at Fort Henry and Fort Donelson and the capture of Nashville, and the whole State of Tennessee having fallen into their hands, victory was again to perch upon their banners, for Buell's army, by forced marches, had come to Grant's assistance at the eleventh hour.

One incident I recollect very well. A Yankee colonel, riding a fine gray mare, was sitting on his horse looking at our advance as if we were on review. W. H. rushed forward and grabbed his horse by the bridle, telling him at the same time to surrender. The Yankee seized the reins, set himself back in the saddle, put the muzzle of his pistol in W. H.'s face and fired. About the time he pulled trigger, a stray ball from some direction struck him in the side and he fell off dead, and his horse becoming frightened, galloped off, dragging him through the Confederate lines. His pistol had missed its aim.

I have heard hundreds of old soldiers tell of the amount of greenback money they saw and picked up on the battlefield of Shiloh, but they thought it valueless [i.e. not legal tender in the South] and did not trouble themselves with bringing it off with them.

One fellow, a courier, who had had his horse killed, got on a mule he had captured, and in the last charge, before the final and fatal halt was made, just charged right ahead by his lone self, and the soldiers said, 'Just look at that brave man, charging right in the jaws of death.' He began to seesaw the mule and grit his teeth, and finally yelled out, 'It arn't me, boys, it's this blarsted old mule. Whoa! Whoa!'

'The dead shall not have died in vain': The Gettysburg Address

Abraham Lincoln, Gettysburg, Pennsylvania,
19 November 1863

At 5 p.m. on 18 November 1863, President Abraham Lincoln arrived by train at Gettysburg, Pennsylvania, having journeyed from the White House in Washington D.C. He had been invited to dedicate the new Union cemetery the next day. The cemetery contained many of the 3,512 Union dead of the Battle of Gettysburg (1–3 July 1863). The rebel dead lay in field burial plots until disinterred and reburied, mostly in Richmond, Virginia, between 1870 and 1873. Human remains were still being found on the battlefield in the 1950s.

The battle had been decisive in its result – the Confederate General Robert E. Lee had gambled that his invasion of the northern states would force Lincoln to negotiate a compromise peace, but, in the bloody three-day battle, General George G. Meade's Army of the Potomac repulsed Lee's Army of Northern Virginia. On a rain-swept 4 July the rebel army started its retreat south-west towards Virginia, leaving many of its wounded on the battlefield. The South lost 4,637 killed out of total southern casualties – dead, wounded, captured – of 28,000. Northern casualties were 23,000. Lee offered to resign. Confederate President Jefferson Davis refused his resignation saying that finding a better commander was 'an impossibility'. Lincoln felt that Meade had failed to exploit his victory:

> *'I was deeply mortified by the escape of Lee across the Potomac, because the substantial destruction of his army would have ended the war, and because I believed such destruction was perfectly easy.'*
>
> [Letter to General Oliver Howard, 21 July 1863]

A few days after the battle, Pennsylvania Governor Andrew Curtin asked David Wills, a rich local citizen and judge, to clean up the bloody detritus of the battle, to care for the wounded soldiers in the barns and farms, and remove the bloated dead. Wills acquired seventeen acres for the national cemetery and commissioned the Germantown landscape architect, William Saunders, to lay it out. Wills invited Edward Everett, the country's foremost rhetorician, to give an oration at the dedication ceremony, and asked President Lincoln to make a 'few appropriate remarks'. The President, Curtin and Everett were also invited by Wills to stay at his house on the public square in Gettysburg.

Lincoln accepted, seeing it as an appropriate moment both to honour the dead of the Civil War, and to air his belief that the war was a fight not just to preserve the Union, but for freedom and equality for all, under God and under the law. The use of the word 'nation' is significant. In his inaugural address on 4 March 1861, before the war had begun, he had spoken of the 'Union' twenty times, of the 'nation' not at all. Now the President mentions the 'Union' not once, but the word 'nation' five times, invoking a sense of nationalism and 'a new birth of freedom'.

Lincoln brought the first part of the speech with him, either composed on the train or in the White House. It was written in ink on Executive Mansion stationery. He wrote the second part in pencil on lined paper before the dedication; both pages survive. They were given to one of his private secretaries, John

Nicolay, and are in the Library of Congress. But the text differs from that heard by several witnesses at Gettysburg – the words 'under God' do not appear, for example. So Lincoln probably rewrote the Nicolay version as Everett droned on, presenting that first draft to Nicolay. When Lincoln returned to Washington he wrote out a fair copy – of the actual words delivered – for John Hay, another private secretary, presumably copied from the crumpled pages he read from at Gettysburg, which he subsequently destroyed.

A crowd of about 6,000 came to hear the speeches on 19 November. Local entrepreneurs sold battle relics such as buttons and canteens and spent musket balls. Edward Everett declaimed for an agonising two hours. Then Lincoln rose.

The photographer was still adjusting his apparatus when Lincoln sat down again. No photograph therefore exists of him speaking. Lincoln himself was displeased with his performance: 'a flat failure', he called it. The London *Times* agreed: 'The ceremony was rendered ludicrous... by the sallies of that poor President Lincoln... Anyone more dull and commonplace it would not be easy to produce.'

His delivery may indeed have been poor. As for his words, opinion was divided on party lines. Democratic newspapers savaged the speech, while Republican editors applauded it. The great American journalist H.L. Mencken (1880–1956) wrote of the Address:

'The Gettysburg speech is at once the shortest and the most famous oration in American history... It is eloquence brought to a pellucid and almost gem-like perfection – the highest emotion reduced to a few poetical phrases. Nothing else precisely like it is to be found in the whole range of oratory. Lincoln himself never even remotely approached it. It is genuinely stupendous.'

But the libertarian and advocate of states' rights went on to say:

> 'But let us not forget that it is poetry, not logic; beauty, not sense. Think of the argument in it. Put it into the cold words of everyday. The doctrine is simply this: that the Union soldiers who died at Gettysburg sacrificed their lives to the cause of self-determination – 'that government of the people, by the people, for the people,' should not perish from the earth. It is difficult to imagine anything more untrue. The Union soldiers in that battle actually fought against self-determination; it was the Confederates who fought for the right of their people to govern themselves.'

In a letter to the President, Edward Everett wrote: 'I should be glad if I could flatter myself that I came as near to the central idea of the occasion, in two hours, as you did in two minutes.' Lincoln was not an eyewitness to the battle, but as an eyewitness to the war and architect of its direction, he was uniquely placed to see Gettysburg's significance to liberty and the union.

FOUR SCORE and seven years ago our fathers brought forth on this continent, a new nation, conceived in Liberty, and dedicated to the proposition that all men are created equal.

Now we are engaged in a great civil war, testing whether that nation, or any nation so conceived and so dedicated, can long endure. We are met on a great battlefield of that war. We have come to dedicate a portion of that field, as a final resting place for those who here gave their lives that that nation might live. It is altogether fitting and proper that we should do this.

But, in a larger sense, we cannot dedicate – we cannot consecrate – we cannot hallow – this ground. The brave men, living and dead, who struggled here, have consecrated it, far above our poor power to add or detract. The world will little note, nor long remember what we say here, but it can never forget what they did here. It is for us the living, rather, to be dedicated here to the unfinished work which they who fought here have thus far so nobly advanced. It is rather for us to be here dedicated to the great task remaining before us – that from these honored dead we take increased devotion to that cause for which they gave the last full measure of devotion – that we here highly resolve that these dead shall not have died in vain – that this nation, under God, shall have a new birth of freedom – and that government of the people, by the people, for the people, shall not perish from the earth.

The plight of the wounded, the Wilderness, 1864

Clara Barton [from her *War Diary*]

Clara Harlowe Barton (1821–1912) from Oxford, Massachusetts, previously a teacher who had learnt the rudiments of medicine from nursing a sick brother for two years, was working as a clerk in the Patent Office in Washington when the American Civil War broke out. She looked on in horror at the plight of the wounded after the first Battle of Bull Run (21 July 1861) and wrote an anguished letter to the *Worcester Spy* (Mass.) pleading for food, clothing and bandages for the soldiers. They poured in; and thus began her relief organisation, which was to see her administer to the wounded – even as the shells burst around her – at the battles of Cedar Mountain, Second Bull Run, Chantilly, South Mountain and Antietam. One surgeon called her 'the angel of the battlefield'. She was a tiny, forceful woman, a sort of American Florence Nightingale, who invariably considered her superiors and colleagues incompetent or wrong. Her place, she said, 'was anywhere between the bullet and the battlefield'. She was instrumental in founding the American Red Cross (1881).

The Battle of the Wilderness (5–7 May 1864) in Virginia was fought between Confederate forces under Lee's overall command and Union forces under Grant. It was a Union reverse, but not a defeat. The Confederate General Longstreet described the Wilderness as 'a forest land of about fifteen miles square, lying between and equidistant from Orange Court House and Fredericksburg. It is broken occasionally by small farms and abandoned clearings, and two roads.' Southern troops broke Grant's right and nearly cut off his supply line. The Federals lost 2,246 killed and 12,073 wounded out of 116,886 engaged. Confederate strength was 61,025 and they lost about 7,750 killed and wounded. Several generals on both sides were killed, leading their men as in Napoleonic times. On the night of the 7th, as bushfires raged burning the wounded, Grant whittled in his tent, and wept. But next day he advanced towards Richmond, pursuing Lee to Spotsylvania (8–21 May 1864), an inconclusive battle, where Major General John Sedgwick famously exclaimed that Confederate snipers 'couldn't hit an elephant at this distance' before being shot and killed. Grant was checked at Cold Harbor (31 May–12 June 1864), described by the Confederate General Law as 'not war, but murder'. Grant lost around 6,000 men in one futile assault, the only attack he ever regretted ordering. But this was attritional warfare and Grant was wearing Lee's forces down.

This episode at the Wilderness illustrates the suffering that often followed a great battle, as the authorities failed to cope with the inevitable chaos, made worse by the amateurs suddenly thrust into positions of power and responsibility for which they were both untrained and unsuited.

————◆◈◆————

No one has forgotten the heart-sickness which spread over the entire country as the busy wires flashed the dire tidings of the terrible destitution and suffering of the wounded of the Wilderness whom I attended as they lay in Fredericksburg. But… these ills were augmented by the conduct of improper, heartless, unfaithful officers in the immediate command of the city and upon whose actions and indecisions depended entirely the care, food, shelter, comfort, and lives of that whole city…

A little dapper captain quartered with the owners of one of the finest mansions in the town, boasted that he had changed his opinion since entering the city the day before; that it was in fact a pretty hard thing for refined people like the people of Fredericksburg to be compelled to open their homes and admit these 'dirty, lousy, common soldiers', and that he was not going to compel it.

This I heard him say, and waited until I saw him make his words good, till I saw, crowded into one old sunken hotel, lying helpless upon its bare, wet, bloody floors, five hundred fainting men hold up their cold, bloodless, dingy hands, as I passed, and beg me in Heaven's name for a cracker to keep them from starving (and I had none); or to give them a cup that they might have something to drink water from, if they could get it (and I had no cup and could get none); till I saw two hundred six-mule army wagons in a line, ranged down the street to headquarters, and reaching so far out on the Wilderness road that I never found the end of it; every wagon crowded with wounded men, stopped, standing in the rain and mud, wrenched back and forth by the restless, hungry animals all night from four o'clock in the afternoon till eight next morning and how much longer, I know not. The dark spot in the mud under many a wagon told only too plainly where some poor fellow's life had dripped out in those dreadful hours.

I remembered one man who would set it right, if he knew it, who possessed the power and who would believe me if I told him I commanded immediate conveyance back to Belle Plain. With difficulty I obtained it, and four stout horses with a light army wagon took me ten miles at an unbroken gallop, through field and swamp and stumps and mud to Belle Plain and a steam tug at once to Washington. Landing at dusk I sent for Henry Wilson, chairman of the Military Committee of the Senate. A messenger brought him at eight, saddened and appalled like every other patriot in that fearful hour, at the weight of woe under which the Nation staggered, groaned, and wept.

He listened to the story of suffering and faithlessness, and hurried from my presence, with lips compressed and face like ashes. At ten he stood in the War Department. They could not credit his report. He must have been deceived by some frightened villain. No official report of unusual suffering had reached them. Nothing had been called for by the military authorities commanding Fredericksburg.

Mr. Wilson assured them that the officers in trust there were not to be relied upon. They were faithless, overcome by the blandishments of the wily inhabitants. Still the Department doubted. It was then that he proved that my confidence in his firmness was not misplaced, as, facing his doubters he replies: 'One of two things will have to be done – either you will send some one to-night with the power to investigate and correct the abuses of our wounded men at Fredericksburg, or the Senate will send some one tomorrow.'

This threat recalled their scattered senses.

At two o'clock in the morning the Quartermaster-General and staff galloped to the 6th Street wharf under orders; at ten they were in Fredericksburg. At noon the wounded men were fed from the food of the city and the houses were opened to the 'dirty, lousy soldiers' of the Union Army.

Both railroad and canal were opened. In three days I returned with carloads of supplies.

No more jolting in army wagons! And every man who left Fredericksburg by boat or by car owes it to the firm decision of one man that his grating bones were not dragged ten miles across the country or left to bleach in the sands of that city.

'The close of the war': Lee's surrender at Appomattox, 9 April 1865

General Ulysses S. Grant
[from *Personal Memoirs*, New York, 1885]

General Robert E. Lee (1807–70) surrendered his Army of Northern Virginia to General Ulysses S. Grant (1822–85), commanding the northern forces, in the McLean House in the hamlet of Appomattox Court House, Virginia, on 9 April 1865. Surrender had become inevitable – specifically because the Confederate army's last trainload of supplies had been captured by General Phil Sheridan's cavalry, leaving Lee without food; and because 'Lee couldn't go backward, he couldn't go forward, and he couldn't go sideways' as a private in his army said. He was boxed in. 'There was but one outlet,' wrote a Confederate general – Appomattox Court House – 'and to that General Grant had the shortest road'. But more generally surrender was inevitable because the Army of Northern Virginia was, like the rest of the South, exhausted, starving, defeated. Lee had received a message from Grant at 5 p.m. on 7 April 1865 referring to 'the hopelessness of further resistance' and asking him to surrender. The North had one million men under arms, the South less than 100,000. Lee accepted the inevitable and sent a white flag (actually a towel) into the Union lines. He then dispatched an aide to find a suitable house for the meeting with Grant. The first civilian the aide encountered was Wilmer McLean, whose house proved ideal. McLean had moved to this backwater to escape the war – the first major battle of the Civil War, Bull Run, had been fought literally across his backyard. He was thus the reluctant witness of the first and last battles.

Lee's prestige and nobility remained undimmed by failure at Gettysburg, where his launching of 'Pickett's Charge' was fatal, or by his costly frontal assaults and misguided offensives elsewhere. But the American historian and philosopher Henry Brooks Adams struck a dissenting note: 'Lee should have been hanged. It was all the worse that he was a good man and a fine character and acted conscientiously. It's always the good men who do the most harm in the world.'

Lee's surrender effectively ended the American Civil War. After over four years' fighting the South succumbed to the industrial strength and mass armies of the North. Lee and his beaten army were fortunate in finding Grant a magnanimous victor. As the surrender approached, Lincoln, wishing to 'bind up the nation's wounds' had told Grant at a meeting at City Point, Virginia, to 'let them down easy'. General Sherman, also present at that meeting, offered yet more generous terms, effectively an armistice rather than a surrender, to the Confederate General Joseph E. Johnston in Raleigh, North Carolina, infuriating Sherman's Washington masters and earning him a humiliating rebuke. Lee would have preferred to consult his political master, the Confederate President Jefferson Davis, over surrender terms for all men under arms in the South, but as Grant pointed out in this extract, Davis 'was a fugitive in the woods'.

After a two-term Presidency (1869–77), Grant became a partner in a financial firm that went bankrupt. Although scrupulously honest himself, he was tolerant of failings in others and was never a good judge of character. His other weakness was occasional drinking bouts. During the Civil War he had remained mostly sober but lapses were brought on, it has been suggested, by enforced sexual abstinence. He was devoted and loyal to his wife at home. At the same time as losing his money he learned that he had cancer of the throat. He started writing his memoirs to pay off his debts and provide for his family, racing against declining health to complete a book that ultimately earned nearly $450,000. A few days after writing the last page he died. Mark Twain called the book 'a great, unique and unapproachable literary masterpiece'. Sherman, who had cherished the lucidity of Grant's wartime orders, wrote: 'Other books of the war will be forgotten, mislaid, dismissed. Millions will read Grant's *Memoirs* and remember them. His expertise as a writer does not surprise me, for I have read hundreds of his letters and know too well his style and flawless effort at turning a phrase.' Below Grant recalls the details and decorum of the surrender at Appomattox.

ON THE NIGHT before Lee's surrender, I had a wretched headache – headaches to which I have been subject – nervous prostration, intense personal suffering. But, suffer or not, I had to keep moving. The object of my campaign was not Richmond, not the defeat of Lee in actual fight, but to remove him and his army out of the contest. You see the war was an enormous strain upon the country. Rich as we were I do not see how we could have endured it another year, even from a financial point of view. So with these views I wrote Lee…

I received word that Lee would meet me at a point within our lines near Sheridan's headquarters. I had to ride quite a distance through a muddy area. I remember now that I was concerned with my personal appearance. I had an old suit on, without my sword, and without any distinguishing mark of rank except the shoulder straps of a Lieutenant-general on a woolen blouse. I was splashed with mud in my long ride. I was afraid Lee might think I meant to show him studied discourtesy by so coming – at least I thought so.

I went up to the house where Lee was waiting. I found him in a new, splendid uniform, which only recalled my anxiety as to my own clothes while on my way to meet him. I expressed my regret that I was compelled to meet him in so unceremonious a manner, and he replied that the only suit he had available was one which had been sent him by some admirers in Baltimore, and which he then wore for the first time. We spoke of old friends in the army. I remembered having seen Lee in Mexico. He was so much higher in rank than myself at the time that I supposed he had no recollection of me. But he said he remembered me very well. We talked about old times and exchanged inquiries about friends.

Lee then broached the subject of our meeting. I told him my terms, and Lee, listening attentively, asked me to write them down. I took out my manifold order book and pencil and wrote them down. General Lee put on his glasses and read them over. The conditions gave the officers their side-arms, private horses, and personal baggage. I said to Lee that I hoped and believed this would be the close of the war; that it was most important that the men should go home and go to work, and the government would not throw any obstacles in the way. Lee answered that it would have the most happy effect, and accepted the terms. I handed over my penciled memorandum to an aide to put into ink, and we resumed our conversation about old times and friends in the army. Various officers came in – Longstreet, Gordon, Pickett, from the South; Sheridan, Ord and others from our side. Some were old friends – Longstreet and myself for instance, and we had a general talk. Lee no doubt expected me to ask for his sword but I did not want his sword. It would only have gone to the Patent Office to be worshipped by the Washington Rebels.

There was a pause, when General Lee said that most of the animals in his cavalry and artillery were owned by the privates, and he would like to know, under the terms, whether they would be regarded as private property or the property of the government. I said that under the terms of surrender they belonged to the government. General Lee read over the letters and said that was so. I then said to the General that I believed and hoped this was the last battle of the war; that I saw the wisdom of these men getting home and to work as soon as possible, and that I would give orders to allow any soldier or officer claiming a horse or mule to take it. General Lee showed some emotion at this – a feeling which I also shared – and said it would have a most happy effect.

The interview ended, and I gave orders for rationing his troops. The next day I met Lee on horseback and we had a long talk. In that conversation I urged upon him the wisdom of ending the war by the surrender of the other armies. I asked him to use his influence with the people of the South – an influence that was supreme – to bring the war to an end. General Lee said that his campaign in Virginia was the last organized resistance which the South was capable of making – that I might have to march a good deal and encounter isolated commands here and there but there was no longer any army which could make a stand. I told Lee that this fact only made his responsibility greater, and any further war would be a crime.

I asked him to go among the Southern people and use his influence to have all men under arms surrender to the same terms given to the army of Northern Virginia. He replied that he could not do so without consultation with President Davis. I was sorry. I saw that the Confederacy had gone beyond the reach of President Davis, and that there was nothing that could be done except what Lee could do to benefit the Southern people. I was anxious to get them home and have our armies go to their homes and fields. But Lee would not move without Davis, and as a matter of fact at that time, or soon after, Davis was a fugitive in the woods.

The Charge of the 21st Lancers at Omdurman

Winston Churchill
[from *My Early Life*, London, 1930]

Sudanese nationalist and fundamentalist Muhammad Ahmad (1844–85) had proclaimed himself the Mahdi ('Expected Guide' or 'Chosen One') on 29 June 1881. He exhorted his Dervishes to overthrow Sudan's occupying Egyptian forces. 'Dervish', the name the British gave to the Mahdi's followers (the Sudanese referred to them as Ansar, 'supporters'), derived from the Persian 'darvish' meaning 'poor man', with an additional sense of being poor for faith's sake, because riches impeded spirituality. Although unschooled in military science, being a carpenter and boat builder by trade, and lacking modern weapons, the Mahdi nevertheless won victories that gained him one million square miles of territory.

Egypt's financial collapse had resulted in 1879 in her being controlled by her principal creditors Great Britain and France. After a brief revolt against these foreigners, the Egyptian army was defeated by General Wolseley at Tel-el-Kebir (13 September 1882) and Britain assumed command of the country and its forces, France refusing to co-operate and withdrawing. Thus Egyptian Sudan became Britain's responsibility. Britain decided in 1884 to leave the Sudan, but General Charles Gordon disobeyed orders to supervise the evacuation of all Egyptian garrisons, and stayed to defend Khartoum. The public at home bayed for his relief and finally a reluctant government sent an army to Khartoum, but it was too slow and too late. Omdurman, the Dervish capital on the Nile opposite Khartoum, was the scene of Gordon's death at the hands of the Mahdi's men on 26 January 1885. For the next ten years the Sudan was free from foreign domination. Then in 1895 Britain, fearful of Italian and French interference in the Sudan, decided on its re-conquest. A retrained and reorganised Egyptian army under its British Commander-in-Chief, General Horario Herbert Kitchener (1850–1916), began a slow advance, building a railway as it went.

On 1 September 1898 Kitchener camped on the Nile near Omdurman, facing 50,000 Mahdists under Khalifa Abdullah, the Mahdi's successor. The Khalifa's only hope was a night attack, when his enemy's repeating rifles, artillery and machine guns would have been blind. But he chose to fight by day and was destroyed. Thus ended the Sudanese jihadist independence movement (Sudan eventually became independent in 1956).

A squad of 20 water-cooled Maxim machine-guns ensured victory for Kitchener. Only a few thousand of the Khalifa's soldiers had rifles; the rest were armed with spears, swords and daggers and protected only by shields. Hilaire Belloc penned a couplet after Omdurman –

> *'Whatever happens we have got*
> *The Maxim gun and they have not.'*

An estimated 11,000 or 90 per cent of the Dervishes were killed in the battle; the Anglo Egyptian army of 25,000 lost only 48 men. Thousands of Mahdist wounded were butchered, because these fanatical jihadists would attempt to fight even when wounded, disarmed, and lying bleeding on the 'hard, crisp desert'. Churchill does not mention this disgraceful act. The charge of the 21st Lancers, the stuff of legend and heroes at home, was however condemned in military circles as a blunder. The *Daily Mail's* correspondent G.W. Steevens wrote:

'For cavalry to charge unbroken infantry, of unknown strength, over unknown ground, within a mile of their advancing infantry, was as grave a tactical crime as cavalry could possibly commit… the British cavalry in the charge itself suffered far heavier losses [22 killed] than it inflicted. And by its loss in horses practically put itself out of action for the rest of the day…'

Winston Churchill (1874–1965) served in the 1897 Malakand expedition but his combining soldierly duties with those of a war correspondent aroused Kitchener's suspicion, and it was only through his American mother, Lady Randolph Churchill, that he subsequently managed to join the 21st Lancers. He first described the charge in *The River War* (1899) but rewrote it for *My Early Life* (1930). His vivid description reeks of a thirst for adventure – and fame – and no awkward facts concerning the virtue or wisdom of the action and battle sully the pure excitement and romance of it all. In *The River War* he called the battle 'the most signal triumph ever gained by the arms of science over barbarians'. But he paid tribute to his foe: 'these were as brave men as ever walked the earth'.

The trumpet sounded 'Right wheel into line', and all the sixteen troops swung round towards the blue-black riflemen. Almost immediately the regiment broke into gallop, and the 21st Lancers were committed to their first charge in war!

I propose to describe exactly what happened to me; what I saw and what I felt. The troop I commanded was, when we wheeled into line, the second from the right of the regiment. I was riding a handy, sure-footed, grey Arab polo pony. Before we wheeled and began to gallop, the officers had been marching with drawn swords. On account of my shoulder I had always decided that if I were involved in hand-to-hand fighting, I must use a pistol and not a sword. I had purchased in London a Mauser automatic pistol, then the newest and latest design. I had practised carefully with this during our march and journey up the river. This then was the weapon, with which I determined to fight. I had first of all to return my sword into its scabbard, which is not the easiest thing to do at a gallop. I had then to draw my pistol from its wooden holster and bring it to full cock. This dual operation took an appreciable time, and until it was finished, apart from a few glances to my left to see what effect the fire was producing, I did not look up at the general scene.

Then I saw immediately before me, and now only half the length of a polo ground away, the row of crouching blue figures firing frantically, wreathed in white smoke. On my right and left my neighbouring troop leaders made a good line. Immediately behind was a long dancing row of lances couched for the charge. We were going at a fast but steady gallop. There was too much trampling and rifle fire to hear any bullets. After this glance to the right and left and at my troop, I looked again towards the enemy. The scene appeared to be suddenly transformed. The blue-black men were still firing, but behind them there now came into view a depression like a shallow sunken road. This was crowded and crammed with men rising up from the ground where they had hidden. Bright flags appeared as if by magic, and I saw arriving from nowhere Emirs on horseback among and around the mass of the enemy. The Dervishes appeared to be ten or twelve deep at the thickest, a great grey mass gleaming with steel, filling the dry watercourse. In the same twinkling of an eye I saw also that our right overlapped their left, that my troop would just strike the edge of their array, and that the troop on my right would charge into air. My subaltern comrade on the right, Wormald of the 7th Hussars, could see the situation too; and we both increased our speed to the very fast gallop and curved inwards like the horns of the moon. One really had not time to be frightened or to think of anything else but these particular necessary actions which I have described. They completely occupied mind and senses.

The collision was now very near. I saw immediately before me, not ten yards away, the two blue men who lay in my path. They were perhaps a couple of yards apart. I rode at the interval between them. They both fired. I passed through the smoke conscious that I was unhurt. The trooper immediately behind me was killed at this place and at this moment, whether by these shots or not I do not know. I checked my pony as the ground began to fall away beneath his feet. The clever animal dropped like a cat four or five feet down on the sandy bed of the watercourse, and in this sand bed I found myself surrounded by what seemed to be dozens of men. They were not thickly packed enough at this point for me to experience any actual collision with them. Whereas Grenfell's troop next but one on my left was brought to a complete standstill and suffered very heavy losses, we seemed to push our way through as one has sometimes seen mounted policemen break up a crowd. In less time than it takes to relate, my pony had scrambled up the other side of the ditch. I looked round.

Once again I was on the hard, crisp desert, my horse at a trot. I had the impression of scattered Dervishes running to and fro in all directions. Straight before me a man threw himself on the ground. The reader must remember that I had been trained as a cavalry soldier to believe that if ever cavalry broke into a mass of infantry, the latter would be at their mercy. My first idea therefore was that the man was terrified. But simultaneously I saw the gleam of his curved sword as he drew it back for a ham-stringing cut. I had room and time enough to turn my pony out of his reach, and leaning over on the off side I fired two shots into him at about three yards. As I straightened myself in the saddle, I saw before me another figure with uplifted sword. I raised my pistol and fired. So close were we that the pistol itself actually struck him. Man and sword disappeared below and behind me. On my left, ten yards away, was an Arab horseman in a bright-coloured tunic and steel helmet, with chain-mail hangings. I fired at him. He turned aside. I pulled my horse into a walk and looked around again … There was a mass of Dervishes about forty of fifty yards away on my left. They were huddling and clumping themselves together, rallying for mutual protection. They seemed wild with excitement, dancing about on their feet, shaking their spears up and down. The whole scene seemed to flicker. I have an impression, but it is too fleeting to define, of brown-clad Lancers mixed up here and there with this surging mob. The scattered individuals in my immediate neighbourhood made no attempt to molest me. Where was my troop? Where were the other troops of the squadron? Within a hundred yards of me I could not see a single officer or man. I looked back at the Dervish mass. I saw two or three riflemen crouching and aiming their rifles at me from the fringe of it. Then for the first time that morning I experienced a sudden sensation of fear. I felt myself absolutely alone. I thought these riflemen would hit me and the rest devour me like wolves. What a fool I was to loiter like this in the midst of the enemy! I crouched over the saddle, spurred my horse into a gallop and drew clear of the *mêlée*.

Sir John French struggles with his French

Edward Spears [from *Liaison, 1914*, London, 1930]

The reasons for the outbreak of war in 1914 are complex. The spark was the assassination on 28 June 1914 of the heir to the Austro-Hungarian throne, Franz Ferdinand, and his wife by a Bosnian Serb nationalist in Sarajevo, capital of Bosnia. Franz Ferdinand was seen as an obstacle to the union of Austrian-ruled Bosnia with an independent Serbia. The assassination provoked ultimatums and the momentum for war. But the underlying causes were many: Germany's desire for empire – her 'place in the sun', the arms race of the preceding years, a series of ensnaring treaties and alliances, Austrian insecurity and German's violation of neutral Belgium. Social turmoil and nationalist movements played a part, as did terrible miscalculations by political and military leaders, the complacent diplomacy of Great Britain, the belligerence of the Kaiser and troop mobilisations that created an irreversible timetable towards war.

Edward Spears (1886–1974) was brought up in France and became an outstanding liaison officer between the French and the British during the Great War. A close friend of Churchill, he was eventually to be his representative to the doomed French government in 1940, escaping to England with de Gaulle to raise the Free French standard.

In August 1914 he was attached – in the formal capacity of a subaltern in the 11th Hussars – to General Lanrezac's Fifth French Army. This excerpt gives some indication of the disastrous relations between Lanrezac and BEF (British Expeditionary Force) Commander Sir John French. Neither could speak the other's language and matters were not helped by the absence of interpreters at key meetings because of an obsession with secrecy. They soon ignored each other, acting as if each other's armies did not exist. Spears was thus an essential conduit between the two. When, on the night of 23 August 1914, Lanrezac decided to withdraw without informing Sir John French at Le Cateau, the BEF seemed doomed. But Spears discovered the planned withdrawal and drove through the night to alert French, who immediately ordered a retreat. Spears, an acting captain, saved the British Expeditionary Force from being isolated and surrounded. The following conversation took place during the German breakthrough at Sedan in the first days of the war.

Sir John, stepping up to a map in the 3ème Bureau, took out his glasses, located a place with his finger, and said to Lanrezac: 'Mon General, est-çe-que —' His French then gave out, and turning to one of his staff, he asked: 'How do you say "to cross the river" in French?' He was told, and proceeded: 'Est-çe que les Allemands vont traverser la Meuse à – à —' Then he fumbled over the pronunciation of the name. 'Huy' was the place, unfortunately one of the most difficult words imaginable to pronounce, the 'u' having practically to be whistled. It was quite beyond Sir John. 'Hoy', he said at last, triumphantly. 'What does he say? What does he say?' exclaimed Lanrezac. Somebody explained that the Marshal wanted to know whether in his opinion the Germans were going to cross the river at Huy? Lanrezac shrugged his shoulders impatiently. 'Tell the Marshal,' he said curtly, 'that in my opinion the Germans have merely gone to the Meuse to fish.'

The Retreat from Mons,
24 August–5 September 1914

Frank Richards [from *Old Soldiers Never Die*, London, 1933]

In the opening days of war in 1914 Germany advanced through neutral Belgium, as part of the Schlieffen Plan, towards the French border, aiming to knock out France before dealing with Russia in the east. The Plan was, however, fatally compromised in scope and direction, and it did not work. France stopped the Germans at the Battle of the Marne (6–12 September 1914), north-east of Paris. They were saved in part by 600 Paris taxis rushing 6,000 troops to stop a German breakthrough.

Mons, the scene of the British Expeditionary Force's first battle in the Great War, was a small Belgian mining town. The BEF were there because the Allied plan called for the British to support the extreme left of the French line. The defensive Battle of Mons was fought on 23 August 1914, when the Germans attacked with massed infantry 'in solid square blocks' making 'the most perfect targets', and were severely mauled. The Germans had not known the British were there. Some 30,000 British faced 90,000 Germans. But the weight of attacks forced a British withdrawal. British casualties were 1,600; German losses were about 15,000, a tribute to the superb marksmanship of Britain's small, professional army. Their rate of fire led the Germans to believe that 'each English soldier was armed with his own Maxim'. In fact there were only two Vickers-Maxim machine guns per battalion.

A defensive position was prepared for the anticipated battle next day, but at 11.00 p.m. it was learnt (through the British liaison officer Spears) that General Lanrezac of the French Fifth Army had – 'in a supremely uncoordinated move' – broken off fighting and retreated, without telling either his own French Commander, Joffre, or the British to his immediate left, who were now alone, isolated and vulnerable. Sir John French ordered a withdrawal and the 'Retreat from Mons' had begun.

Frank Richards (1883–1961), whose real name was Francis Philip Woodruff, served as a regular soldier in India and Burma from 1901–9, and as a reservist until the Great War when he rejoined the regiment. He was one of the very few who fought from 1914 to the Armistice, in many of the major battles and campaigns, and survived uninjured. He was awarded the Distinguished Conduct Medal and the Military Medal for his gallantry. He wrote *Old Soldiers Never Die* with Robert Graves' assistance; Graves was an officer in the same regiment, the Royal Welch Fusiliers. Richards steadfastly refused promotion even to NCO. The occasional grammar of the ranks ('without no halt', 'we were woke up') was actually Graves' insertion; he thought it sounded authentic.

We retired all night with fixed bayonets, many sleeping as they were marching along. If any angels were seen on the Retirement, as the newspaper accounts said they were, they were seen that night. March, march, for hour after hour, without no halt: we were now breaking into the fifth day of continuous marching with practically no sleep in between. We were carrying our rifles all shapes and it was only by luck that many a man didn't receive a severe bayonet wound during the night. Stevens said: 'There's a fine castle there, see?' pointing to one side of the road. But there was nothing there. Very nearly everyone were seeing things, we were all so dead-beat.

At last we were halted and told that we would rest for a couple of hours. Outposts and sentries were posted and we sank down just off the road and were soon fast asleep. Fifteen minutes later we were woke up, and on the march again. We had great difficulty in waking some of the men. About ten yards from the side of the road was a straw rick, and about half a dozen men had got down the other side of it. I slipped over and woke them up. One man we had a job with but we got him going at last. By this time the Company had moved off, so we were stragglers. We came to some crossroads and didn't know which way to go. Somehow we decided to take the road to the right.

Dawn was now breaking. Along the road we took were broken-down motor lorries, motor cycles, dead horses and broken wagons. In a field were dumped a lot of rations. We had a feed, crammed some biscuits into our haversacks and moved along again. After a few minutes, by picking up more stragglers, we were twenty strong, men of several different battalions. I inquired if anyone had seen the 2nd Royal Welch Fusiliers, but nobody had. By the time that it was full daylight there were thirty-five of us marching along, including two sergeants. We got into a small village – I had long since lost interest in the names of the places we came to, so I don't know where it was – where we met a staff-officer who took charge of us. He marched us out of the village and up a hill and told us to extend ourselves in skirmishing order at two paces interval and lie down and be prepared to stop an attack at any moment. About five hundred yards in front of us was a wood, and the attack would come from that direction. The enemy commenced shelling our position, but the shells were falling about fifteen yards short. The man on my left was sleeping: he was so dead-beat that the shelling didn't worry him in the least and the majority of us were not much better. We lay there for about half an hour but saw no signs of the enemy. The staff-officer then lined us up and told us to attach ourselves to the first battalion we came across. I had to shake and thump the man on my left before I could wake him up. We marched off again and came across lots of people who had left their homes. Four ladies in an open carriage insisted on getting out to let some of our crippled and dead-beat men have a ride. We packed as many as we could into the carriage and moved along, the ladies marching with us. Late in the afternoon we took leave of the ladies. The men who had been riding had a good day's rest and sleep. If the ladies had all our wishes they would be riding in a Rolls-Royce for the rest of their lives.

In Flanders Fields

John McCrae

John McCrae, MD (1872–1918) was a doctor in the Canadian Army Medical Corps, who graduated from the University of Toronto, saw war and suffering in the Boer War and subsequently taught at McGill University. During the Great War of 1914–18 he was attached as a surgeon to the 1st Field Brigade, RCFA (Royal Canadian Field Ambulance), and served in the Ypres Salient and on the Somme. At the time of writing his most famous poem he had spent seventeen consecutive days treating the injured and the dying in an advanced dressing station on the west side of the Canal de l'Yser, just a few hundred yards north of the main square in Ypres. It was a terrible and exhausting ordeal. He was used to death, but not on this scale. He wrote:

> *'I wish I could embody on paper some of the varied sensations of that seventeen days... Seventeen days of Hades! At the end of the first day if anyone had told us we had to spend seventeen days there, we would have folded our hands and said it could not have been done.'*

Among the dead buried in the small adjacent cemetery was a young friend and former student, Lieutenant Alexis Helmer of Ottawa,

who had been killed by shell-fire on 2 May 1915. McCrae himself
had performed the funeral ceremony in the absence of the chaplain.
He was much affected by Helmer's death.

The next day, sitting on the back of an ambulance near the graves,
and looking towards the wooden crosses, McCrae expressed his
sadness and sense of loss and anger in a short poem. Sergeant Major
Cyril Allinson, aged 22, who was delivering mail, watched him write
it. 'His face was very tired but calm as he wrote,' Allinson recalled.
'He looked around from time to time, his eyes straying to Helmer's
grave.' When Major McCrae finished five minutes later, he took his
mail from Allinson and silently handed him his pad. Allinson was
much moved:

> *'The poem was an exact description of the scene in front
> of us both. He used the word blow in that line because
> the poppies actually were being blown that morning by a
> gentle east wind. It never occurred to me at that time that
> it would ever be published. It seemed to me just an exact
> description of the scene.'*

McCrae tossed his poem away, but a fellow officer retrieved it and
sent it to newspapers in England. It was rejected by *The Spectator*
but published by *Punch* on 6 December 1915.

The poem's last verse is often omitted in recitations or anthologies
because it seems too bellicose for modern taste. But the poem sounds
painfully unfinished without it, and the last three lines give exhortation
to the living, purpose to the death of those beneath the crosses, and a
resonant closing echo of the first line. One critic, Paul Fussell, writing
in *The Great War and Modern Memory* (Oxford, 1975), condemned its
'vicious', 'stupid', 'recruiting-poster rhetoric', but his objections are
political, not literary. Lieutenant Colonel McCrae died on 28 January,
1918, aged 45, from complications after contracting pneumonia
and meningitis. He was buried with military honours at Wimereaux
Communal Cemetery. 75 nursing sisters attended McCrae's funeral

procession, and McCrae's horse, Bonfire, carried his master's boots backwards in the stirrups, according to military tradition.

In Flanders fields the poppies blow
Between the crosses, row on row,
That mark our place: and in the sky
The larks, still bravely singing, fly
Scarce heard amid the guns below.

We are the Dead. Short days ago
We lived, felt dawn, saw sunset glow,
Loved and were loved, and now we lie,
In Flanders fields.

Take up our quarrel with the foe:
To you from failing hands we throw
The torch: be yours to hold it high.
If ye break faith with us who die
We shall not sleep, though poppies grow
In Flanders fields.

A Subaltern has his introduction to the Trenches

Guy Chapman [from *A Passionate Prodigality*, London, 1933]

Guy Chapman (1889–1972), who later had a varied and successful career in the law and academia, arrived on the Franco-Belgian border in July 1915. His battalion was the 13th Royal Fusiliers, a raw New Army unit composed of volunteers. It was a period of relative quiet after the 2nd Battle of Ypres (22 April–25 May 1915), the only major attack launched by the German forces on the Western Front in 1915, to divert Allied attention from the Eastern Front and to test chlorine gas.

A Passionate Prodigality is undoubtedly one of the great books to come out of the war. Edmund Blunden wrote of Chapman:

'I doubt if any man has recollected better the ironies, the panoramas, the inventions and the mirages of those years.'

Is this the front line?' I asked. 'That's it.' He pointed to a dark wall. Someone else bustled out of the darkness. 'What platoon are you? No. 2. Send your men up to the right, two by two. Your platoon sergeant? He'll go with mine.'

The men moved on, and someone guided me to a clean and pleasant summer-house with boarded walls, decorated with Kirchner drawings and portraits of English beauties torn from the *Tatler*. 'We'll find you a dugout later,' said the company commander. 'Drop your pack and come round.'

The trench was not a trench at all. The bottom may have been two feet below ground level. An enormous breastwork rose in the darkness some ten or more feet high. All about was an air of bustle. Men came and went bearing mysterious burdens. Men were lifting filled sandbags on to the parapet and beating them into the wall with shovels. Bullets cracked in the darkness. Flares from the German side, thrown further than usual, illuminated a shoulder, a cheekbone, a straining thigh. Every now and then a figure would appear on the skyline and drop skilfully on to the firestep. 'Be careful coming in over the top,' said my guide. 'One of my blighters sat on a bayonet the other night. Care to see the wire?'

I followed him gingerly over the edge of the wall, and slid clumsily down a ramp of greasy sandbags. A small party was working swiftly over a tangle of some dark stuff. Two of my own were being inducted into the ceremony of wiring. ''Old it tight, chum,' growled one figure. He proceeded to smite a heavy baulk of timber with a gigantic maul, the head of which had been cunningly muffled in sandbags. The noise seemed enough to waken the German army, but there was no answering excitement from the dull hummock across the way. One of our machine guns broke into Aristophanic chorus over our heads, which roused an acquaintance opposite. But the party in the wire went on with its work unmoved. 'He's shooting at our parapet,' said my guide, in a loud voice. 'We're quite all right down here.'

As the night passed, the labour grew less and less tumultuous. Men came in over the parapet, settled down in the corners of firebays and dropped asleep. A sentry in each embrasure, with one of the 13th, watched raptly over the top. Here and there a man boiled up a can of tea over a tiny fire skilfully dug in the side of a traverse. This domesticity seemed completely fantastic.

About two o'clock I was shown a doorway. 'You can sleep in there. The roof's quite good.' I found myself in a tiny cell, six foot by four. A stump of candle burned in a niche carved out of the clay wall. Half the space was occupied by a bed of wire stretched on poles. I lay down and blew out the light. Mysterious rustlings became audible, grew louder; there was a scamper of little feet. Rats, I guessed and shuddered. I relit my stump. The rustling abruptly ceased, and I dozed off.... I came back to the surface with a jerk. I could hear something scrabbling beside my ear. I turned my head and caught a glimpse of what looked like a small pink monkey, clambering up the wall. With a spasm of disgust, I threw myself off the bed and bolted into the mess, where I sat shuddering and retching until the subaltern on duty pushed his head in and called 'Stand-to'. I was not yet hardened to rats.

I felt my way behind him into the darkness. Over the breastwork, the blackness was fading. The desultory shooting of the early hours of the night had died away to an occasional shot. On the duckboards there was the sound of feet stamping to restore the circulation and put to flight the dawn chill that strikes a man who has slept in his clothes. As the light hardened, I looked over the parapet. What I had expected, I do not know; certainly not this derelict dump which lay between us and the inert sandbag wall two hundred yards away, the German line, guarded by its leaf-brown belt of patched and rusty wire; not the diseased stumpy trees in the orchard behind; not the tumbled-down gape-roofed house over there on the left, nor the unkempt skyline, growing stronger every moment as the sun rose.

'We'd better get down,' said my companion. 'Their snipers will start soon. You can't show your head in day-light.' 'Stand down,' he passed along the line. In five minutes, little fires of dry chips were brisking up along the trench. In alternate bays, men pitched their eyes to periscopes. Looking through one, you could see patches of smoke rising from the line opposite. The war lapsed and men broke their fast.

The morning passed quietly. A rare rifle shot echoed. A few shells passed overhead travelling to the back areas. Parties came and went with wood, wire, and sandbags. The sanitary men bent over their malodorous task. Presently Blake came along. His battered clown's face was that of a man who has discovered an awful joy. 'Seen – ? It's the funniest sight in France. He's as nervous as a cat and speaks in a hoarse whisper for fear the enemy will overhear him. The men can't make him out.'

The afternoon passed even more quietly than the morning. At dark, Walter Spencer arrived with No. 4 and we dragged ourselves back through the mud to Houplines. Two nights later we returned. We arrived in what to some veteran of Albuera [a famously bloody battle of the Peninsular War] might have seemed a battle. As we reached the front line a deafening noise broke out. From both sides machine guns racketed, rifle-fire crashed. Bullets cracked overhead or came spinning past with a sharp whine. The men were crowded on the fire-step, blazing off S.A.A. [small arms ammunition] as if victory dwelt in their exertions. There was a certain air of levity about the performance, a bank holiday spirit. The men were cheering and cheering: it was very like a football match. After two minutes, it died down, and we were left in an empty world, in which, so sudden was the stoppage, the only movement seemed to be the Boche machine-gun bullets racing overhead.

'We're just giving them two minutes' rapid,' it was explained, 'a kind of celebration for the gun-boats they've lost off Riga.'

The next days passed exactly as the first. We learned trench routine; and so far as my company was concerned, not one shell was aimed at the acre of barren earth on which we squatted. We bade our instructors good-bye and marched for the last time down the Houplines road. Orders came for us to rendezvous at Bailleul. The next morning we set out, our term of finishing school over, nominally trained soldiers. I tried to reckon up what we had learned. It was very little. We could put up wire, keep ourselves clean. We knew something about ration parties and other fatigues, and we had learned to build sandbags into a wall which looked strong, a seductive art, too seductive, as we were soon to learn. I think that most of us had been disappointed. We had keyed ourselves to such a pitch of expectation that the reality proved a trifle flat. For my own part, I was vastly relieved.

'They're all f*cking dead': Battle of Loos, Sept. 1915

Robert Graves [from *Goodbye to All That*, London, 1929]

Robert Graves (1895–1985) was educated at Charterhouse and St. John's College, Oxford. He was commissioned into the Royal Welch Fusiliers where the elder Siegfried Sassoon, although in a different battalion, was a fellow subaltern and became a friend. They encouraged each other's writing. Graves was urged by Sassoon to write more realistic verse. Like Sassoon, Graves was a brave and conscientious officer.

On 20 July 1915, Robert Graves was severely wounded in trenches at Bazentin cemetery. He was carried into Mametz Wood, and placed on a stretcher in an old German Dressing Station. His wounds were considered fatal. Orderlies of the Royal Army Medical Corps then did what many thought they did best – they robbed him. Graves said that their initials stood for 'Rob All My Comrades'. They stole everything on him apart from a ring, which was too tight to wrench off his finger. The next morning an orderly was clearing away the dead for burial, when he spotted Graves breathing. Graves was evacuated and recovered. But the Battalion CO, Lieutenant-Colonel Crawshay, had seen the badly wounded Graves and thought he was as good as dead. He wrote a letter of condolence to Graves' mother. *The Times* reported his death.

Graves was amused by a letter of apology he later received from their advertising manager, stating that no charge would be made for the second announcement printed, that Graves had not in fact died of his wounds.

Goodbye to All That was one of a number of Great War memoirs by junior officers, written some ten years after the Armistice, which described the war in terms of the soldier in the trenches, and redefined it as one of suffering and futility; an image that lasted a generation and influenced the British response to the new German threat.

The incident below was told to Graves by a fellow officer. It describes a moment on the first day of the Battle of Loos (25 September–4 November 1915), in the 2nd Division sector. The battle was demanded by French C-in-C Joffre as part of a joint Franco-British assault on the German salient in the centre of the Western Front. It was a disaster: too many British shells were duds and chlorine gas, supposed to incapacitate the Germans, blew the wrong way. Gas was used because of the dearth of artillery; the Germans had tried it with mixed results at Ypres 10 days before. Although gas *projectiles* were outlawed by the Hague Declaration of 1899, gas canisters were not. But Graves thought the use of gas 'damnable'.

'It's not soldiering to use stuff like that, even if the Germans start it. It's dirty, and it will bring us bad luck. We're sure to bungle it. Take those new gas companies – their very look makes me tremble. Chemistry dons from London University, a few lads straight from school… Of course they'll bungle it. How could they do anything else?'

In the south, however, Loos was taken and the outskirts of Lens reached, but reserves to exploit this success were released too late. A second attack on 13 October was a bloody failure. The British suffered 60,000 casualties before bad weather put an end to the offensive; the British had gained a couple of miles but were in a worse, more vulnerable position, overlooked by slagheaps and a prominent ridge. German losses were about 20,000, reflecting the dominance of German defensive tactics over British infantry-based attacks.

When his platoon had gone about twenty yards, he signalled them to lie down and open covering fire. The din was tremendous. He saw the platoon on his left flopping down too, so he whistled the advance again. Nobody seemed to hear. He jumped up from his shell-hole, waved, and signalled 'Forward!'

Nobody stirred.

He shouted: 'You bloody cowards, are you leaving me to go on alone?'

His platoon-sergeant, groaning with a broken shoulder, gasped, 'Not cowards, sir. Willing enough. But they're all f*cking dead.' The Pope's Nose machine-gun, traversing, had caught them as they rose to the whistle.

Night patrol in No Man's Land

Robert Graves [from *Goodbye to All That*, London, 1929]

Laventie, where this episode took place, lies before Fromelles near Bethune. Patrolling at night was popular with generals, less so with the men. It was deemed essential to send out patrols at night to find out the strength of units and defences opposite, and to 'keep the men on their toes'. Capturing a dozy enemy sentry could be a priceless source of intelligence.

Many men who fought in France never saw the enemy, for it was largely an artillery war after 1916. But some glimpsed the enemy on night patrol, fleetingly or closer. It could be salutary. Sidney Rogerson wrote in *Twelve Days*:

> '*The enemy early became a legend. The well-wired trenches that faced ours frequently at a distance of only a few yards, gave shelter, we understood, to a race of savages, Huns, blond beasts who gave no quarter, who crucified Canadians and bayoneted babies, raped Belgian women… Many of us had never seen any Germans… Except… for an occasional miserable prisoner dragged back half-dead with fright from some raid… But were these pallid, serious youths really capable of such enormities?*'

A junior officer usually accompanied a patrol, which would rarely number more than 12, usually less. Mostly they did not attack – throwing bombs into an enemy trench would attract a star-shell and machine-gun fire. Men tended to crawl through the foul detritus of No Man's Land, only walking at a stoop on moonless nights and ready to drop instantly when a flare shot up. The most dangerous part of patrolling was getting back to your own trench when jumpy sentries could loose off.

Sergeant Townsend and I went out from Red Lamp Corner at about ten o'clock; both carrying revolvers. We had pulled socks, with the toes cut off, over our bare knees, to prevent them showing up in the dark and to make crawling easier. We went ten yards at a time, slowly, not on all fours, but wriggling flat along the ground. After each movement we lay and watched for about ten minutes. We crawled through our own wire entanglements and along a dry ditch; ripping our clothes on more barbed-wire, glaring into the darkness until it began turning round and round. Once I snatched my fingers in horror from where I had planted them on the slimy body of an old corpse. We nudged each other with rapidly beating hearts at the slightest noise or suspicion: crawling, watching, crawling, shamming dead under the blinding light of enemy flares, and again crawling, watching, crawling. A Second Battalion officer, who revisited these Laventie trenches after the war ended, told me the other day of the ridiculously small area of No Man's Land compared with its seeming immensity on the long, painful journeys that he had made over it. 'It was like the real size of a hollow in one's tooth compared with how it feels to the tongue.'

We found the gap in the German wire and at last came within five yards of the sap-head. We waited quite twenty minutes, listening for any signs of its occupation. Then I nudged Sergeant Townsend and, revolver in hand, we wriggled quickly forward and slid into it. It was about three feet deep and unoccupied. On the floor were a few empty cartridges and a wicker basket containing something large and smooth and round, twice the size of a football. Very, very carefully I groped and felt all around it in the dark. I was afraid that it might be some sort of infernal machine. Eventually I dared lift it out and carry it back, suspecting that it might be one of the German gas-cylinders we had heard so much about.

We got home after making a journey of perhaps two hundred yards in rather more than two hours. The sentries passed along the word that we were in again. Our prize proved to be a large glass container quarter-filled with some pale yellow liquid. This was sent down to battalion headquarters, and from there to the divisional intelligence officer. Everybody seemed greatly interested in it. The theory was that the vessel contained a chemical for re-damping gas-masks, though it may well have been dregs of country wine mixed with rain water. I never heard the official report. The colonel, however, told Captain Thomas in the hearing of the Surrey-man: 'Your new wart [subaltern] seems to have more guts than the others.'

A bird sings in No Man's Land,
Somme, June 1916

Private Albert Conn, 8th Devonshires, 20th Brigade,
7th Div. [Oral history, Imperial War Museum]

Superstition was rife in the Great War, men turned to rubbing rabbits' feet and crucifixes, touching lucky charms and seeing portends of doom in strange or unusual happenings. Here the killing of a bird is a harbinger of death. A running motif or refrain through Western Front letters and memoirs is the strange, wondrous singing of larks and other birds, heard during brief lulls between the firing of the guns.

The 8th Devonshires were slaughtered three weeks later on 1 July, the first day of the Battle of the Somme. Many lie buried in Devonshire Cemetery in Mansell Copse opposite Mametz, buried in the trench which they had left at dawn.

———◆◆◆———

A small bird sang on a stunted tree in Mansell Copse. At the break of dawn we used to listen to it and wonder that amongst so much misery and death a bird could sing. One morning a corporal visiting the fire posts heard the bird singing and muttering, 'What the hell have you got to sing about?' fired and killed it. A couple of the lads told him to fuck off out of it. We missed the bird.

Going Over the Top, 1 July 1916

George Ashurst [from *My Bit*, Ramsbury, 1987]

I July 1916, the first day of the Battle of the Somme (fought to relieve the French at Verdun) is a date etched into a nation's consciousness and into a thousand war memorials. It was a defeat of terrible proportions, 20,000 British dead in one day with negligible enemy casualties; no amount of revisionism can explain it away as 'necessary' or 'inevitable'. Tactics varied – some divisions, even New Army ones, adopted proto-infiltration tactics ('worms not waves') that anticipated the more complex and successful assault tactics of 1917 and 1918, but most walked in line across No Man's Land with full packs – because, as their Commander-in-Chief Douglas Haig emphasised, troops were still 'untrained' and more sophisticated tactics were beyond eager but raw volunteers. He believed too readily in Intelligence reports about the state of the enemy, the wire opposite, the effect of 1.6 million shells fired during the week-long bombardment (up to a third have since been estimated to have been duds). Co-ordination of infantry attack and artillery was poor and inflexible; the creeping barrage was only just being developed. Staff work was inadequate, perhaps a forgivable fault given the unprecedented nature of such a mass attack by 11 divisions on a 15 mile front. Most staff officers were amateurs too. Communications broke down. Some junior officers saved men's lives by using initiative and disregarding impossible orders. But in the main, Tommies were cut down by well-placed machine gunners, untouched by the bombardment in their deep dug-outs. German artillery and counter-attacks did the rest. This account makes it clear that Ashurst and his bombing party had only a few moments' grace before the German machine gunners opened fire. The 'bombs' referred to here are hand grenades. The Colonel who ordered the survivors out of the sunken road into a futile attack bears the name Magniac.

George Ashurst (1895–1985) joined the Lancashire Fusiliers in 1913 to escape unemployment and a drunken father. His service in the Great War included 1st Ypres, Gallipoli and the Somme, making his survival little short of miraculous. His memoir *My Bit* is that rare thing, a genuine unadorned story from the ranks – Ashurst never rose above corporal.

We had all received our special instructions and been informed that the huge mine under Beaumont Hamel which the Sappers had been preparing for weeks would be blown up at 7.30 a.m., and the great explosion would be the signal to go over the top. We had all received a stiff tot of rum and some of the officers and NCOs had certainly had a very stiff tot, which was very plain to some of us who did not have access to the stone jar, or carry flasks. I was detailed off in charge of a party of eight bombers and we were supposed to be the colonel's bodyguard. We took up our position in a communication trench leading into the front line. There we stood, rather silently leaning against the side of the trench, wondering if we had much longer to live and suddenly brushing the ugly thought of death away and thinking that a nice Blighty would come to us quickly. As a huge German shrapnel shell burst overhead we came to earth again and openly expressed the view to each other that we might get it sharp, whether it was Blighty or death.

Fritz's guns seemed to be coming to life now; his shells were dropping over pretty merrily and machine-gun bullets whistled over our heads, just as if he knew as well as we did that the time was near. Just as the waiting was becoming unbearable and the terrible strain causing some men to utter almost unnatural noises, we felt a queer dull thud and our trench fairly rocked, and a great blue flame shot into the sky, carrying with it hundreds of tons of bricks and stone and great chunks of earth mingled with wood and wire and fragments of sandbags.

The great mine had gone up. It was 7.30, zero hour. We set our teeth; we seemed to say to ourselves all in a moment, 'To hell with life', and, as the shout of our comrades in the front line leaping over the top reached us above the din of battle, we bent low in the trench and moved forward. Fritz's shells were screaming down on us fast now; huge black shrapnel shells seemed to burst on top of us. Shouts of pain and calls for help could be heard on all sides; as we pushed forward, we stepped over mortally wounded men who tried to grab our legs as we passed them, or we squeezed to one side of the trench while wounded men struggled by us anxious to get gaping wounds dressed and reach the safety of the dug-outs in rear.

In a few minutes the whole atmosphere of the place had taken on a fearful change. One felt like stopping to help a badly wounded comrade but to stop at such a time was to be accused of cowardice. Men uttered terrible curses even as they lay dying from terrible wounds, and others sat at the bottom on the trench shaking and shouting, not wounded but unable to bear the noise, the smell and the horrible sights.

When we reached the front line trench there was no need to climb out on top. It was already battered flat and our wire entanglements blown to fragments. Instantly I jumped on top and ran as fast as I could through the powder smoke towards the sunken road, two-thirds of the way across No Man's Land, holding down my head as I ran to shield my face as much as possible with my tin hat. The bullets made a horrible hissing noise all round me; shrapnel shells seemed to rend the sky and huge shells screamed down on us, shaking the ground under my feet and blowing to pieces both dead and wounded men who were lying about. Even in that mad dash I could plainly hear the sickly thud as a bullet struck some comrade close by me, and every moment I fully expected a bullet to tear through my body.

Miraculously, I breathlessly reached the sunken road, practically leaping the last yard or two and almost diving into its shelter. Picking myself up and looking round, my God, what a sight! The whole of the road was strewn with dead and dying men. Some were talking deliriously, others calling for help and asking for water.

Some other fit men like myself were bandaging wounded comrades or holding a water bottle to some poor fellow's lips. As the thumping of my heart steadied down a bit and my breathing eased I heard a faint voice quite close to me calling 'Corporal'. There I recognised one of my boys, his face deathly pale and his tunic saturated in blood. Quickly I held my water bottle to his lips. He drank just a little and then as he smiled up at me I heard the colonel calling out for all fit men to line the bank of the road, waving his revolver menacingly as he did so. Then he called for a signaller. One stepped up to him. 'Get to the top of that road and signal for reinforcements quickly,' he thundered. Without a moment's hesitation the signaller obeyed, but as he raised his flags to send the first letter the brave fellow dropped back into the road, riddled with bullets. The picture of that gallant hero's brave act will never leave my memory, but no sooner had the signaller's body crashed back into the road than the colonel's voice rang out again – 'Now men, as soon as I give the word over you go again, and this time don't stop until you reach that front line.' Then quickly jumping up out of the road he called at the top of his voice, 'Come on.'

Once more we sprang into that fusillade of bullets. In a few moments I must have been alone and quickly decided to drop into a shell-hole. I felt almost certain that most of the men had been killed or wounded. Anyhow, I was quite safe from Fritz's bullets, at least in my shell-hole, and I could look back over No Man's Land towards our own trenches. Hundreds of dead lay about and wounded men were trying to crawl back to safety; their heart rending cries for help could be heard above the noise of rifle fire and bursting shells.

As I lay there watching their painful efforts to get back to our line I noticed these poor fellows suddenly try to rise on their feet and then fall in a heap and lie very still. Surely Fritz wasn't killing these unfortunate men. Shells whistled over my head and dropped amongst the poor fellows, blowing dead men into the air and putting others out of their agony. As I gazed on this awful scene and realised my own terrible danger I asked God to help me. I did not know if the others had reached the German line or not and if Englishmen or Germans were in front of me, and to venture to look might mean certain death.

Now I seemed to have time to think. I suddenly remembered that I had water and was thirsty, and taking my water bottle from its carrier I rolled over on my back and drank. I also thought of the biscuits in my haversack but I was not feeling hungry somehow. I would have loved a smoke but one puff of smoke floating out of my shallow shell-hole might have brought a dozen German bombs in my direction for I was only a few yards from Fritz's line, if he still held it.

Then I began to try and decide my next move. God help me if Fritz decided to counter-attack; our artillery, in shelling Fritz, would blow me to bits, and if I escaped that Fritz would find me there, and would he trouble to take me prisoner or give me a bullet, or, even worse, the bayonet? If only darkness would come, then I could move, but it was still only morning on a summer's day and darkness was a long way off.

Over to the right I could see where our neighbouring battalion, The Royal Fusiliers, had gone over the top. Suddenly I noticed a few of them running for their lives back to their front line. This made me think that Fritz was counter-attacking and I fully expected to hear him coming at the double for my shell-hole. Sudden fear must have spurred me to action, for in a flash I sprang out of my shell-hole and dashed madly for the sunken road, flinging myself into it as Fritz's bullets whistled all about me, and almost jumping on to two of our men who were busy making a firing step in the side of the road.

The Somme 1916:
A treasure hunt in No Man's Land

Sidney Rogerson [from *Twelve Days*, London, 1933]

Sidney Rogerson (1894–1968) was commissioned in the West Yorkshire Regiment and served on the Western Front from 1916 to the end of the War, afterwards enjoying a distinguished career in public relations. He was also an ornithologist and artist. His book *Propaganda in the Next War* (1938) drew on his expertise in warfare, art and the media, and impressed Churchill among others with its somewhat Machiavellian tone and espousal of black propaganda.

But *Twelve Days* (1933) and *The Last of the Ebb* (1937) were his finest works, the former a classic account of 12 uneventful but typical days in the front line. In his foreword Rogerson wrote –

> *'This narrative... embraces no action that history is likely to deem worth recording; no epic fact of attack or defence. It deals with the 'fag-end' of the Battles of the Somme in 1916, and concerns merely the uneventful part of one Battalion in one sector – one among several hundred Battalions.'*

It describes the everyday experiences – dirt, fear, fatigue – of the man in the trenches.

Corporal Robinson's first request to me on my return to headquarters was to be allowed to go out and resume the treasure hunt which had been so rudely interrupted the night previously. My reply was the same as before – that I would not see him go, and that he had to bring in the pay-books or other valuables of any British dead he might stumble across. With a very brisk, 'Very good, sir! Thank you, sir!' he scrambled out of the trench and disappeared into the murk.

About midnight Robinson reappeared, looking like some vendor of cheap jewellery at a fair. He was garlanded with watch-chains, and his pockets and haversack bulged with the haul of his gruesome search. He reported his return to me and added, 'You know that shell-hole with two dead Jerries in it where I had to shelter last night, sir? Well, there aren't two. It's the same Jerry, sir, only his head has been blown across the other side of the hole!'

This news he gave me with the cheerful air of one correcting a piece of false information, with no hint of either horror or disgust.

Forthwith he proceeded to spread out his trophies on the fire-step as if arranging a shop-counter, and hissed like a groom does when curry-combing a horse – for many of the exhibits belonged to owners long deceased – as he made an inventory of them. There were six or seven German watches complete with chains, two gold rings, an automatic pistol, several pocket-books, which were found to contain nothing more valuable than letters and some vulgar comic post-cards, two tins of 'rindfleisch' ('the poor b____'s iron rations,' commented Robinson), and a pair of gloves. As he sorted them out, he kept up a running commentary in the curious barrack slang he had picked up in Malta. I interrupted him to know what he had done about the English dead, whereupon he produced from his haversack about twenty pay-books, and other articles. He made to hand these over, but I bluntly reminded him that it was his affair entirely, and that he would have to take these out with him and hand them to the Quartermaster himself. I added, 'And I think it would be only decent of you to write to the relatives yourself.'

The sequel has a moral. Robinson did write to several wives and mothers only to get letters back asking, for example, if he could please forward our Jim's watch, or 'what became of the money my Albert had on him when he was killed.' I can swear that Robinson took nothing from those bodies except the pay-books, etc., which were the price he paid for his evening's 'scrounge.' My aim in making him do this was to establish the identity of the nameless corpses, many of whom would certainly be reported 'missing.' It was a dirty and dangerous task to set a man to do – C and D Companies had on both nights sent out burying parties which had accomplished little, since the men on them had been too sick to dig! – and as it proved, a thankless one. The requests from relatives received by Robinson showed clearly how little idea they had of the circumstances in which the identity of their lost loved ones was established – hurriedly, and under shell-fire, by a corporal grubbing about in the darkness for souvenirs.

Death on a trench raid

Frederic Manning
[from *Her Privates We,* first published as
The Middle Parts to Fortune, 1929]

Frederic Manning (1882–1935) was a wealthy Australian by birth but educated in England. He joined the King's Shropshire Light Infantry in early 1916 and was sent to Oxford for officer training but never completed the course. He went to France as a private and was immediately plunged into the Battle of the Somme. His war lasted just over four months and it is this that provides the background for *Her Privates We*. In the preface Manning explains that it is 'a record of experience on the Somme and Ancre fronts, with an interval behind the lines, during the latter half of the year 1916; and the events described in it actually happened; the characters are fictitious'.

Arnold Bennett and Ernest Hemingway, who re-read it every year, both thought it the finest of war novels. T. E. Lawrence and Ezra Pound praised it lavishly. It is rare to have such a literary work written from the perspective of a private by a highly educated and sensitive man. The novel was first published in England in 1929 as *The Middle Parts to Fortune* with no author's name on the title page. Only 520 copies were privately printed because of the 'direct' language. A year later a bowdlerised trade edition appeared as written by 'Private 19022'. Manning appeared as author only in 1943.

———◆◆×◆●———

THE PARTY UNDER MR CROSS had made a slight encircling movement, and then, after creeping forward until within striking distance, rushed the trench. As the sentry turned, one of the maces crashed into his temple, and another man finished him with a bayonet. There were two other Huns in the same bay, and one had his arm broken with a mace, and screamed. Simultaneously the dug-out was bombed, and a couple of men hurled themselves on the third Hun, a Prussian sergeant, who put up a fight, but was overmastered, and lifted, booted, hustled out of the trench. They killed any survivors in the dug-out, and another Prussian had been killed in the next bay. While they were forcing the sergeant and the man with the broken arm towards the wire, they heard Weeper and Bourne bombing the machine-gun post, and Mr Cross blow his whistle. Almost immediately a star-shell went up, and there was some blind desultory rifle fire. They had got their men through the wire. Suddenly the Hun sergeant, with a desperate effort, wrenched himself free, and faced them with lifted hand:

'*Halte!*' he shouted, and flung himself on Sergeant Morgan. They went down together. Mr Cross fired, and fortunately killed the Prussian.

'I hope you'll never do that again, sir!' said Sergeant Morgan, rising.

'Get his helmet off.'

The chain was tight in the thick fat under the chin. Taking his bayonet, the sergeant tried to prise it off, and cut through all the soft part of the neck so that the head fell back. The helmet came away in the end, and they pushed on, with their other moaning prisoner.

Weeper was ahead when he and Bourne reached the gap in the wire. Star-shell after star-shell was going up now, and the whole line had woken up. Machine-guns were talking; but there was one that would not talk. The rattle of musketry continued, but the mist was kindly to them, and had thickened again. As they got beyond the trammelling, clutching wire, Bourne saw Weeper a couple of paces ahead of him, and what he thought was the last of their party disappearing into the mist about twenty yards away. He was glad to be clear of the wire. Another star-shell went up, and they both froze into stillness under its glare. Then they moved again, hurrying for all they were worth. Bourne felt a sense of triumph and escape thrill in him. Anyway the Hun couldn't see them now. Something kicked him in the upper part of the chest, rending its way through him, and his agonised cry was scarcely audible in the rush of blood from his mouth, as he collapsed and fell.

Weeper turned his head over his shoulder, listened, stopped, and went back. He found Bourne trying to lift himself; and Bourne spoke, gasping, suffocating.

'Go on. I'm scuppered.'

'A'll not leave thee,' said Weeper.

He stooped and lifted the other in his huge, ungainly arms, carrying him as tenderly as though he were a child. Bourne struggled wearily to speak, and the blood, filling his mouth, prevented him. Sometimes his head fell on Weeper's shoulder. At last, barely articulate, a few words came.

'I'm finished. Le' me in peace, for God's sake. You can't...'

'A'll not leave thee,' said Weeper in an infuriate rage.

He felt Bourne stretch himself in a convulsive shudder, and relax, becoming suddenly heavier in his arms. He struggled on, stumbling over the shell-ploughed ground through that fantastic mist, which moved like an army of wraiths, hurrying away from him. Then he stopped, and, taking the body by the waist with his left arm, flung it over his shoulder, steadying it with his right. He could see their wire now, and presently he was challenged, and replied. He found the way through the wire, and staggered into the trench with his burden. Then he turned down the short stretch of Delauney to Monk Trench, and came on the rest of the party outside A Company's dug-out.

'A've brought 'im back,' he cried desperately, and collapsed with the body on the duck-boards. Picking himself up again, he told his story incoherently, mixed with raving curses.

'What are you gibbering about?' said Sergeant Morgan. "aven't you ever seen a dead man before?'

Sergeant-Major Tozer, who was standing outside the dug-out, looked at Morgan with a dangerous eye. Then he put a hand on Weeper's shoulder.

'Go down an' get some 'ot tea and rum, ol' man. That'll do you good. I'd like to 'ave a talk with you when you're feelin' better.'

'We had better move-on, Sergeant,' said Mr Cross, quietly.

'Very good, sir.'

The party moved off, and for a moment Sergeant-Major Tozer was alone in the trench with Sergeant Morgan.

'I saw him this side of their wire, Sergeant-Major, and thought everything would be all right. 'pon, my word, I would 'ave gone back for 'im myself, if I'd known.'

'It was hard luck,' said Sergeant-Major Tozer with a quiet fatalism.

Sergeant Morgan left him; and the Sergeant-Major looked at the dead body propped against the side of the trench. He would have to have it moved; it wasn't a pleasant sight, and he bared his teeth in the pitiful repulsion with which it filled him. Bourne was sitting: his head back, his face plastered with mud, and blood drying thickly about his mouth and chin, while the glazed eyes stared up at the moon. Tozer moved away, with a quiet acceptance of the fact. It was finished. He was sorry about Bourne, he thought, more sorry than he could say. He was a queer chap, he said to himself, as he felt for the dug-out steps. There was a bit of a mystery about him; but then, when you come to think of it, there's a bit of a mystery about all of us. He pushed aside the blanket screening the entrance, and in the murky light he saw all the men lift their faces, and look at him with patient, almost animal eyes.

Then they all bowed over their own thoughts again, listening to the shells bumping heavily outside, as Fritz began to send a lot of stuff over in retaliation for the raid. They sat there silently; each man keeping his own secret.

Pill Box

Edmund Blunden

Edmund Blunden (1896–1974) was born in London but raised in Yalding in Kent. He served throughout the First World War in the Royal Sussex Regiment, having enlisted in 1915. He fought at both Ypres and the Somme, winning an MC. His famous, restrained memoir of trench life, *Undertones of War*, was published in 1928. The book laments the loss of optimism and betrayal of promise the war wrought, but finds solace and hope in the natural landscape. Passchendaele he calls 'murder, not only to the troops, but to their singing faiths and hopes'. It is a tale of endurance, heroism and despair. He became a great friend of Sassoon, who shared his passion for English rural life and the countryside of Kent, and championed his poetry. According to Sassoon's most recent biographer, theirs was the most enduring of all the friendships between war poets. Sassoon thought Blunden the most deeply affected by the War.

'Pill Box' refers to an incident during the Battle of the Somme on 3 September 1916, when Blunden's battalion of the 11th Royal Sussex were part of the 39th Division attack towards Beaumont Hamel from almost the same start line as 1 July. Blunden's men were employed bringing up buckets of Mills bombs, a type of grenade, for troops defending captured trenches. The pill box was a German one and thus its entrance pointed the wrong way, i.e. towards the German

lines. One of the men who lost his life in this engagement was Sgt.
F. A. Hoad. The attack failed and they were forced to leave Hoad's
body behind. He is commemorated on the Thiepval Memorial.

Just see what's happening, Worley. – Worley rose
And round the angled doorway thrust his nose,
And Sergeant Hoad went, too, to snuff the air.
Then war brought down his fist, and missed the pair!
Yet Hoad was scratched by a splinter, the blood came,
And out burst terrors that he'd striven to tame,
A good man, Hoad, for weeks. I'm blown to bits.
He groans, he screams. Come, Bluffer, where's your wits?
Says Worley. Bluffer, you've a blighty, man!
All in the pillbox urged him, here began
His freedom: Think of Eastbourne and your dad.
The poor man lay at length and brief and mad
Flung out his cry of doom; soon ebbed and dumb
He yielded. Worley with a tot of rum
And shouting in his face could not restore him.
The ship of Charon over channel bore him.
All marvelled even on that most deathly day
To see this life so spirited away.

'A formal execution': Arabia 1917
T. E. Lawrence (Lawrence of Arabia)
[from *Seven Pillars of Wisdom,* London, 1926]

Seven Pillars of Wisdom is Lawrence's account of his 1916–1918 Arab
campaign. Turkey was allied to Germany, and Britain needed a proxy
force of Arab fighters to defend its flank in Palestine. Britain was also
bent on knocking Turkey out of the war. There was a theory that if
Germany's props were defeated then Germany would collapse; but
others saw that Germany was propping up Turkey, not the other
way round, and that there was no cheap backdoor strategy which
would win the war; Germany's army had to be beaten in the field.

Thomas Edward Lawrence (1888–1935), an Oxford educated
archaeologist of Anglo-Irish stock, was familiar with Arab customs
and languages, having excavated extensively in the Middle East
before the war. In 1914 he joined the Intelligence branch of the
Arab Bureau in Cairo, monitoring Arab nationalism, and was
commissioned after the army lowered height restrictions. He
was sent to liaise with the leader of the Arab Revolt, Feisal Ibn
Hussein. They forged an immediate bond. Fertile Anglo-Arab
communication led to an effective alliance and together they seized
the Red Sea port of Aqaba, by land and on camels, and mounted
an increasingly successful guerrilla war against Turkish bridges and
railways, of great assistance to the British General Allenby in his
victorious Palestine campaign.

Lawrence did not change the map of Arabia – the spheres of influence had been drawn up secretly between Britain and France in the 1916 Sykes-Picot Agreement. Nevertheless he was ideologically committed to Arab self-rule and independence, promoting Arab regimes in captured towns like Dera, against stiff British local opposition. At the Paris Peace Conference, where he was Feisal's advisor and strutted about in full Arab dress, his pledges to Arab leaders about independence were thwarted by the extension of imperial control over much of the former Turkish empire. Vain, complex, deeply affected by his illegitimacy and – after Paris – bitter, he never recovered from his wartime experience.

Seven Pillars was printed privately (1926) and sold by subscription, but only published in full after his death following a motorcycle accident near his cottage, Clouds Hill, in Dorset. Lawrence's stated ambition had been to write a *Moby Dick* or *Brothers Karamazov*, although he wrote to Robert Graves in 1922, 'The thing was not written for anyone to read'. Historians are divided about the book, some regarding it as an historical novel with the author as semi-fictional hero; others – like Lawrence's authorised biographer Jeremy Wilson – consider it 'extremely accurate, historically' but incomplete. Wilson concedes he had 'a talent for self-invention' but calls the book 'true in essence', perhaps wrong in detail. An enigma, Lawrence actually plays down some things he did, while exaggerating others. Part of his wartime posturing was deliberate – he understood the psychological impact of a hero-figure on contemporary Arab culture. *Seven Pillars* may or may not be reliable history but as literature it remains a classic.

MY FOLLOWERS had been quarrelling all day; and while I was lying near the rocks a shot was fired. I paid no attention; for there were hares and birds in the valley; but a little later Suleiman roused me and made me follow him across the valley to an opposite bay in the rocks, where one of the Ageyl, a Boreida man, was lying stone dead with a bullet through his temples. The shot must have been fired from close by; because the skin was burnt about one wound. The remaining Ageyl were running frantically about; and when I asked what it was Ali, their head man, said that Hamed the Moor had done the murder. I suspected Suleiman, because of the feud between the Atban and Ageyl which had burned up in Yenbo and Wejh; but Ali assured me that Suleiman had been with him three hundred yards further up the valley gathering sticks when the shot was fired. I sent all out to search for Hamed, and crawled back to the baggage, feeling that it need not have happened this day of all days when I was in pain.

As I lay there I heard a rustle, and opened my eyes slowly upon Hamed's back as he stooped over his saddle-bags, which lay just beyond my rock. I covered him with a pistol and then spoke. He had put down his rifle to lift the gear; and was at my mercy till the others came. We held a court at once, and after a while Hamed confessed that, he and Salem having had words, he had seen red and shot him suddenly. Our inquiry ended. The Ageyl, as relatives of the dead man, demanded blood for blood. The others supported them; and I tried vainly to talk the gentle Ali round. My head was aching with fever and I could not think; but hardly even in health, with all eloquence, could I have begged Hamed off; for Salem had been a friendly fellow and his sudden murder a wanton crime.

Then rose up the horror which would make civilised man shun justice like a plague if he had not the needy to serve him as hangmen for wages. There were other Moroccans in our army; and let the Ageyl kill one if feud meant reprisals by which our unity would have been endangered. It must be a formal execution, and at last, desperately, I told Hamed that he must die for punishment, and laid the burden of his killing on myself. Perhaps they would count me not qualified for feud. At least no revenge could lie against my followers; for I was a stranger and kinless.

I made him enter a narrow gully of the spur, a dank twilight place overgrown with weeds. Its sandy bed had been pitted by trickles of water down the cliffs in the late rain. At the end it shrank to a crack a few inches wide. The walls were vertical. I stood in the entrance and gave him a few moments' delay which he spent crying on the ground. Then I made him rise and shot him through the chest. He fell down on the weeds shrieking, with the blood coming out in spurts over his clothes, and jerked about till he rolled nearly to where I was. I fired again, but was shaking so that I only broke his wrist. He went on calling out, less loudly, now lying on his back with his feet towards me, and I leant forward and shot him for the last time in the thick of his neck under the jaw. His body shivered a little, and I called the Ageyl; who buried him in the gully where he was. Afterwards the wakeful night dragged over me, till, hours before dawn, I had the men up and made them load, in my longing to be set free of Wadi Kitan. They had to lift me into the saddle.

Strange Meeting
Wilfred Owen

Wilfred Owen (1893–1918) was born in Oswestry, Shropshire. When war broke out in 1914 Owen was a private tutor in Bordeaux, and was much influenced by modern French poetry. In 1915 he enlisted in the Artists' Rifles but was commissioned in the Manchester Regiment. He served on the Western Front from January to June 1917 when his nerves collapsed. The breakdown began when he fell into a cellar through a hole in the floor, hitting his head. He was there for two days. He was rescued but shortly afterwards he was heavily shelled in a railway cutting; a brother officer's body was splattered all over him. His CO later noticed he was shaking, stammering and behaving oddly. He was taken to a first aid post where he was diagnosed as shell-shocked.

He was sent to Craiglockhart War Hospital near Edinburgh. There he met Siegfried Sassoon, whom he revered. Sassoon introduced him to Robert Graves. Graves wrote of Owen that he was 'a real find, not a sudden lo here! or lo there!... but the real thing, when we've educated him a trifle more'.

Owen was killed on the Oise-Sambre Canal on 4 November 1918, leading his men in a vain attempt to cross the canal while under heavy enemy fire. A visit to this place is to see an almost physical metaphor of 'Futility'; for a crossing under fire from hills opposite appears well-nigh impossible. A successful crossing was made later a mile or so away. He is buried nearby in the village cemetery at Ors. A week after he was killed, on the day the Armistice was signed, his mother received the telegram while church bells rang deliriously.

It seemed that out of battle I escaped
Down some profound dull tunnel, long since scooped
Through granites which titanic wars had groined.
Yet also there encumbered sleepers groaned,
Too fast in thought or death to be bestirred.
Then, as I probed them, one sprang up, and stared
With piteous recognition in fixed eyes,
Lifting distressful hands, as if to bless.
And by his smile, I knew that sullen hall, –
By his dead smile I knew we stood in Hell.
With a thousand pains that vision's face was grained;
Yet no blood reached there from the upper ground,
And no guns thumped, or down the flues made moan.
'Strange friend,' I said, 'here is no cause to mourn.'
'None,' said that other, 'save the undone years,
The hopelessness. Whatever hope is yours,
Was my life also; I went hunting wild
After the wildest beauty in the world,
Which lies not calm in eyes, or braided hair,
But mocks the steady running of the hour,
And if it grieves, grieves richlier than here.
For by my glee might many men have laughed,
And of my weeping something had been left,
Which must die now. I mean the truth untold,
The pity of war, the pity war distilled.
Now men will go content with what we spoiled,
Or, discontent, boil bloody, and be spilled.

They will be swift with swiftness of the tigress.
None will break ranks, though nations trek from
progress.
Courage was mine, and I had mystery,
Wisdom was mine, and I had mastery:
To miss the march of this retreating world
Into vain citadels that are not walled.
Then, when much blood had clogged their chariot-
wheels,
I would go up and wash them from sweet wells
Even with truths that lie too deep for taint.
I would have poured my spirit without stint
But not through wounds; not on the cess of war.
Foreheads of men have bled where no wounds were.
'I am the enemy you killed, my friend.
I knew you in this dark: for so you frowned
Yesterday through me as you jabbed and killed.
I parried; but my hands were loath and cold.
Let us sleep now…'

Futility

Wilfred Owen

Move him into the sun
Gently its touch awoke him once,
At home, whispering of fields unsown.
Always it woke him, even in France,
Until this morning and this snow.
If anything might rouse him now
The kind old sun will know.

Think how it wakes the seeds,
Woke, once, the clays of a cold star.
Are limbs, so dear-achieved, are sides
Full-nerved – still warm, – too hard to stir?
Was it for this the clay grew tall?
O what made fatuous sunbeams toil
To break earth's sleep at all?

Anthem For Doomed Youth

Wilfred Owen

What passing-bells for these who die as cattle?
Only the monstrous anger of the guns.
Only the stuttering rifles' rapid rattle
Can patter out their hasty orisons.
No mockeries now for them; no prayers nor bells;
Nor any voice of mourning save the choirs, –
The shrill, demented choirs of wailing shells;
And bugles calling for them from sad shires.
What candles may be held to speed them all?
Not in the hands of boys but in their eyes
Shall shine the holy glimmers of goodbyes.
The pallor of girls' brows shall be their pall;
Their flowers the tenderness of patient minds,
And each slow dusk a drawing-down of blinds.

Shute

A. P. Herbert

A. P. Herbert (1890–1971), MP, barrister, novelist, tireless advocate for good English, was above all a humourist. Herbert fought with the 63rd (Royal Naval) Division in the Great War. After Gallipoli, the Division moved to France where it took part in the later stages of the first Battle of the Somme. In October 1916 a new CO was appointed, Major-General Shute. He commanded the RND until February 1917, a grim four months for all who served under him, as he regarded the Division's nautical traditions as unsoldierly and grotesque. He became known as 'Shultz the Hun' for his insistence on 'spit and polish'.

He inspected the trenches when the Division took over a sector at Souchez (near Arras) from the Portuguese. The trenches were a mess, but the sailors had no time to tidy and clean before Shute turned up. He was appalled, and sent a critical report to Corps about the filth. Herbert's poem was turned into a song, sung by the entire BEF to the tune of 'Wrap me up in my tarpaulin jacket'.

Major-General 'Tiger' Shute was transferred by the C-in-C to the 32nd Division following his unjustified disciplinary measures imposed on the reservist sailors of the 63rd. He did well and was promoted to command V Corps, which performed admirably in late 1918 on the Somme and Canal du Nord.

A. P. Herbert successfully prosecuted an RND deserter in 1918, and the man was sentenced to death (later commuted); whereas Lieutenant-General Shute commuted an Able Seaman's death sentence on the grounds that he was suffering from 'nervous shock'. So Shute was not a complete shit. But that is forgotten – his epitaph, unfortunately, is this vulgar, witty poem.

The General inspecting the trenches
Exclaimed with a horrified shout
'I refuse to command a division
Which leaves its excreta about.'

But nobody took any notice
No one was prepared to refute,
That the presence of shit was congenial
Compared to the presence of Shute.

And certain responsible critics
Made haste to reply to his words
Observing that his staff advisors
Consisted entirely of turds.

For shit may be shot at odd corners
And paper supplied there to suit,
But a shit would be shot without mourners
If someone shot that shit Shute.

Threat of a German Attack, 1918

Sidney Rogerson
[from *Last of the Ebb*, London and Edinburgh, 1937]

The Last of the Ebb is Rogerson's memorable account of the German offensive on the Aisne, near Reims, in May 1918. His 8th Division had been sent to a 'quiet sector' to recover from being 'terribly shattered' in March and April on the Somme and at Villers Bretonneux, where the German March 1918 offensive was halted. He described his fortnight's fighting on the Aisne as 'very strenuous' but 'cheery', which sums up his selfless resilience.

A day later the Intelligence Officer of the 24th Brigade reported the presence of a number of black boards between the German trenches. These could only be the direction boards known to be used for the guidance of tanks or heavy transport.

Then from the French on the left came the final blow. News that a great enemy attack was impending was elicited from three members of a German patrol captured on the Chemin des Dames. On further special examination, the prisoners confessed that this would open at midnight, 26–27 May, by German time.

The first news of this reached us about 3.45 pm on 26 May. In a shallow trench outside the mess dug-out, Millis and I were stretching ourselves in the sun. A signaller came up and handed Millis the little pink telephone slip. He read it and without a word passed it to me. 'The enemy will attack on a wide front at 01.00 hours tomorrow, 27th inst.: A.A.A.' – then followed orders for taking up battle stations.

For a second we looked at each other in silence. In a flash the whole world had changed. The landscape around us smiled no longer. It was all a grinning reality, a mockery designed to raise our hopes so that they could be shattered the more pitilessly. The sun still blazed down but it had lost its heat. Millis said something like 'Oh, well, it can't be helped. We're for it again,' and went off to break the news to the General.

So the blow had fallen. For the third time we were to bear the brunt of an enemy offensive. Surely we who had suffered so much already might have been spared this! It was too much to hope that those of us who had come through so far would again escape. The mercy was that we had little time to indulge in self-pity. Everything was haste and energy. Moments were of importance. Much has to be done before zero hour; the biggest single item being to reconnoitre dug-out accommodation for the 2nd Devons, who would form the garrison of the reserve or battle line which ran on a level with the Bois des Buttes. This task was left to Ledward and me and a hot and tiring one it was, involving much climbing of crazy stairs and hurrying, bent double, along low corridors. We were staggered at the size and extent of this underground village, and more than once lost our way. The Devons had never seen the position or been in the tunnels, and as they would only arrive after dark we dared not imagine how they were likely to fare.

About 6.30pm there arrived from French Army Headquarters a signal officer to inspect communications in the Brigade area. He was informed that our signal officer, Prance, was busy up the line supervising arrangements for the morrow's attack. This was apparently the first intimation that the Frenchman had had of the impending offensive, but the news merely caused a smile. What, the enemy attack? Nonsense, they had been *going* to attack for four months on this front, but of course everyone knew they never would. 'Ils sont plus sages que ça. On ne passerait jamais ici.' [They are too wise for that. They would never come here.] It is more than probable that he left Bois des Buttes convinced that the English were very 'windy'.

His departure coincided with the arrival of the officer in charge of the French 'mitrailleuses de position,' heavy Etienne machine-guns which had been left as an additional garrison to the line. None of us knew their locations, but the grey haired old French captain called to the place himself under British command and assure the British general of his unswerving obedience – a pleasant interlude, reminiscent of more chivalrous days, at a time when chivalry was at a discount.

It was a splendid evening, and as the sun waned and we stood on our hillock waiting for dinner we looked down on the scene around us, across the green shrubbery where the smoke from the Middlesex cook-houses rose in thin blue pillars through the still air, and over to the trees and reeds that marked the course of the Aisne river. It was all so peaceful and so vibrant with life, yet by tomorrow's light what would have happened? High overhead, mere black spots in the soft amber haze were two German planes quartering the ground like hovering kestrels and noting the every movement of the tiny mice below. Not a gun fired at them, nor friendly aeroplane went to drive them off, for the French, it seemed, had neither 'Archies' [anti-aircraft guns] nor aircraft available.

For the first time in the war I had the feeling that there was no one behind us, no help which could be relied upon in case of need to stem a breach or retake a vital point.

Dinner was not an enjoyable meal, and as soon at it was over the more prudent, or the more pessimistic, as it then seemed, set to work to pack up everything not absolutely necessary. I was one who had a horror of being caught short of minor necessities, so carefully crammed into a pack a spare pair of boots and socks, a shirt, vest, tin of cigarettes, matches, and a bottle of whisky. I got definite satisfaction out of this, as I felt that somehow it was the only preparation it lay in my power to make against any eventuality the next morning might bring, and it was not till months later that I realised how futile it must have appeared in the eyes of Heaven – as well might I have buttoned my overcoat to ward off the lightening! Most of the others took a more sanguine or more fatalistic view and did not bother. This cost General Grogan a beautiful brand-new uniform and many items of out-of-the-trenches apparel that he had had sent up to the Bois des Buttes preparatory to going on short leave to Paris!

A message came in about 9 o'clock giving the names of a number of men who had been sent up that night to rejoin their units from hospital, leave, or other duties. Among these was my servant, Private Briggs, posted back to the West Yorkshires from hospital. He had been with me since October 1916, but had gone sick early in March, and I had temporarily taken on the venerable Mr Parkin, my one-time cook, in his place. It would happen, I thought, that Briggs should have been sent to the regiment direct on the eve of a battle, when I had no chance of applying for him back again! It was fifteen years before I was to see him again.

Meanwhile it was growing dark. The transport arrived early, bringing rations and ammunition and taking away any surplus kit that was ready to be moved, but they did not tarry long. The Devons began moving into their tunnels. With the coming of night, an uncanny silence settled over the countryside, a silence such as can only prevail in crowded places. About nine o'clock 'harassing' fire was opened on enemy communications and assembly points. All along our line the batteries gave tongue, the sharp bang of eighteen-pounders mingling with the hoarse reports of the field howitzers. Behind the river the few old French 'heavies,' regular museum pieces, coughed asthmatically now and again, while the intermittent dry rattle of machine-guns came as a staccato punctuation. Still, the feeling of silence persisted. Not a gun was fired by the enemy, and his quietness dispelled any last lingering hopes we might have cherished. How that evening dragged! The minutes crept slowly towards zero hour. I had gone into the mess to inquire from Johns, our imperturbable mess-corporal, whether he was all packed-up ready to move if necessary. I took a whisky-and-soda and was standing talking to him when suddenly whizz – plop! whizz – plop! Two German gas shells burst close at hand, punctual heralds of the storm. Within a second a thousand guns roared out their iron hurricane. The night was rent with sheets of flame. The earth shuddered under the avalanche of missiles: leapt skywards in dust and tumult.

Ever above the din screamed the fierce crescendo of approaching shells, ear-splitting crashes as they burst: all the time the dull thud, thud, thud of detonations – drumfire… Inferno raged and whirled round the Bois des Buttes. The dug-outs rocked, filled with the acrid fumes of cordite, the sickly-sweet tang of gas. Timbers started. Earth showered from the roof. Men rushed for shelter, seizing kits, weapons, gas-masks, message-pads as they dived to safety. It was a descent into hell. Crowded with jostling, sweating humanity, the deep dug-outs reeked, and to make matters worse, we had no sooner got below than gas began to filter down. Gas-masks were hurriedly donned and anti-gas precautions taken – the entrances closed by saturated blankets, braziers lighted on the stairs. If gas could not enter, neither could air – though the fact was that in small quantities both did. Mercifully that night was short in time however long it seemed, otherwise we could not have endured, crammed as we were into stinking, overcrowded holes, forty feet below ground, all the entrances sealed up and charcoal braziers burning, heaving to get a breath of oxygen through the gas-mask with its clip on nostrils and its gag between teeth. At first my heart thumped and my head swam distressingly, but I found if I kept still I could just bear it.

Down below the clamour of the barrage was muted, but even so far underground the walls shivered every few minutes as a heavy shell burst directly overhead. The Brigadier, Millis, Ledward, Prance and I were together, Thompson having already gone to his observation post. Prance's signallers at once made contact with the battalions and the flank brigades – 149th on the left and 24th on the right – both by 'phone and wire. The other Brigade Headquarters were undergoing experiences like our own, but the West Yorkshires reported cheerily, 'We're all right. You're getting the worst of it. It's going over us' – then the line went dead, and we heard no more from the front line battalion. The Middlesex, close to us, were being terribly pounded, though they were reasonably safe so long as they kept below ground. Up to then the gunners had come off worst. The first surge of the barrage had overwhelmed them, the 24th Brigade's (Ballard) emplacements having been so accurately registered that after half an hour they had only one gun left in action.

These and other messages from 8th Division reached us as we sat huddled up on the frame beds round the dug-out walls. Prance had soon grown restless and, clapping on his helmet, had gone out to be with his men who were working to keep the wires intact. He would not take an orderly, saying he felt happier without one – a point of view I could not understand. The Brigadier was also, very naturally restless. He too would have preferred it be out and alone in danger, rather than cooped up, inactive but in safety, but his place was for the moment at the end of the telephone. Millis was calmness itself, and I was too nearly stifled and too busy to feel more than usually fearful. I had been given the job of keeping a diary of the action, to include every outgoing and incoming message. This had been declared necessary because the absence of such records in the two earlier offensives had made it impossible to trace the sequence of events of even to tell what had happened. So I wrote messages at Millis's dictation, and passed them to Signals, keeping a copy for myself. Similarly I collected every incoming message, whether verbal or Morse.

Dawn began to break outside, but no news reached us that the enemy had yet attacked. Thompson reported that a very heavy ground mist, joined with the smoke and dust of the bombardment, made observation impossible over a few yards. The thump! – thud! – thump! – thud! overhead told us the barrage continued. Perhaps the Germans were not going to attack on our front after all! Vain hope! Not five minutes after his first statement Thompson sent the amazing message: 'Can see enemy balloons rising from our front line!' Hot upon this came another from the 24th Brigade on our right: 'Enemy advancing up Miette stream. Close to Brigade Headquarters. Cannot hold out without reinforcements.' Such news was startling enough, but worse was yet to come, and shortly afterwards – at about 5.30am – the left flank brigade, 149th reported, 'Enemy has broken our battle-line and is advancing on Ville au Bois.'

'With our backs to the wall': SPECIAL ORDER OF THE DAY

Field Marshal Sir Douglas Haig,
Western Front, 11 April 1918

Field Marshal Sir Douglas Haig, later Earl Haig (1861–1928), commanded the BEF from December 1915 to November 1918. Not averse to new ideas like tanks, he was however stubborn, inarticulate and too ready to believe his own propaganda that the enemy was on the point of collapse. He persisted with the Somme and Passchendaele battles long after the ground and weather made offensive operations futile. Of Haig's refusal to abort the misery of Passchendaele, Leon Wolff wrote (*In Flanders Fields*, New York, 1958):

> *'The element of surprise was irretrievably gone. Haig's own generals wanted him to stop… The morale of his own armies was sinking into the swamps of the Salient. What Haig hoped to achieve… and what he was trying to prove, are perhaps questions more appropriate to a psychiatrist than to the student of military history.'*

Haig's apologists argue that he had no alternative. He could not stay put 'along a very bad line' for the winter (admitted Wolff), could not 'retreat to a decent one' for political reasons, so had to slog up to the higher ground of the Ridge. Haig had boxed himself into this corner by his ambitious goal of sweeping to the coast, and not making the temporary halt of 28 August permanent (the attack resumed on 20 September). Yet he won the victories of 1918 with sound staff work and all-arms co-ordination, though at a cost. He was an inveterate intriguer, having had a quiet word with his friend King George V about Sir John French, Haig's predecessor as BEF commander, and French's fatal failure to rush up reserves at Loos (1915). He loathed Prime Minister Lloyd George (1863–1945) for his duplicity, not without reason, disliked politicians generally, and scorned French excitability. 'All would be so easy if I only had to deal with the Germans!' he confided to his diary.

The *Special Order of the Day* (a regular bulletin read out to all troops) was greeted with some cynicism – a corporal of the East Surreys would have welcomed 'anything as solid as a wall behind us. So far as we could see, all there was behind us was a diminishing bit of France and the cold, wet channel.' The German offensive of 21 March was made possible by divisions released from the East, and its timing was prompted by the imminent arrival of the Americans in force. Lloyd George, unimpressed with Haig's butcher's bill, starved him of troops; Haig thus had to weaken his line somewhere. He chose the 40-mile front that abutted the French, partly because he considered 12 miles 'impassable' to the Germans due to the obstacles of the River Oise and its marshes. He was wrong, due to an unusually dry winter. He also anticipated, again wrongly, that the French might extend their line into the weakened sector. Nevertheless he felt confident that his 'defence in depth' would prevail and even welcomed a German attack. In the face of whirlwind barrages, German storm-troopers and fog, Gough's Fifth Army was routed.

FIELD MARSHAL SIR DOUGLAS HAIG

SPECIAL ORDER OF THE DAY

By FIELD MARSHAL SIR DOUGLAS HAIG
K.T., G.C.B., G.C.V.O., K.C.I.E.
Commander-in-Chief, British Armies in France

To ALL RANKS OF THE BRITISH ARMY IN FRANCE AND FLANDERS

THREE WEEKS ago to-day the enemy began his terrific attacks against us on a fifty-mile front. His objects are to separate us from the French, to take the Channel Ports and destroy the British Army.

In spite of throwing already 106 Divisions into the battle and enduring the most reckless sacrifice of human life, he has as yet made little progress towards his goals.

We owe this to the determined fighting and self-sacrifice of our troops. Words fail me to express the admiration which I feel for the splendid resistance offered by all ranks of our Army under the most trying circumstances.

Many amongst us now are tired. To those I would say that Victory will belong to the side which holds out the longest. The French Army is moving rapidly and in great force to our support.

There is no other course open to us but to fight it out. Every position must be held to the last man: there must be no retirement. With our backs to the wall and believing in the justice of our cause each one of us must fight on to the end. The safety of our homes and the Freedom of mankind alike depend upon the conduct of each one of us at this critical moment.

(Signed) D. Haig F.M.
Commander-in-Chief
British Armies in France
General Headquarters
Tuesday, April 11th, 1918

Attack

Siegfried Sassoon

Siegfried Sassoon (1886–1967) was born in rural Kent. After Cambridge, which he left without taking a degree, Sassoon lived a careless sporting life, hunting, riding in point-to-points and playing cricket until the outbreak of war.

Sassoon was a minor poet before the War. The suffering and kinship of the trenches provoked a sense of outrage and an outpouring of bitter, unpretentious verse that became much admired for its directness and satirical lampooning of 'scarlet majors'. Sassoon served with the Royal Welch Fusiliers on the Western Front and briefly in Mesopotamia. He was particularly affected by his brother Hamo's death at Gallipoli and, in early 1916, by his friend 'Tommy' Thomas's death ('Dick Tiltwood' of *Memoirs of a Fox-hunting Man*) on the Somme. He determined to 'get his revenge' on the Germans. He became recklessly bold, careless of his life, patrolling No Man's Land on his own initiative. He earned the nickname 'Mad Jack'. He won an MC for bringing in a wounded Lance-Corporal lying close to the German lines, under heavy fire. He was fortunate to be in reserve on 1 July 1916, the disastrous first day of the Battle of the Somme, when the British dead numbered 20,000. On 4 July he calmly read a copy of *The London Mail* before going over the top opposite Fricourt. During the action, he single-handedly attacked a German trench by Mametz Wood where a sniper lurked, worked his way up it with hand grenades and was surprised to see about 60 Germans running 'hell for leather' into the Wood. He sat down and read a volume of poetry. Sassoon was recommended for a VC, but – typically – as the action itself was a failure he only received a bar to his Military Cross.

Sassoon was wounded in the shoulder during the Second Battle of the Scarpe in 1917. While convalescing in England he met prominent pacifists including Bertrand Russell. His 'Soldier's Declaration' of 'wilful defiance' was written during this time. Symbolically, and melodramatically, he threw his MC ribbon into the River Mersey, protesting that the war, originally one of defence and liberation, was now a war of conquest. He attacked 'the political errors and insincerities for which the fighting men are being sacrificed...' He expected a court martial and serious punishment but his friend and fellow Welch Fusilier, Robert Graves, unprompted, pulled strings. Sassoon was sent in late July to Craiglockhart War Hospital, Edinburgh, officially suffering from shell-shock, where he was both stimulated and influenced by long talks with the innovative psychiatrist Dr W. H. Rivers, and where he met and was a dominant influence on Wilfred Owen.

On 13 July 1918, back on the Western Front and now a Company Commander, his recklessness returned and together with a young corporal he attacked the German trenches opposite. He was wounded in the head and his war ended. 'Bombs' here means hand grenades, 'bombers' being men trained in their use. 'Five-nines' are German shells fired from one of four versions of their 15 cm (5.9 inches) Heavy Field Howitzer.

At dawn the ridge emerges massed and dun
In the wild purple of the glow'ring sun,
Smouldering through spouts of drifting smoke that shroud
The menacing scarred slope; and, one by one,
Tanks creep and topple forward to the wire.
The barrage roars and lifts. Then, clumsily bowed
With bombs and guns and shovels and battle-gear,
Men jostle and climb to meet the bristling fire.
Lines of grey, muttering faces, masked with fear,
They leave their trenches, going over the top,
While time ticks blank and busy on their wrists,
And hope, with furtive eyes and grappling fists,
Flounders in mud. O Jesus, make it stop!

Counter-Attack

Siegfried Sassoon

We'd gained our first objective hours before
While dawn broke like a face with blinking eyes,
Pallid, unshaved and thirsty, blind with smoke.
Things seemed all right at first. We held their line,
With bombers posted, Lewis guns well placed,
And clink of shovels deepening the shallow trench.
The place was rotten with dead; green clumsy legs
High-booted, sprawled and grovelled along the saps
And trunks, face downward, in the sucking mud,
Wallowed like trodden sand-bags loosely filled;
And naked sodden buttocks, mats of hair,
Bulged, clotted heads slept in the plastering slime.
And then the rain began, – the jolly old rain!
A yawning soldier knelt against the bank,
Staring across the morning blear with fog;
He wondered when the Allemands would get busy;
And then, of course, they started with five-nines
Traversing, sure as fate, and never a dud.
Mute in the clamour of shells he watched them burst
Spouting dark earth and wire with gusts from hell,

While posturing giants dissolved in drifts of smoke.
He crouched and flinched, dizzy with galloping fear,
Sick for escape, – loathing the strangled horror
And butchered, frantic gestures of the dead.
An officer came blundering down the trench:
'Stand-to and man the fire-step!' On he went…
Gasping and bawling, 'Fire- step… counter-attack!'
Then the haze lifted. Bombing on the right
Down the old sap: machine-guns on the left;
And stumbling figures looming out in front.
'O Christ, they're coming at us!' Bullets spat,
And he remembered his rifle… rapid fire…
And started blazing wildly… then a bang
Crumpled and spun him sideways, knocked him out
To grunt and wriggle: none heeded him; he choked
And fought the flapping veils of smothering gloom,
Lost in a blurred confusion of yells and groans…
Down, and down, and down, he sank and drowned,
Bleeding to death. The counter-attack had failed.

The Happy Warrior

Herbert Read

Herbert Read (1893–1968) served in France with the Green Howards, winning a DSO and MC. After the war he became an influential critic and art historian. His modernist poems were among the first bitter verses to appear. The poem below refers to Wordsworth's *The Character of the Happy Warrior*; it answers Wordsworth's questions –

'Who is the happy Warrior? Who is he
That every man in arms should wish to be?'

His wild heart beats with painful sobs,
His strin'd hands clench an ice-cold rifle,
His aching jaws grip a hot parch'd tongue,
His wide eyes search unconsciously.
He cannot shriek.
Bloody saliva
Dribbles down his shapeless jacket.
I saw him stab
And stab again

A well-killed Boche.
This is the happy warrior,
This is he...

Bombed Last Night

World War I Song

This and the songs that follow were mostly conceived as marching songs, something to distract from the physical ghastliness of marching with maybe 60 pounds on your back, in hob-nailed boots and perhaps on cobbled roads. The beat and repetition help keep in step.

Although they are British Great War songs, singing while marching is not primarily a British tradition. Complaining is. German armies have been much keener on stirring oom-pah-pah marching tunes with bands accompanying, and far less cynical or profane in their lyrics. Patriotic and stirring songs were approved and encouraged by German commanders and officers. American soldiers and marines inherited the Germanic tradition and rousing refrains have been the stuff of boot camp and the long trail a-winding since the Civil War. British songs fall into two camps: pop songs of the day, with spiced-up lyrics; and good, robust whinges at everything grim about the army, sergeant-majors, lice, whizz-bangs, chateau generals, rotten beer and rotten pay (compared to the Yanks). And being killed. At the risk of pointing out the obvious, 'bombed' in the song below is a pun on the dual meaning: getting drunk or, in this context, being literally bombed from the air or mortared.

Mustard gas (dichloroethylsulphide) was used by both sides. The writer Vera Brittain (1893–1970) nursed the victims and described the symptoms in *Testament of Youth* (1933): 'Great mustard-coloured blisters, blind eyes, all sticky and stuck together, always fighting for breath, with voices a mere whisper, saying that their throats are closing and they know they will choke.' Some died. More died from phosgene gas (carbonyl chloride), also used by both sides, an asphyxiant, often fatal if gas masks were not to hand. Wilfred Owen described its effects in *Dulce Et Decorum Est*:

> '… the white eyes writhing in his face,
> His hanging face, like a devil's sick of sin;
> If you could hear, at every jolt, the blood
> Come gargling from the froth-corrupted lungs…'

Bombed last night, and bombed the night before,
Going to get bombed tonight
If we never get bombed any more.
When we're bombed, we're scared as we can be;
Can't stop the bombing sent from higher Germany.

They're over us, they're over us,
One shell hole for just the four of us.
Thank your lucky stars there are no more of us,
'Cause one of us can fill it all alone.

Gassed last night, and gassed the night before,
Going to get gassed tonight
If we never get gassed anymore.
When we're gassed, were sick as we can be
For Phosgene and Mustard Gas is much too much for me.
They're warning us, they're warning us,
One respirator for the four of us.
Thank your lucky stars that three of us can run,
So one of us can use it all alone.

When Very Lights Are Shining

World War 1 Song

Sung to the tune of 'When Irish Eyes Are Smiling'. A Very (or sometimes Verey) light was invented by a US naval officer E. W. Very (1852–1910). It was a coloured flare like a roman candle shot from a special pistol, used mostly as a signal or to illuminate an area. 'Five-nines' were German shells fired from one of four versions of their 15 cm (5.9 inches) Heavy Field Howitzer.

When Very lights are shining,
Sure they're like the morning light,
And when the guns begin to thunder,
You can hear the angel's shite.
Then the Maxims start to chatter
And trench mortars send a few,
And when Very lights are shining
'Tis time for a rum issue.

When Very lights are shining
Sure 'tis like the morning dew,
And when shells begin a bursting

It makes you think your times come too.
And when you start advancing
Five nines and gas comes through,
Sure when Very lights are shining
'Tis rum or lead for you.

Forward Joe Soap's Army

World War 1 Song

Sung to the tune of 'Onward Christian Soldiers'.

Forward Joe Soap's army, marching without fear,
With our old commander, safely in the rear.
He boasts and shites from morn till night,
And thinks he's very brave,
But the men who really did the job are dead and in their grave.
Forward Joe Soap's army, marching without fear,
With our old commander, safely in the rear.
Amen.

When This F*cking War is Over

World War 1 Song

In printed versions the word 'f*cking' is replaced with 'lousy'. Not a word that Tommy would have used in this context. The song was sung to the tune of 'What a Friend We Have in Jesus'. 'Tickler's Marmalade' was produced in Tickler's jam factory in Grimsby and was standard ration, so standard that it became monotonous. Occasionally Tickler's Plum & Apple Jam enlivened the menu.

When this f*cking war is over, no more soldiering for me,
When I get my civvy clothes on, oh how happy I shall be.
No more church parades on Sunday, no more putting in
for leave,
I will miss the Sergeant-Major,
How he'll miss me how he'll grieve.

No more standing to in trenches,
Only one more church parade,
No more NCOs to curse us,
No more Tickler's Marmalade.

When this f*cking war is over,
No more soldiering for me,
When I get my civvy clothes on,
Oh how happy I shall be.
People said when we enlisted,
Fame and medals we would win,
But the fame is in the guardroom,
And the medals made of tin.

When this f*cking war is over,
No more soldiering for me,
When I get my civvy clothes on
Oh how happy I shall be.

'The end of a frightful four years':
The Armistice

Brigadier-General Jack
[from *General Jack's Diary 1914–18*, London, 1964]

James Jack (1880–1962) was a regular soldier who had fought with both the Argylls, a Scottish infantry regiment, and the Scottish Horse in the South African War (1899–1902), between Britain and the Boer Republics (Boers being settlers of Dutch descent). He fought throughout the Great War, with the Cameronians and the West Yorks, from Mons to the Armistice, being wounded twice. He won the DSO and Bar and was twice Mentioned in Despatches. He was a fighting soldier, unusually without a period as a staff officer. Sidney Rogerson, a fellow West Yorks officer, but junior, described him as extremely reserved, not without a sense of humour, and deeply immersed in military life and lore. He never 'got on a train', he 'entrained'. But Jack was by no means aloof from concern for his men. An extract from his diary (29 April 1916), written while preparing for the Somme offensive, reveals how the reticent manner of a Regular officer concealed a loathing for war as deep as any volunteer's:

> '… the remark of my friend George Boyd rather nettled me. He said 'I suppose you Regulars like this sort of life?'

*Hating it, and dreading the approaching battle, I replied
'As much as you do, I suppose...'*

A photograph of Captain Jack in 1914 and another of him in 1918
(now a Brigadier-General) show a man who seems to have aged
twenty years in four.

●━━━━━●

11 NOVEMBER 1918: CUERNE

A 'priority' message states that an Armistice has been
concluded with Germany, to take effect from 11 o'c this
morning. What a relief!

On a short parade of battalions in fatigue dress at their
billets I congratulate them on their services, shake hands
with all recipients of decorations during my period of
command, and express the hope that the behaviour of the
Brigade under Peace conditions will remain unsullied as it
has been in the field.

In the evening I and many officers are most hospitably
entertained to dinner by the Burgomaster of Cuerne and his
Council. The town band, having hurriedly disinterred and
cleaned their blue, silver-laced uniforms and instruments
after four years' burial, is in grand form. Champagne and
other wines flow generously but not in excess. The healths
of King George and King Albert [of Belgium] are drunk. A
few speeches are made in spite of linguistic difficulties – what
does that matter on an occasion like this? The Allies toast
one another cordially; the enthusiasm passes description.

Throughout the night the noise of singing, the shrill
hooting of railway whistles, and the blast of factory sirens
might awaken the dead. Rockets hiss skywards as long as the

supply lasts. Officers' pickets in the town ensure that there is no other kind of disturbance, and when the celebrations are concluded we have only one or two cases of simple drunkenness to report.

At last I lie down tired and very happy, but sleep is elusive. How far away is that 22 August 1914, when I heard with a shudder, as a platoon commander at Valenciennes, that real live German troops, armed to the teeth, were close at hand – one has been hardened since then. Incidents flash through the memory: the battles of the first four months: the awful winters in waterlogged trenches, cold and miserable: the terrible trench-war assaults and shell fire of the next three years: loss of friends, exhaustion and wounds: the stupendous victories of the last few months: our enemies all beaten to their knees.

Thank God! the end of a frightful four years, thirty-four months of them at the front with the infantry, whose company officers, rank and file, together with other front-line units, have suffered bravely, patiently and unselfishly, hardships and perils beyond even the imagination of those, including soldiers, who have not shared them.

When They Ask Us

World War 1 Song

And when they ask us
How dangerous it was,
Oh! We'll never tell them,
No, we'll never tell them.
We spent our pay in some café
And f*cked wild women night and day,
T'was the cushiest job we ever had.

And when they ask us,
And they're certainly going to ask us,
The reason why we didn't win the
Croix de Guerre,
Oh! We'll never tell them,
No! We'll never tell them...
There was a front but f*cked if we knew where.

High Wood

Philip Johnstone

This amusing poem was published in *The Nation* on 16 February 1918. It has been credited, probably wrongly, to Lieutenant John Stanley Purvis of the 5th Battalion, Yorkshire Regiment, writing under a pseudonym. But Purvis's known poems show a completely different style, and moreover he wrote under the pseudonym Philip Johnson, not Johnstone. Purvis, later a canon of York Minster, reveals not a trace of humour or irony in his published work.

This poem was prophetic. After the war, veterans, relatives and the curious tramped the desecrated woods and fields of Flanders and the Somme. The Michelin Tyre Co. started to produce illustrated guides for these battlefield tourists in 1919, their concise historical commentary being based on official records that were subsequently closed to others.

High Wood in the Somme is still a place of pilgrimage. Now privately owned, its pitted depths should not be trespassed as it has never been fully cleared of debris and explosives. The remains of more than 8,000 German and British soldiers lie under the trees, now grown back.

The British called it High Wood because of its position on the top of a slope. The French called it 'Bois des Foureaux' (a local corruption of 'fourreaux' – scabbard – perhaps), not 'Furneaux' as in the poem. In flat Somme country every little incline offered crucial advantages to defenders. For attackers, trudging uphill with pack and entrenching tool, it could be lethal.

High Wood was a major German stronghold. First attacked on 14 July 1916, optimism was such that cavalry stood waiting for the great breakthrough. Over the next two months the British tried frontal assaults, gas, flame throwers, machine gun barrages, tanks, even a desperate cavalry charge – and mines (craters are still there today). Robert Graves, serving with the 2nd Battalion, Royal Welch Fusiliers, was badly injured in an attack on the wood on 20 July. The Hill was eventually captured, at great loss, on 15 September 1916 during the Battle of Flers-Courcelette, when the 47th London Division (men of the Post Office Rifles and Civil Service Rifles among them) took it. An initial attack with four tanks failed but after a hurricane mortar bombardment (the front lines were too close for artillery) the Wood fell. But the Division failed to reach its other objectives that day and its Commander was relieved for, surprisingly, both 'lack of push' and 'wanton waste of men'. Certainly the 'waste' was evident even to a humble private:

'We were sent in to High Wood in broad daylight in the face of heavy machine-gun fire and shellfire, and everywhere there was dead bodies all over the place where previous battalions had taken part in attacks. We went in there and we got a terrible bashing... It was criminal to send men in broad daylight, into machine-gun fire, without any cover of any sort whatsoever... There was one particular place just before we got to High Wood which was a crossroads [this was 'Crucifix Corner' – the crucifix is still there], and it was really hell there, they shelled it like anything, you couldn't get past it... There were men everywhere, heaps of men... all dead.'

[quoted in Lyn Macdonald's *Somme*, London, 1983]

Ladies and gentlemen, this is High Wood,
Called by the French, Bois des Furneaux,
The famous spot which in Nineteen-Sixteen,
July, August and September was the scene
Of long and bitterly contested strife,
By reason of its High commanding site.
Observe the effect of shell-fire in the trees
Standing and fallen; here is wire; this trench
For months inhabited, twelve times changed hands;
(They soon fall in), used later as a grave.
It has been said on good authority
That in the fighting for this patch of wood
Were killed somewhere above eight thousand men,
Of whom the greater part were buried here,
This mound on which you stand being... Madame, please,
You are requested kindly not to touch
Or take away the Company's property
As souvenirs; you'll find we have on sale
A large variety, all guaranteed.
As I was saying, all is as it was,
This is an unknown British officer,
The tunic having lately rotted off.
Please follow me – this way..... the *path*, sir, *please*,
The ground which was secured at great expense
The Company keeps absolutely untouched,
And in that dug-out (genuine) we provide
Refreshments at a reasonable rate.
You are requested not to leave about
Paper, or ginger-beer bottles, or orange peel,
There are waste-paper baskets at the gate.

A Raid

George Orwell, Huesca, Spain, 1936
[from *Homage to Catalonia*, London, 1937]

George Orwell (1903–50) – real name Eric Blair – was born in Bengal and educated at Eton. He moved to Burma in 1922 where he joined the Indian Imperial Police in Burma for five years, resigning because he became disillusioned with imperialism. *Burmese Days* (London, 1934) describes his experience. He moved to France where a succession of menial jobs both there and latterly in London formed the basis of his wry and observant *Down and Out in Paris and London* (London, 1933), his first book.

In Britain, Orwell, now a convert to socialism, contacted the ILP (Independent Labour Party) about fighting for the Republican Loyalists against Franco's Fascists in the Spanish Civil War, having been rejected as politically unreliable by the Communists. General Franco had led an insurrection in July 1936 against the elected Republican government. The Fascists regarded the Republicans as threatening the vested interests of the Church, military and landed classes. Franco and the nucleus of his army had been ferried across to the mainland from Morocco by the German *Luftwaffe*, which was to be vital to his eventual victory (and responsible for the bombing of Guernica on 26 April 1937). To combat Franco a new political structure had spontaneously emerged with a plethora of committees and workers' councils. The fight against Franco

169

developed into a revolutionary mass movement with agriculture and industry collectivised.

In December 1936 Orwell joined the Lenin Division of the anti-Stalinist, revolutionary POUM (Partido Obrero de Unificación Marxista) in Barcelona. He was immediately excited by the revolutionary atmosphere, by Socialism in action:

> *'It was the first time that I had ever been in a town where the working class was in the saddle. Practically every building of any size had been seized by the workers and was draped with red flags or the red and black flag of the Anarchists... even the bootblacks had been collectivised... Waiters and shop-walkers looked you in the face and treated you as an equal... I recognized it immediately as a state of affairs worth fighting for...'*

After the most rudimentary training, he was sent in January 1937 to join the party's militia on the Aragon front. He was appalled by their lack of weapons and supplies. He learnt later that it was because the authorities withheld arms and munitions from revolutionary forces that did not toe the correct political line, notwithstanding their commitment to anti-Fascism. The corruption of the socialist ideal, the reality and consequence of political infighting depressed and enraged him, but he still regarded the militia as an example of how socialism itself could be organised: truly democratic, decisions taken by the group, everyone paid the same, discipline self-imposed. 'Here', he wrote, 'I became a real socialist.'

Orwell was back in Barcelona in May 1937 and witnessed the murderous street fighting between leftist factions. The POUM were later blamed. 'Internal order had been handed over to Communist ministers, and no one doubted that they would smash their political rivals as soon as they got a quarter of a chance', he acknowledged. After the May fighting, Orwell transferred to the front at Huesca in Aragona where he was promoted to Second Lieutenant, commanding a unit of 30 men. He was shot in the neck by a sniper and temporarily paralysed. While recuperating in hospital Orwell heard that the POUM had been declared an illegal organization, and he was therefore in danger of being imprisoned or murdered like many of his compatriots. The British consul in Barcelona helped him escape to France on 23 June 1937, pursued by the secret police.

Orwell had sensed the coming of the totalitarian state. He saw no distinction between the brutality of fascism and that of Soviet communism. Commenting on the Communist regime in Spain (*New English Weekly*, 1937) Orwell wrote:

> *'The logical end is a régime in which every opposition party and newspaper is suppressed and every dissentient of any importance is in jail. Of course, such a régime will be Fascism... Only, being operated by Communists and Liberals, it will be called something different.'*

In *Homage to Catalonia* Orwell exposed the nonsense and propaganda disseminated by gullible or conniving British newspapers of all political persuasions. English newspapers, especially but not exclusively left-wing ones, repeated the lies of the Spanish press. Without having read the manuscript, his left-wing publisher Victor Gollancz refused to publish it, fearful of Orwell's exposure of Stalinist manipulation and murder. Orthodoxy among the left ruled. It was eventually published by Secker & Warburg but sold a meagre 1,500 copies in the next 12 years.

One afternoon Benjamin told us that he wanted fifteen volunteers. The attack on the Fascist redoubt which had been called off on the previous occasion was to be carried out tonight. I oiled my ten Mexican cartridges, dirtied my bayonet (the things give your position away if they flash too much), and packed up a hunk of bread, three inches of red sausage, and a cigar which my wife had sent from Barcelona and which I had been hoarding for a long time. Bombs [hand grenades] were served out, three to a man. The Spanish Government had at last succeeded in producing a decent bomb. It was on the principle of a Mills bomb, but with two pins instead of one. After you had pulled the pins out there was an interval of seven seconds before the bomb exploded. Its chief disadvantage was that one pin was very stiff and the other very loose, so that you had the choice of leaving both pins in place and being unable to pull the stiff one out in a moment of emergency, or pulling out the stiff one beforehand and being in a constant stew lest the thing should explode in your pocket. But it was a handy little bomb to throw.

... Kopp addressed us, first in Spanish, then in English, and explained the plan of attack... To prevent us from shooting each other in the darkness white armlets would be worn. At this moment a messenger arrived to say that there were no white armlets. Out of the darkness a plaintive voice suggested: 'Couldn't we arrange for the Fascists to wear white armlets instead?'

... We filed through the gap in the parapet and waded through another irrigation ditch. Splash-gurgle! Once again in water up to your waist, with the filthy, slimy mud oozing over your boot-tops. On the grass outside Jorge [battalion commander] waited till we were all through. Then, bent almost double, he began creeping slowly forward. The Fascist parapet was about a hundred and fifty yards away. Our one chance of getting there was to move without noise.

... every time I raised my head Benjamin, close beside me, whispered fiercely in my ear: 'To keep ze head down! To keep ze head down!' I could have told him that he needn't worry. I knew by experiment that on a dark night you can never see a man at twenty paces. It was far more important to go quietly. If they once heard us we were done for. They had only to spray the darkness with their machine-gun and there was nothing for it but to run or be massacred.

But on the sodden ground it was almost impossible to move quietly. Do what you would your feet stuck to the mud, and every step you took was slop-slop, slop-slop. And the devil of it was that the wind had dropped, and in spite of the rain it was a very quiet night. Sounds would carry a long way. There was a dreadful moment when I kicked against a tin and thought every Fascist within miles must have heard it.

… Once I raised my head; in silence Benjamin put his hand behind my neck and pulled it violently down. I knew that the inner wire was barely twenty yards from the parapet. It seemed to me inconceivable that thirty men could get there unheard. Our breathing was enough to give us away. Yet somehow we did get there. The Fascist parapet was visible now, a dim black mound, looming high above us. Once again Jorge knelt and fumbled. Snip, snip. There was no way of cutting the stuff silently.

…The sentry had heard us at last. Jorge poised himself on one knee and swung his arm like a bowler. Crash! His bomb burst somewhere over the parapet. At once, far more promptly than one would have thought possible, a roar of fire, ten or twenty rifles, burst out from the Fascist parapet. They had been waiting for us after all… Every loophole seemed to be spouting jets of flame. It is always hateful to be shot at in the dark – every rifle-flash seems to be pointed straight at yourself – but it was the bombs that were the worst. You cannot conceive the horror of these things till you have seen one burst close to you in darkness; in the daytime there is only the crash of the explosion, in the darkness there is the blinding red glare as well. I had flung myself down at the first volley. All this while I was lying on my side in the greasy mud, wrestling savagely with the pin of a bomb. The damned thing *would* not come out. Finally I realized that I was twisting it in the wrong direction. I got the pin out, rose to my knees, hurled the bomb, and threw myself down again. The bomb burst over to the right, outside the parapet; fright had spoiled my aim. Just at this moment another bomb burst right in front of me, so close that I could feel the heat of the explosion. I flattened myself out and dug my face into the mud so hard that I hurt my neck and thought that I was wounded. Through the din I heard an English voice behind me say quietly: 'I'm hit.' The bomb had, in fact, wounded several people round about me without touching myself. I rose to my knees and flung my second bomb. I forget where that one went.

The Fascists were firing, our people behind were firing, and I was very conscious of being in the middle. I felt the blast of a shot and realized that a man was firing from immediately behind me. I stood up and shouted at him: 'Don't shoot at me, you bloody fool!'

… The Fascist fire seemed to have slackened very suddenly. Benjamin leapt to his feet and shouted: 'Forward! Charge!' We dashed up the short steep slope on which the parapet stood. I say 'dashed'; 'lumbered' would be a better word; the fact is that you can't move fast when you are sodden and mudded from head to foot and weighted down with a heavy rifle and bayonet and a hundred and fifty cartridges. I took it for granted that there would be a Fascist waiting for me at the top. If he fired at that range he could not miss me, and yet somehow I never expected him to fire, only to try for me with his bayonet. I seemed to feel in advance the sensation of our bayonets crossing, and I wondered whether his arm would be stronger than mine. However, there was no Fascist waiting…

… Then a man, a shadowy figure in the half-light, skipped over the roof of one of the ruined huts and dashed away to the left. I started after him, prodding my bayonet ineffectually into the darkness. As I rounded the corner of the hut I saw a man – I don't know whether or not it was the same man as I had seen before – fleeing up the communication-trench that led to the other Fascist position. I must have been very close to him, for I could see him clearly. He was bareheaded and seemed to have nothing on except a blanket which he was clutching round his shoulders. If I had fired I could have blown him to pieces. But for fear of shooting one another we had been ordered to use only bayonets once we were inside the parapet, and in any case I never even thought of firing. Instead, my mind leapt backwards twenty years, to our boxing instructor at school, showing me in vivid pantomime how he had bayoneted a Turk at the Dardanelles. I gripped my rifle by the small of the butt and lunged at the man's back. He was just out of my reach. Another lunge: still out of reach. And for a little distance we proceeded like this, he rushing up the trench and I after him on the ground above, prodding at his shoulder-blades and never quite getting there – a comic memory for me to look back upon, though I suppose it seemed less comic to him.

We began searching the position. There were several dead men lying about, but I did not stop to examine them. The thing I was after was the machine-gun. All the while when we were lying outside I had been wondering vaguely why the gun did not fire. I flashed my torch inside the machine-gun nest. A bitter disappointment! The gun was not there… We were furious. We had set our hearts on capturing a machine-gun.

… Up at the far end there was a small dug-out which was partly above ground and had a tiny window. We flashed the torch through the window and instantly raised a cheer. A cylindrical object in a leather case, four feet high and six inches in diameter, was leaning against the wall. Obviously the machine-gun barrel. We dashed round and got in at the doorway, to find that the thing in the leather case was not a machine-gun but something which, in our weapon-starved army, was even more precious. It was an enormous telescope, probably of at least sixty or seventy magnifications, with a folding tripod. Such telescopes simply did not exist on our side of the line and they were desperately needed. We brought it out in triumph and leaned it against the parapet, to be carried off after.

At this moment someone shouted that the Fascists were closing in. Certainly the din of firing had grown very much louder…

… I remember feeling a deep horror at everything: the chaos, the darkness, the frightful din, the slithering to and fro in the mud, the struggles with the bursting sand-bags – all the time encumbered with my rifle, which I dared not put down for fear of losing it. I even shouted to someone as we staggered along with a bag between us: 'This is war! Isn't it bloody?'

… I saw a flash hardly twenty yards away. Obviously they were working their way up the communication-trench. At twenty yards they were within easy bombing range; there were eight or nine of us bunched together and a single well-placed bomb would blow us all to fragments… I had no bombs left except the Fascist ones and I was not certain how these worked. I shouted to the others to know if anyone had a bomb to spare. Douglas Moyle felt in his pocket and passed one across. I flung it and threw myself on my face. By one of those strokes of luck that happen about once in a year I had managed to drop the bomb almost exactly where the rifle had flashed. There was the roar of the explosion and then, instantly, a diabolical outcry of screams and groans. We had got one of them, anyway; I don't know whether he was killed, but certainly he was badly hurt. Poor wretch, poor wretch! I felt a vague sorrow as I heard him screaming. But at the same instant, in the dim light of the rifle-flashes, I saw or thought I saw a figure standing near the place where the rifle had flashed. I threw up my rifle and let fly. Another scream, but I think it was still the effect of the bomb. Several more bombs were thrown. The next rifle-flashes we saw were a long way off, a hundred yards or more. So we had driven them back, temporarily at least.

… At this moment Paddy Donovan, who was second-in-command to Benjamin and had been sent back for orders, climbed over the front parapet.

'Hi! Come on out of it! All men to retire at once!'

'What?' 'Retire! Get out of it!' 'Why?' 'Orders. Back to our own lines double-quick.'

People were already climbing over the front parapet. Several of them were struggling with a heavy ammunition box. My mind flew to the telescope which I had left leaning against the parapet on the other side of the position… Paddy was waiting at the parapet.

'Come on, hurry up.' 'But the telescope!' 'B— the telescope! Benjamin's waiting outside.'

We climbed out. Paddy held the wire aside for me. As soon as we got away from the shelter of the Fascist parapet we were under a devilish fire that seemed to be coming at us from every direction. Part of it, I do not doubt, came from our own side, for everyone was firing all along the line. Whichever way we turned a fresh stream of bullets swept past; we were driven this way and that in the darkness like a flock of sheep… At last we saw the low flat line of a parapet looming in front of us. It might be ours or it might be the Fascists'; nobody had the dimmest idea which way we were going. Benjamin crawled on his belly through some tall whitish weed till he was about twenty yards from the parapet and tried a challenge. A shout of 'Poum!' answered him. We jumped to our feet, found our way along the parapet, slopped once more through the irrigation ditch – splash – gurgle! – and were in safety.

Kopp was waiting inside the parapet with a few Spaniards. The doctor and the stretchers were gone. It appeared that all the wounded had been got in except Jorge and one of our own men, Hiddlestone by name, who were missing. Kopp was pacing up and down, very pale. Even the fat folds at the back of his neck were pale; he was paying no attention to the bullets that streamed over the low parapet and cracked close to his head. Most of us were squatting behind the parapet for cover. Kopp was muttering. 'Jorge! *Cogño!* Jorge!' And then in English. 'If Jorge is gone it is terreeble, terreeble!' Jorge was his personal friend and one of his best officers. Suddenly he turned to us and asked for five volunteers, two English and three Spanish, to go and look for the missing men. Moyle and I volunteered with three Spaniards.

… There was a tremendous noise of excited voices coming from the Fascist redoubt… One of them flung a bomb over the parapet – a sure sign of panic. We were lying in the grass, waiting for an opportunity to move on, when we heard or thought we heard… that the Fascist voices were much closer. They had left the parapet and were coming after us. 'Run!' I yelled to Moyle, and jumped to my feet. And heavens, how I ran! I had thought earlier in the night that you can't run when you are sodden from head to foot and weighted down with a rifle and cartridges; I learned now you can always run when you think you have fifty or a hundred armed men after you. But if I could run fast, others could run faster. In my flight something that might have been a shower of meteors sped past me. It was the three Spaniards, who had been in front. They were back to our own parapet before they stopped and I could catch up with them. The truth was that our nerves were all to pieces. I knew, however, that in a half light one man is invisible where five are clearly visible, so I went back alone. I managed to get to the outer wire and searched the ground as well as I could, which was not very well, for I had to lie on my belly. There was no sign of Jorge or Hiddlestone, so I crept back.

… It was getting light now… When I got back to my dug-out the three men I shared it with were already fast asleep. They had flung themselves down with all their equipment on and their muddy rifles clutched against them… By long searching I managed to collect enough chips of dry wood to make a tiny fire. Then I smoked the cigar which I had been hoarding and which, surprisingly enough, had not got broken during the night.

Afterwards we learned that the action had been a success, as such things go. It was merely a raid to make the Fascists divert troops from the other side of Huesca, where the Anarchists were attacking again. I had judged that the Fascists had thrown a hundred or two hundred men into the counter-attack, but a deserter told us later on that it was six hundred. I dare say he was lying – deserters, for obvious reasons, often try to curry favour. It was a great pity about the telescope. The thought of losing that beautiful bit of loot worries me even now.

Shot

George Orwell, Huesca, Spain, 1937
[from *Homage to Catalonia,* London, 1938]

This extract from an article by Albert Weisbord (1900–77), an American Communist who visited the Loyalist troops on the Aragon Front at Huesca when Orwell was fighting there, appeared in the magazine *Class Struggle* in 1937, which Weisbord published. It provides an appropriate background to Orwell's piece that follows.

'The six thousand men of the P.O.U.M. with two thousand others in reserve, held about 46 kilometers. For the entire force around Huesca [17,000 men] *there were only five effective cannon of 70–75 mm., about sixty machine guns, and one airplane (not in use). The soldiers complained to me that... the men had only twenty cartridges apiece... Since no bayonets had been issued until very late in the struggle, hand to hand charges to drive the enemy out of their positions were not to be thought of. Headquarters estimated they had no more than 3 per cent of the material they actually needed.*

Opposed to the Loyalists the fascists had placed around Huesca some ten thousand trained soldiers supplied with at least six batteries of 100–105 mm. The Loyalists, however, had been instructed not to fire their largest cannon because they might damage the 'famous Cathedral in Huesca' which, as a matter of fact, was now used for military purposes by the fascists. For similar delicate scruples, when a few airplanes were loaned to the Aragon Front, they, too, were instructed not to bomb the Cathedral which was a 'work of art.'

… Behind the trenches, only a few hundred yards away, life was going on as normally as though nothing in the world was taking place. Men and women were swimming in the river, farmers were busy with their ploughing and planting. And even in the trenches phonographs were playing and men were dancing one with the other. Some went about in shorts as though they were in some vacationist camp. Only the vicious crack of some sharpshooter's bullet from time to time reminded one that it was war.'

They had promised us a trench-mortar for the company; I was looking forward to it greatly. At nights we patrolled as usual – more dangerous than it used to be, because the Fascist trenches were better manned and they had grown more alert; they had scattered tin cans just outside their wire and used to open up with the machine-guns when they heard a clank. In the daytime we sniped from No Man's Land. By crawling a hundred yards you could get to a ditch, hidden by tall grasses, which commanded a gap in the Fascist parapet. We had set up a rifle-rest in the ditch. If you waited long enough you generally saw a khaki-clad figure slip hurriedly across the gap. I had several shots. I don't know whether I hit anyone – it is most unlikely; I am a very poor shot with a rifle. But it was rather fun, the Fascists did not know where the shots were coming from, and I made sure I would get one of them sooner or later. However, the dog it was that died – a Fascist sniper got me instead. I had been about ten days at the front when it happened. The whole experience of being hit by a bullet is very interesting and I think it is worth describing in detail.

It was at the corner of the parapet, at five o'clock in the morning. This was always a dangerous time, because we had the dawn at our backs, and if you stuck your head above the parapet it was clearly outlined against the sky. I was talking to the sentries preparatory to changing the guard. Suddenly, in the very middle of saying something, I felt – it is very hard to describe what I felt, though I remember it with the utmost vividness.

Roughly speaking it was the sensation of being *at the centre* of an explosion. There seemed to be a loud bang and a blinding flash of light all round me, and I felt a tremendous shock – no pain, only a violent shock, such as you get from an electric terminal; with it a sense of utter weakness, a feeling of being stricken and shrivelled up to nothing. The sandbags in front of me receded into immense distance. I fancy you would feel much the same if you were struck by lightning. I knew immediately that I was hit, but because of the seeming bang and flash I thought it was a rifle nearby that had gone off accidentally and shot me. All this happened in a space of time much less than a second. The next moment my knees crumpled up and I was falling, my head hitting the ground with a violent bang which, to my relief, did not hurt. I had a numb, dazed feeling, a consciousness of being very badly hurt, but no pain in the ordinary sense.

The American sentry I had been talking to had started forward. 'Gosh! Are you hit?' People gathered round. There was the usual fuss – 'Lift him up! Where's he hit? Get his shirt open!' etc. etc. The American called for a knife to cut my shirt open. I knew that there was one in my pocket and tried to get it out, but discovered that my right arm was paralysed. Not being in pain, I felt a vague satisfaction. This ought to please my wife, I thought; she had always wanted me to be wounded, which would save me from being killed when the great battle came. It was only now that it occurred to me to wonder where I was hit, and how badly; I could feel nothing, but I was conscious that the bullet had struck me somewhere in the front of the body. When I tried to speak I found that I had no voice, only a faint squeak, but at the second attempt I managed to ask where I was hit. In the throat, they said. Harry Webb, our stretcher-bearer, had brought a bandage and one of the little bottles of alcohol they gave us for field-dressings. As they lifted me up a lot of blood poured out of my mouth, and I heard a Spaniard behind me say that the bullet had gone clean through my neck. I felt the alcohol, which at ordinary times would sting like the devil, splash onto the wound as a pleasant coolness.

They laid me down again while somebody fetched a stretcher. As soon as I knew that the bullet had gone clean through my neck I took it for granted that I was done for. I had never heard of a man or an animal getting a bullet through the middle of the neck and surviving it. The blood was dribbling out of the corner of my mouth. 'The artery's gone,' I thought. I wondered how long you last when your carotid artery is cut; not many minutes, presumably. Everything was very blurry. There must have been about two minutes during which I assumed that I was killed. And that too was interesting – I mean it is interesting to know what your thoughts would be at such a time. My first thought, conventionally enough, was for my wife. My second was a violent resentment at having to leave this world which, when all is said and done, suits me so well. I had time to feel this very vividly. The stupid mischance infuriated me. The meaninglessness of it! To be bumped off, not even in battle, but in this stale corner of the trenches, thanks to a moment's carelessness! I thought, too, of the man who had shot me – wondered what he was like, whether he was a Spaniard or a foreigner, whether he knew he had got me, and so forth. I could not feel any resentment against him. I reflected that as he was a Fascist I would have killed him if I could, but that if he had been taken prisoner and brought before me at this moment I would merely have congratulated him on his good shooting. It may be, though, that if you were really dying your thoughts would be quite different.

They had just got me onto the stretcher when my paralysed right arm came to life and began hurting damnably. At the time I imagined that I must have broken it in falling; but the pain reassured me, for I knew that your sensations do not become more acute when you are dying. I began to feel more normal and to be sorry for the four poor devils who were sweating and slithering with the stretcher on their shoulders. It was a mile and a half to the ambulance, and vile going, over lumpy, slippery tracks. I knew what a sweat it was, having helped to carry a wounded man down a day or two earlier. The leaves of the silver poplars which, in places fringed our trenches brushed against my face; I thought what a good thing it was to be alive in a world where silver poplars grow. But all the while the pain in my arm was diabolical, making me swear and then try not to swear, because every time I breathed too hard the blood bubbled out of my mouth.

The doctor re-bandaged the wound, gave me a shot of morphia, and sent me off to Siétamo. The hospitals at Siétamo were hurriedly constructed wooden huts where the wounded were, as a rule, only kept for a few hours before being sent on to Barbastro or Lérida. I was dopey from morphia but still in great pain, practically unable to move and swallowing blood constantly. It was typical of Spanish hospital methods that while I was in this state the untrained nurse tried to force the regulation hospital meal – a huge meal of soup, eggs, greasy stew and so forth – down my throat and seemed surprised when I would not take it. I asked for a cigarette, but this was one of the periods of tobacco famine and there was not a cigarette in the place. Presently two comrades who had got permission to leave the line for a few hours appeared at my bedside.

'Hullo! You're alive, are you? Good. We want your watch and your revolver and your electric torch. And your knife, if you've got one.'

They made off with all my portable possessions. This always happened when a man was wounded – everything he possessed was promptly divided up; quite rightly, for watches, revolvers, and so forth were precious at the front and if they went down the line in a wounded man's kit they were certain to be stolen somewhere on the way.

'Guernica is destroyed', 26 April 1937

Noel Monks [from *Eyewitness*, London, 1955]

Hitler gave crucial military aid to Franco's Fascists in the Spanish Civil War (1936–1939). Franco had no airforce to speak of, and was wholly dependent for his dominance of the air on Hitler's Condor Legion, which arrived in August 1936. By November the Legion boasted 100 planes and 5,000 German air and ground crew, under Hugo Sperrle (1885–1953). A total of around 20,000 Germans eventually served in Spain. Hitler maintained the fiction that the men serving in Spain were volunteers for the Fascist fight against Bolshevism. Germany tested new weapons like the Me 109 fighter, Heinkel III bomber and Ju 87 Stuka dive-bomber, and the *Luftwaffe* undoubtedly benefitted from experimenting with new tactics. Mussolini gave yet more aid to the Fascists, twice as much in terms of money spent, and considerably more in manpower – 50,000 in mid-1937 against the peak strength of 10,000 Germans in late 1936.

Guernica, the spiritual capital of the Basque people, lies 30 km east of Bilbao, and was held by the Republicans on 26 April 1937, when an attack by about 40 planes was launched. It was market day and the town's population of 7,000 was swelled by traders and buyers. First explosive bombs, then incendiaries rained down. Fighters machine-gunned indiscriminately. Both German and Italian aircraft were involved. George Steer, the *Times* correspondent, wrote: 'The object of the bombardment was seemingly the demoralization of the civil population and the destruction of the cradle of the Basque race.'

Franco claimed that Guernica had been dynamited and then burnt by anarchists. But the Condor Legion's own operations log reveals their presence over Guernica. And General Wolfram Von Richtofen, Sperrle's Chief of Staff (the Red Baron's cousin and later the commander of Fliegerkorps VIII at Stalingrad) who executed the order for the raid, recorded in his diary for 26 April that the Guernica attack was part of a plan to corner the Loyalists. A telegram from Franco's headquarters has also been discovered requesting that the Condor Legion bomb the town. The motive was in part to instil terror. It was successful. Incendiaries were dropped in huge numbers, not as target indicators but as a means of destruction by fire. The low-level daylight raid continued for over three hours unopposed and destroyed the town. The Fascists walked in three days later, the defenders having panicked and run. The Republicans claimed that 1,654 people were killed and 889 wounded. Recent estimates put a more likely death toll at about 300. Nevertheless Guernica's destruction had a profound effect on the democracies – fear of aerial obliteration hastening the slide towards appeasement. 271 buildings were destroyed, 75 per cent of those that had stood that morning.

Noel Monks (1906–1960) was born in Hobart, Tasmania, the youngest of 13. He ran away to sea aged 15, then returned to live in Melbourne for several years, working on the *Melbourne Sun* and surviving two plane crashes in one week. Monks began his long career as a war correspondent when he paid his own way to Abyssinia and began sending dispatches to the London *Daily Express*. Delighted at Monks' exclusive reports of Italian forces shelling and bombing spear-carrying natives, the *Express*'s proprietor Lord Beaverbrook had him taken onto the staff of the mass circulation daily. Monks' friend and colleague Evelyn Waugh, who was also covering the war, wrote his great comic novel *Scoop*, with 'The Beast' newspaper based on Lord

('Copper') Beaverbrook's *Daily Express*, and the fast-learning novice reporter, 'Boot', partly based on Monks (and W. F. Deedes).

Monks was a brave and resourceful war correspondent who covered Abyssinia, Spain and many of the campaigns of World War 2. He jumped from a landing craft just after H-Hour on D-Day. As a reporter, he was committed both to truth and a cause. In his autobiography *Eyewitness* (London, 1955) he writes of leaving the besieged city of Madrid: 'And yet when my time came for relief, I felt... I were deserting a cause... Republican Spain had the greatest cause of all – freedom.'

Mola, referred to in this extract, was General Emilio Mola (1887–1937). He led the army coup, but in September 1936 agreed to serve under Franco, becoming commander of the Army of the North. Mola was to die on 3 June 1937 when his plane crashed during bad weather. Franco was rumoured to be responsible.

I passed through Guernica at about 3.30pm. The time is approximate, based on the fact that I left Bilbao at 2.30. Guernica was busy. It was market day. We passed through the town and took a road that Anton said would take us close to Marquina, where, as far as I knew, the front was. The front was there, all right, but Marquina was not. It had been smashed flat by bombers.

We were about eighteen miles east of Guernica when Anton pulled to the side of the road, jammed on the brakes and started shouting. He pointed wildly ahead, and my heart shot into my mouth when I looked. Over the tops of some hills appeared a flock of planes. A dozen or so bombers were flying high. But down much lower, seeming just to skim the treetops were six Heinkels, out for random plunder, spotted our car, and, wheeling like a block of homing pigeons, they lined up the road – and our car.

Anton and I flung ourselves into a bomb hole, twenty yards to the side of the road. It was half filled with water, and we sprawled in mud. We half knelt, half stood, with our heads buried in the muddy side of the crater.

After one good look at the Heinkels, I didn't look up again until they had gone. That seemed hours later, but it was probably less than twenty minutes. The planes made several runs along the road. Machine-gun bullets plopped onto the mud ahead, behind, all around us. I began to shiver from sheer fright. Only the day before Steer, an old hand now, had 'briefed' me about being strafed. 'Lie still and as flat as you can. But don't get up and start running, or you'll be bowled over for certain.'

When the Heinkels departed, out of ammunition I presumed, Anton and I ran back to our car. Nearby a military car was burning fiercely. All we could do was drag two riddled bodies to the side of the road. I was trembling all over now, in the grip of the first real fear I'd ever experienced… Then suddenly the quaking passed and I felt exhilarated. These were the days in foreign reporting when personal experiences were copy, for there hadn't been a war for eighteen years, long enough for those who went through the last one to forget, and for a generation and a half who knew nothing of war to be interested. We used to call them 'I' stories, and when the Spanish War ended in 1939 we were as heartily sick of writing them as the public must have been of reading them.

At the foot of the hills leading to Guernica we turned off the main road and took another back to Bilbao. Over to our left, in the direction of Guernica, we could hear the crump of bombs. I thought the Germans had located reinforcements moving up from Santander to stem the retreat. We drove on to Bilbao.

At the Presidencia, Steer and Holme were writing dispatches. They asked me to join them at dinner at Steer's hotel…

We'd eaten our first course of beans and were waiting for our bully beef when a government official, tears streaming down his face, burst into the dismal dining room crying, 'Guernica is destroyed. The Germans bombed and bombed and bombed.'

The time was about 9.30pm. Captain Roberts banged a huge fist on the table and said, 'Bloody swine.' Five minutes later I was in one of Mendiguren's limousines speeding towards Guernica. We were still a good ten miles away when I saw the reflection of Guernica's flames in the sky. As we drew nearer, on both sides of the road, men, women and children were sitting, dazed. I saw a priest in one group. I stopped the car and went up to him. 'What happened, Father?' I asked. His face was blackened, his clothes in tatters. He couldn't talk. He just pointed to the flames, still about four miles away, then whispered, '*Aviones… bombas… mucho, mucho.*'

In the good 'I' tradition of the day, I was the first correspondent to reach Guernica, and was immediately pressed into service by some Basque soldiers collecting charred bodies that the flames had passed over. Some of the soldiers were sobbing like children. There were flames and smoke and grit, and the smell of burning human flesh was nauseating. Houses were collapsing into the inferno.

In the Plaza, surrounded almost by a wall of fire, were about a hundred refugees. They were wailing and weeping and rocking to and fro. One middle-aged man spoke English. He told me, 'At four, before the market closed, many aeroplanes came. They dropped bombs. Some came low and shot bullets into the streets. Father Aronategui was wonderful. He prayed with the people in the Plaza while the bombs fell.' The man had no idea who I was, as far as I know. He was telling me what had happened to Guernica.

Most of Guernica's streets began or ended at the Plaza. It was impossible to go down many of them, because they were walls of flame. Debris was piled high. I could see shadowy forms, some large, some just ashes. I moved round to the back of the Plaza among survivors. They had the same story to tell, aeroplanes, bullets, bombs, fire.

Within twenty-four hours, when the grim story was told to the world, Franco was going to brand these shocked, homeless people as liars. So-called British experts were going to come to Guernica, weeks afterwards, when the smell of burnt human flesh had been replaced by petrol dumped here and there among the ruins by Mola's men, and deliver pompous judgements: 'Guernica was set on fire wilfully by the Reds.'

London prepares for the worst

Mollie Panter-Downes
[from *London War Notes: 1939–1945,* London, 1972;
an article originally published in *The New Yorker*, 1940]

Britain declared war on Germany on 3 September 1939 following
Germany's unprovoked invasion (1 September) of Poland, whose
independence Britain had guaranteed. With the signing of the Nazi-
Soviet pact on 23 August 1939, Russia had allowed the Nazis a free
hand in Poland. Britain could do nothing militarily to help Poland,
which was quickly overrun.

The Phoney War was a period of calm (Chamberlain thought
Hitler had 'missed the bus') before the German '*blitzkrieg*' shattered
allied complacency on 10 May 1940. It was the same day Churchill
became Prime Minister. At 5.30 a.m., Germany attacked Holland,
Belgium, Luxembourg and France. Of the defending armies, which
included 10 divisions of Lord Gort's British Expeditionary Force
(250,000 men) fighting under French overall command, by far the
largest was the French, with 104 divisions in the north-eastern front
alone. But even the French C-in-C, Gamelin, conceded that there
was a '*défaillance*' (wobbliness) among several French Communist-
infected divisions. Above all, the legacy of the Battle of Verdun
(1916) and its horrors had not dissipated in the intervening years.
At Verdun, Lieutenant Raymond Jubert of the French 151st Infantry
Regiment wrote: 'They will not make us do it again…'

The Dutch army had one tank and was beaten within five days. Only 82 men took up arms to defend Luxembourg; seven were wounded. Belgium's King Léopold III had refused to allow a Franco-British force to enter and defend neutral Belgium for fear of provoking a Nazi invasion. Many Belgian units fought tenaciously but Belgium's earlier refusal to cooperate with Anglo-French forces meant their defensive strategy, uncoordinated with their allies, was doomed; it was overly reliant on forts and defensive positions vulnerable to German glider assault. The German *blitzkrieg* isolated and overwhelmed Belgian troops. Belgium capitulated after 18 days of battle on 28 May, at the height of the Dunkirk evacuation.

The Germans had a total of 141 divisions, the Allies 144. The Allies had twice as many guns – 13,974 to 7,378 – and more tanks, 3,384 to 2,445, but most of these were inferior to the German Mk III and IV Panzers; furthermore, British 2-pdr. anti-tank guns could not stop a Panzer at an acceptable distance. The Allies had more fighters – about 1,590 to Germany's 1,220 – but Britain's 540 or so were mostly home-based which restricted operations, and the French Air Force was described by General Pownall (Chief of the General Staff to the BEF) as 'rotten'. The *Luftwaffe*'s Me 109 and terrifying Ju 87 Stuka dive-bomber dominated the air, and made a nasty habit of strafing and bombing the hordes of refugees clogging the roads to add to the chaos behind Allied lines. Germany had overwhelming bomber superiority, about 1,560 to 700. Their aircraft and tactics had been perfected in the Spanish Civil War, and French and British bombers were no match.

At the time this piece was written, Italy was still neutral. Her army and air force were both large, but lacked effective equipment. The Italian Navy, on the other hand, was both modern and powerful. It was regarded warily by the British. When Italy eventually joined the war its navy obtained, for a time at least, almost total control of the Mediterranean.

On 14 May French Premier Reynaud demanded ten more squadrons of fighter planes from Britain. Ironside, Chief of the Imperial General Staff, thought Reynaud 'a little hysterical' and not helped by his volatile mistress, the fascistic Madame de Portes, who undermined Reynaud's resolve – 'she had the whole night to undo what Reynaud's democratic friends had done in the day' as one French journalist put it. Walter Thompson, Churchill's bodyguard, thwarted a physical attack on the PM: '[Mme. de Portes] came out in a fury of hatred,' Thompson recalled. 'I caught her and silenced her hysterics. She had no gun, though we found a knife on her person...'

Liaison during the battle was not helped by British reserve and French lack of it. 'My God how awful to be allied to so temperamental a race!' wrote Pownall in his diary. The next day, the outwardly imperturbable Dowding, C-in-C Fighter Command, in a dramatic presentation to Churchill and the Cabinet, explained with a simple graph how many Hurricanes would remain, at current loss rates, after a fortnight if further planes were sent to France. Not 'a single Hurricane left in France or this country.' Dowding recalled that the graph 'did the trick'. The fighters would be held back for the defence of Britain. For France, it was clear, was doomed anyway. Pétain replaced Reynaud on 16 June and immediately began negotiating for an armistice.

The English journalist and writer, Mollie Panter-Downes (1906–1997) was the *New Yorker*'s London correspondent during Word War II, and sent weekly or fortnightly dispatches from a battered Home Front. Her articles were understated, reflecting the humour and stoicism of the Londoners she much admired. Occasionally sorrow and anger break through, and determination, as the last line of this extract testifies. She painted a picture beyond the horror – of queues, blackouts, rationing – all far removed from the comfortable world of her audience. The writer C. P. Snow said of her letters home that they 'bring it all back, as though one caught a whiff of brick dust and was transported to the smell after an air raid'. Mrs Panter-Downes wrote her pieces in her country house near Haslemere in Surrey, where she lived with her civil servant husband and two daughters, when she returned from trips to London. To send her copy to New York she had to use a relay, including a delivery boy on a bicycle who wobbled to the railway station, and a friendly railway conductor who popped across to the cable office at Waterloo Station (if he remembered).

The Berchtesgaden referred to was Hitler's mountain retreat. *Francs-tireurs* ('free shooters') were originally French irregulars in the Franco-Prussian War (1870–1), dressed in non-military uniform. Harold Nicolson, later knighted, was at this time National Labour Member of Parliament for West Leicester, a distinguished ex-diplomat and writer.

May 12, 1940
[On 10 May Germany had invaded the Low Countries]

It is difficult to remember that this is Whitsun, the long weekend on which Londoners usually acquire the tan that must last them until their August vacation, and nothing has impressed them more as an indication that the government is really getting a move on than the decision to cut out the sacred holiday. People say that it feels like September all over again – same sort of weather, same sort of posters, same sort of empty sensation as the news came through of the bombing of Brussels, Calais, and Louvain – and the bus changing gear at the corner sounds ridiculously like a siren for a second, as it used to do in the first edgy days of the war.

On the Friday which began with the invasion of Holland, Belgium, and Luxembourg and ended with the resignation of Mr Chamberlain, London itself seemed much the same as usual except that everyone carried a paper and most people for the first time in months carried a gas mask (ladies who felt like taking in a Whit Saturday matinée were warned by the radio that they would probably be refused admittance to the theatres without one). Air Raid Precautions workers, who have spent the last seven months playing darts and making themselves endless cups of tea, stood ready. Householders checked up on their blackout facilities and ran through the instructions for dealing with an incendiary bomb: you shovel sand over it and rush it out of the house in a bucket, after which, as the Ministry of Home Security cheerfully adds, 'you will then have to deal with the fire which the bomb has started.'

This being notoriously an inarticulate nation which likes to express its feelings at home and not in public at a café table, there were no excited crowds in the streets, and the only place where voices were raised above the average British monotone was Soho, where unemployed Italian waiters stood at the street corners or crowded into their favourite bar on Frith Street, vigorously arguing as to whether Mussolini is coming off the fence now, in which case they will be on the wrong side of an internment camp's barbed wire, or will wait for his friend to give him fresh proof of military prowess in the Low Countries.

Events are moving so fast that England acquired a new Premier almost absent-mindedly, without any excessive jubilation from Winston Churchill's supporters, who had been fearful that even at the last moment Mr Chamberlain would hang onto the office, since he was said to feel, in his mystical Berchtesgaden manner, that it was his sacred duty to lead the nation to ultimate victory. Those who still believed him capable of doing so were mostly to be found in the middle class, for the aristocrats and the working people, who frequently plump on the same side in matters of policy, had long been resentful of his habit of surrounding himself with loyal but fumbling yes-men, and of the inflexible provincial caution which caused M. Osusky, the late Czech Minister to Paris, to observe. *'Monsieur Chamberlain n'est pas un homme d'etat; il est un businessman de Birmingham.'* [Mr Chamberlain is not a statesman; he is a Birmingham businessman.]

In Winston Churchill, people feel that they have a leader who understands exactly what risks should be taken and what kind of adversary they are up against; the iron foe of appeasement had burned too deeply into British souls for them ever to be quite sure again of Chamberlain on that second point. Diehard Tories, who once looked on Mr Churchill as 'a dangerous fellow,' now passionately proclaim that he is just what the country needs. It's paradoxical but true that the British, for all their suspicious dislike of brilliance, are beginning to think that they'd be safer with a bit of dynamite around...

Since the public has been asked to look out for parachute troops at dawn and dusk, there has been a great deal of argument as to what a person should do who suddenly sees a German soldier tumbling from the clouds. One publication urged its golfing readers to carry a rifle in their golf bags, but this was not recommended by the *Times*, which observed, 'It would not be correct for country gentlemen to carry their guns with them on their walks, and take flying or running shots as opportunity is offered. Such action would put them into the position of *francs-tireurs* and should therefore be avoided.' The proper procedure, said the *Times*, in case you're worrying, is to telephone the police as calmly as possible.

Britons are certainly calm in the present crisis. They are neither excessively pessimistic nor optimistic over the news as it comes in, because they remember the initial optimism over what turned out to be the Norwegian reverse. It is probable that good will come out of this reverse in the long run, if only because it has stopped people from chirping, 'Ah well, we always start badly' or 'We English always lose every battle but the last.' There's a feeling now that in this war the last battle may not be recognized until it is over, and anyway, after Chamberlain's unfortunate colloquial remark about Hitler's having missed the bus, snappy slogans aren't so popular as they were.

It takes a good, stiff dose of adversity to release the formidable strength in what Harold Nicolson has called 'the slow-grinding will power of the British people.' To that has been added for the first time the quickening realization that they are fighting for their lives.

'Blood, toil, tears and sweat'

Winston Churchill, House of Commons, 13 May 1940

Chamberlain's policy of appeasing Hitler failed. Hitler annexed Austria in March 1938 and a year later on 15 March 1939 grabbed Bohemia and Moravia, the part of Czechoslovakia that he had not already snatched as part of the Munich Agreement ('a total and unmitigated defeat' – Churchill) in September 1938. Hitler invaded Poland on 1 September 1939. But opponents of appeasement in Chamberlain's own Conservative Party were in a minority.

After the debate on the disastrous Norwegian Campaign on 7 May 1940, Chamberlain survived the vote although with a majority of only 81 from its norm of 200, figures which spelt his doom (41 of his own Tories voted with the opposition and about 60 abstained). An all-party government was needed and Labour let it be known they would not serve under Chamberlain. Lord Halifax, then Foreign Secretary and regarded as Chamberlain's deputy, considered that the new leader should be in the Commons and agreed to serve under Churchill. On 10 May 1940, Winston Churchill became Prime Minister. Yet Churchill's maverick reputation persisted, although his bulldog belligerence inspired hope. He himself was only too aware of what lay ahead. He commented to General Ismay, 'Poor people, poor people. They trust me, and I can give them nothing but disaster for quite a long time.' Brendan Bracken described Winston's mood as one of 'profound anxiety'.

This speech was delivered to the House of Commons, but was later repeated as a broadcast on BBC radio.

———◆◇◆———

I would say to the House, as I said to those who have joined this government: 'I have nothing to offer but blood, toil, tears and sweat.'

We have before us an ordeal of the most grievous kind. We have before us many, many long months of struggle and of suffering. You ask, what is our policy? I can say: It is to wage war, by sea, land and air, with all our might and with all the strength that God can give us; to wage war against a monstrous tyranny, never surpassed in the dark, lamentable catalogue of human crime. That is our policy. You ask, what is our aim? I can answer in one word: It is victory, victory at all costs, victory in spite of all terror, victory, however long and hard the road may be; for without victory, there is no survival. Let that be realised; no survival for the British Empire, no survival for all that the British Empire has stood for, no survival for the urge and impulse of the ages, that mankind will move forward towards its goal. But I take up my task with buoyancy and hope. I feel sure that our cause will not be suffered to fail among men. At this time I feel entitled to claim the aid of all, and I say, 'come then, let us go forward together with our united strength.'

Defence of Calais, 23–26 May 1940

Airey Neave [from *The Flames of Calais*, London 1972]

The three-day defence of Calais (23–26 May 1940) was fought to stop the Germans, whose southern armoured pincer had broken through the French 9th Army, from driving towards Dunkirk, towards which the BEF was retreating. According to Churchill, Calais' defence was 'the crux' without which 'all would have been cut off and lost', and evacuation at Dunkirk impossible. Churchill had sent a last message to the British defenders, about 3,000 men, that 'you must continue to fight... Evacuation will not (*repeat* not) take place...' The C.I.G.S. (Chief of the Imperial General Staff), General Ironside, wrote of Calais in his diary: 'A great effort which I hope we will never forget... The most famous regiments in the Army. They fought it out to the end... I was sure they would do their duty and they did it. A fitting finish to their history. Requiescant.'

But Guderian, 10th Panzer Division's commander at Calais, commented after the war, 'The British defence of Calais had no effect on the operations against Dunkirk.' He claimed that his division was not pinned down at Calais, but had been stopped by Hitler's 'Halt Order' of 24 May when Hitler ordered his tanks to rest and refit.

The heroism of the defenders is undoubted. The garrison's commander, Brigadier Nicholson, refused a German appeal to surrender: 'It is the British Army's duty to fight'. He died in a

German P.O.W. camp. What is also undoubted is that the operation was a balls-up; mistakes in both loading and unloading meant that within hours of landing the defenders had little but Bren guns, anti-tank rifles and rifles to beat off attacks, and were woefully short of ammunition. A vehicle ship was sent back to Dover prematurely, laden with wounded but also half 1st Rifle Brigade's weapons and ammunition. The French, responsible for demolishing bridges over canals, had no demolition charges. French Communists added to the misery by cutting all communications with England and France at the quay, and sniping at British troops in the city. French dockers and tug boat crews deserted. It was somehow predictable that when the Royal Navy eventually brought gelignite for demolition, the primers were found to be the wrong size.

Airey Neave (1916–1979) was a subaltern with a searchlight battalion who found himself swept up in the desperate fighting in Calais at the end of May 1940. He was full of admiration for the fighting qualities of the regular battalions and very conscious of his non-combatant status. Neave was the first officer to make a 'home run' from Colditz. Back in England he worked for MI9 (codename 'Saturday') where he helped set up escape lines. After the war, while assistant secretary to the International Military Tribunal, he served the indictments on Nazi leaders at Nuremberg. He was awarded both a DSO and MC. At the time of his murder by the IRA in 1979 he was MP for Abingdon, Mrs Thatcher's closest adviser and principal Conservative spokesman on Northern Ireland.

At the Pont Jourdan, about 4 p.m. [on 24 May], a cruiser tank moved forward to the railway bridge and an officer peered out of the turret. He fired two or three rounds towards Boulogne and then withdrew. The Germans replied with great violence. Tank shells and machine-gun bullets came thick and fast for twenty minutes. Ricochets off the walls and flying glass made my situation in the Rue Edgar Quinet, a side street next to the bridge, rather exposed. The Rue Edgar Quinet was, in normal times, a quiet street with red-brick houses, and a girls' school on the west side. It was now without a sign of life, save for a young girl's white face at a cellar grating. The wall which sheltered me had ragged gaps where mortar bombs had flung bricks into the street. I began to look for a safer position.

The enemy seemed dreadfully close though I could see nothing but clouds of dust and smoke. I was conscious that standing where I was, I could be of little use except to encourage the Searchlight men as they fired bravely, but inexpertly, towards Boulogne. I was concerned for the safety of the 60th on the far side of the bridge as much as for the Germans. A Bren gun in a window, lace curtains flying, fired fitfully then jammed.

As the afternoon wore on, I began to feel my lack of training for battle. The sun shone and the heat from burning buildings led to an intolerable thirst. If only I could get back to the café. I waited for the firing to lift and was about to cross, when I felt a sharp, bruising pain in my left side. I collapsed to the pavement, my rifle clattering. There came a shout of concern from the lace curtains: 'Are you all right, sir?'

I did not reply. I was trying to imagine what had happened. Was it a sniper, or a machine-gun bullet? Then I realised I could still walk. Doubled up, I hurried painfully across to the café and into the safety of a side street. My immediate fear was that the Germans would break through in the next few minutes, that I should be left behind and captured. It was a fear shared by all. We had a confused but horrific picture of what awaited us if we were taken prisoner by the Nazis. Death in action was something everyone faced, but stories of the ill-treatment of prisoners, of concentration camps, made capture seem the worst of all.

While the café proprietor with the Croix de Guerre brought a large helping of cognac, a medical orderly opened my battledress blouse. He was pale, very cheerful and he squinted. From far away, I heard him say: 'You're a lucky one, sir. 'Arf an inch from the 'eart!'

'Finest hour'

Winston Churchill, House of Commons, 18 June 1940

The German *blitzkrieg* in the West was a monstrous gamble. The Maginot Line (which stopped at Belgium's border) was bypassed by Panzers attacking through the 'impassable' Ardennes, with a surprise, swift breakthrough across the Meuse by Army Group A under Von Rundstedt, who was allotted the bulk of the Panzer forces. He advanced on a narrow front with integrated air support, infantry and armour. Tank generals like Guderian and Rommel commanded from their lead tanks, improvising when necessary, and pressing on regardless of their flanks, trusting in speed to overwhelm enemy command and control. The gamble could have been thwarted by swift counter-attacks on these vulnerable flanks with concentrated armour and air-strikes. A British attack south of Arras on 21 May alarmed Rommel, but it was isolated and too late. German Army Group B, under Von Bock, had the important role of drawing the Allied First Army Group into Belgium and holding it there. When Army Group A reached Abbeville on the Channel coast on 19 May, the Allies were trapped in a huge pocket.

The Dunkirk evacuation (26 May–3 June) rescued 338,000 British and French from the coastline and mole, flotillas of small ships ferrying soldiers from the beaches to Royal Navy ships just offshore. The evacuation was successful beyond all expectations, but 'wars are not won by evacuations' as Churchill said. More than 1,000 ships of all sizes were involved. The British lost all their heavy equipment and transport (120,000 vehicles). 97 per cent of the 120,000 French troops rescued from Dunkirk and elsewhere decided not to join de Gaulle's Free French and returned to France after a few months. Some French people made accommodation with the victors, and Paris restaurants put up little notices: '*Ici on parle allemand*'. But a nucleus of internal resistance began, tiny at first, to be swelled by Communists after the June '41 Nazi invasion of Russia, now obeying different instructions.

The French lost 90,000 dead in the Battle of France, the Germans 28,000. Britain's total casualties, including dead, were over 68,000. It was a brilliant German strategic plan, devised essentially by General Manstein and executed with tactical mastery, one of the classic campaigns of history.

In this speech to the House of Commons, Churchill does not dissemble; 'a colossal military disaster' has befallen the nation. He predicts bomber attacks on cities. But he sees hope in the strength of the Royal Navy and in RAF fighters now operating from home airfields within minutes of the fray. He makes a typically Churchillian joke at the Italian navy's expense. But above all, he relishes the grandeur of the moment, of Britain standing alone.

The disastrous military events which have happened during the past fortnight have not come to me with any sense of surprise. Indeed, I indicated a fortnight ago as clearly as I could to the House that the worst possibilities were open; and I made it perfectly clear then that whatever happened in France would make no difference to the resolve of Britain and the British Empire to fight on, if necessary for years, if necessary alone.

During the last few days we have successfully brought off the great majority of the troops we had on the line of communication in France; and seven-eighths of the troops we have sent to France since the beginning of the war – that is to say, about 350,000 out of 400,000 men – are safely back in this country. Others are still fighting with the French, and fighting with considerable success in their local encounters against the enemy. We have also brought back a great mass of stores, rifles and munitions of all kinds, which had been accumulated in France during the last nine months.

... Some people seem to forget that we have a Navy. We must remind them. For the last thirty years I have been concerned in discussions about the possibilities of oversea invasion, and I took the responsibility on behalf of the Admiralty, at the beginning of the last war, of allowing all regular troops to be sent out of the country. That was a very serious step to take, because our Territorials had only just been called up and were quite untrained. Therefore, this Island was for several months particularly denuded of fighting troops. The Admiralty had confidence at that time in their ability to prevent a mass invasion even though at that time the Germans had a magnificent battle fleet in the proportion of 10 to 16, even though they were capable of fighting a general engagement every day and any day, whereas now they have only a couple of heavy ships worth speaking of – the *Scharnhorst* and the *Gneisenau*. We are also told that the Italian Navy is to come out and gain sea superiority in these waters. If they seriously intend it, I shall only say that we shall be delighted to offer Signor Mussolini a free and safeguarded passage through the Strait of Gibraltar in order that he may play the part to which he aspires. There is a general curiosity in the British Fleet to find out whether the Italians are up to the level they were at in the last war or whether they have fallen off at all...

This brings me... to the great question of invasion from the air, and of the impending struggle between the British and German Air Forces. It seems quite clear that no invasion on a scale beyond the capacity of our land forces to crush speedily is likely to take place from the air until our Air Force has been definitely overpowered. In the meantime, there may be raids by parachute troops and attempted descents of airborne soldiers. We should be able to give those gentry a warm reception both in the air and on the ground, if they reach it in any condition to continue the dispute. But the great question is: Can we break Hitler's air weapon?

… During the great battle in France, we gave very powerful and continuous aid to the French Army, both by fighters and bombers; but in spite of every kind of pressure we never would allow the entire metropolitan fighter strength of the Air Force to be consumed… I am happy to inform the House that our fighter strength is stronger at the present time relatively to the Germans, who have suffered terrible losses, than it has ever been; and consequently we believe ourselves possessed of the capacity to continue the war in the air under better conditions than we have ever experienced before. I look forward confidently to the exploits of our fighter pilots – these splendid men, this brilliant youth – who will have the glory of saving their native land, their island home, and all they love, from the most deadly of all attacks…

During the first four years of the last war the Allies experienced nothing but disaster and disappointment. That was our constant fear: one blow after another, terrible losses, frightful dangers. Everything miscarried. And yet at the end of those four years the morale of the Allies was higher than that of the Germans, who had moved from one aggressive triumph to another, and who stood everywhere triumphant invaders of the lands into which they had broken. During that war we repeatedly asked ourselves the question: 'How are we going to win?' And no one was able ever to answer it with much precision, until at the end, quite suddenly, quite unexpectedly, our terrible foe collapsed before us, and we were so glutted with victory that in our folly we threw it away...

What General Weygand called the Battle of France is over. I expect that the Battle of Britain is about to begin. Upon this battle depends the survival of Christian civilization. Upon it depends our own British life, and the long continuity of our institutions and our Empire. The whole fury and might of the enemy must very soon be turned on us.

Hitler knows that he will have to break us in this Island or lose the war. If we can stand up to him, all Europe may be free and the life of the world may move forward into broad, sunlit uplands. But if we fail, then the whole world, including the United States, including all that we have known and cared for, will sink into the abyss of a new Dark Age made more sinister, and perhaps more protracted, by the lights of perverted science.

Let us therefore brace ourselves to our duties, and so bear ourselves that if the British Empire and its Commonwealth last for a thousand years, men will still say, '*This* was their finest hour.'

Return to Namsos: A Memoir of the Norwegian campaign, April 1940

Peter Fleming [*The Spectator*, 16 May 1970]

Norway and Sweden had opted for neutrality in 1939, and supplied Nazi Germany with vital iron ore, mostly through the ice-free Norwegian port of Narvik, in Ofot Fjord. To stop the flow, Britain and France mined Norwegian inland waters, and prepared to land at Narvik and other ports. But Germany beat them to it. On 9 April 1940, the Germans attacked and by midday had captured Oslo and other major towns, including Narvik, with airborne troops. Both the Norwegians and Allies had assumed, until too late, that a German assault was impossible in the face of British naval superiority. Few predicted that German air superiority would be the key.

In mid-April 12,000 Anglo-French and Polish troops landed north and south of Trondheim but the *Luftwaffe* prevented their supply and German ground troops forced their evacuation by 2 May. On 13 May the allies landed in numbers to retake Narvik and – after a fortnight and despite inter-service squabbling and endless changes of command – they did; but unable to sustain the force after the invasion of France and in the face of constant *Luftwaffe* bombardment they withdrew on 8 June. The British lost 4,500 men, 1,500 of whom went down with the carrier *Glorious* and her escorts, sunk by the German pocket battleship *Scharnhorst*. French and Polish combined losses were about

500. Norwegian dead numbered about 1,800. German losses were high – 5,500 men, 200 aircraft, and some of their most modern ships, including 3 cruisers and all 10 of the destroyers that had landed the troops that had taken Narvik, 8 being sunk by the battleship HMS *Warspite*. The German surface navy never really recovered.

Germany's victory gave her a base from which to harry Allied shipping; but it also tied down a garrison of 350,000, required to protect occupied Norway from Allied invasion. The Chamberlain government fell as a direct result of the disastrous Norway campaign.

Valentine Fleming, father of Peter Fleming (1907–1971), was MP for Henley and was killed in action in 1917. Peter's younger brother Ian was the creator of James Bond. Educated at Eton and Christ Church, Oxford, Fleming became literary editor of *The Spectator* and was a much-travelled Special Correspondent for *The Times*, for which he also wrote many witty Fourth Leaders during the later 1930s. He published popular travel books of which *Brazilian Adventure* (1933) is the best known. In 1935 he married the distinguished stage and screen actress Celia Johnson. In 1939 he joined the Grenadier Guards. After Norway, he served in Greece in 1941, in Burma and lastly as head of strategic deception in South East Asia Command. One clever idea he had was to produce thousands of dummy submarine periscopes. They were dropped into Japanese waters, fooling them into wasting a lot of depth charges. After the war he retired to his estate at Nettlebed in the Chilterns, and led a comfortable life as a literary squire.

'PURPOSE OF VISIT...' The last question on the hotel registration form was not easy to answer. In a civilised country like Norway it didn't really matter what one put down, but I felt an odd reluctance to prevaricate, to evade the issue. I was certainly not on business. 'Tourism' is an abject formula indispensable behind the Iron Curtain but unfit for use elsewhere. 'Research' would have given my motives too intellectual, and 'Sentiment' too emotional, a gloss. In the end I wrote 'Curiosity'.

The friendly girl behind the desk took the form without looking at it. 'You notice some changes in Namsos, perhaps?' she asked. It was clear that she knew who I was.

Thirty years earlier almost to the day – on 14 April 1940, to be exact – I had had my first sight of Namsos, a little wooden town tucked under beetling outcrops of rock at the head of a thirteen-mile-long fjord. In the previous week the Germans, in a series of daring operations, had seized the principal Norwegian ports; the Allies, with a recklessness to which the frustrations of the phoney war and the bellicosity of Winston Churchill may have made contributions of roughly equal importance, resolved to challenge the invaders on Norwegian soil; and amid barely describable confusion three separate expeditionary forces were directed on Narvik, Namsos and Aandalsnes.

In London, however, there was some uncertainty (that is to say, nobody had the slightest idea) whether Namsos was or was not in German hands, and it was prudently decided that a reconnaissance of this obscure little town only 125 miles by road north of Trondheim, where the enemy had been installed for a week – should be carried out before an attempt was made to land there. Less prudently, it was also decided that I should carry it out.

As the Sunderland droned towards the Norwegian coast my last-minute orders from the cruiser *Glasgow* ended: *'Essential observe complete secrecy.'* But it is hardly possible to dissemble a four-engined flying-boat, and after circling low over Namsos for ten minutes without seeing – except for some herring gulls – any sign of life, we had no more idea than Neville Chamberlain whether the Germans were in the town or not.

So we veered off southwards, landed in an arm of the fjord at a little place called Bangsund and, after being assured by a Norwegian in a rowing boat that the Germans had not yet arrived, sent an officer ashore to ring up the Namsos telephone exchange and tell them to stop all outgoing calls. Then we took off again, touched down off Namsos and taxied up to the wooden quay, now peopled by an apprehensive crowd. We landed, I made some sort of speech and we tried, unsuccessfully, to contact the Navy on our portable wireless sets.

Today, thirty years later, these events are vividly remembered by the senior citizens: as is the controversy – only resolved by the appearance that evening of four Tribal class destroyers – as to whether or not I was a German officer in disguise. But it was what happened six days later that made the deepest impression.

In the intervening nights, which gave us only about four hours of darkness, a British territorial brigade, cumbered with enormous fur coats but short of transport and totally devoid of any supporting arms, had somehow got ashore and been deployed southwards towards Trondheim without being observed by the Luftwaffe's thrice-daily reconnaissances. On the night of the 19th three battalions of Chasseurs Alpins, less their indispensable mules, were landed; but nobody had told the French that we were playing hide-and-seek, and when the Luftwaffe arrived, bang on time, for their pre-breakfast inspection the Chasseurs engaged them, ineffectively, with machine-guns. By noon the little wooden town was a holocaust; by dusk two-thirds of it had been destroyed. Astonishingly, there were only six fatal casualties – two Norwegian civilians and four French soldiers. I was reported killed, and several American papers published trite but kindly obituaries.

The Allied Force Command was that legendary, admirable character, Adrian Carton de Wiart, VC. He flew out in a Sunderland which came under air attack while rendezvousing with a destroyer, and his only staff officer was wounded: so for some days I found myself acting as his batman, driver, chief of staff and (mercifully on rare occasions) cook.

The Luftwaffe, unopposed save – towards the end – by a very few AA guns, continued to pound Namsos whenever weather permitted. Standing the other day outside the little wooden house which the General and I had shared, high up under the rock-face which dominates the town, I remembered the morning when I had to tell him that Fanny, the beautiful Norwegian girl who did for us, had departed to safer quarters in the countryside.

'Don't blame her,' said the General accepting a mug of melted snow to shave in. The supply of water, as of electricity, no longer existed. 'I'll go and scrounge some of those French rations while you do breakfast.'

Shovelling more snow into the saucepan (it takes an awful lot of snow to produce a very little water), I watched him saunter down the steep hill towards the quay as the church-bells rang and the first air-raid of the day was unleashed. A conspicuous figure in his red hat (Carton de Wiart refused to wear a steel helmet), he maintained an even pace down the centre of the gutted street. Machine-guns chattered; smoke drifted from burning buildings; the Heinkels were flying so low that the bombs had no time to whistle before they burst. Carton de Wiart paid not the slightest attention. From safe bivouacs in the wooded heights around Namsos hundreds or men were watching him – French infantry, British base personnel, all in some degree shaken by their recent ordeals, all (at a guess) becoming a little more war-worthy as they followed his lackadaisical progress.

The Luftwaffe went home with empty bomb-racks. The General returned with some delicious sardines. His single eye surveyed my preparations for breakfast. Devastation was all around us. 'Better get rid of those egg-shells somewhere,' he said. 'Don't want the place in a mess.'

The Allied plans for a pincer movement on Trondheim from Aandalsnes and Namsos were, after much shilly-shallying, abandoned; German air supremacy decisively cancelled what had never been much more than a pipe-dream. On the short night of 2 May the Royal Navy with some help from the French, extricated us from Namsos, a sour, charred, flat mass of rubble, eerily and dangerously illumined by a huge dump of inextinguishably burning coal.

Today these frightful scars have healed. A new, pleasant, unpretentious town has risen on the ruins of thirty years ago. Only one of the massive German barracks still stands, and there is no longer any trace of what the Norwegians called 'the English Channel'. This was an enormous anti-tank ditch, built right across the middle of Namsos by Russian and Yugoslav prisoners of war, who were treated with extreme inhumanity. A main theme of the Allied deception plans in the last war was the simulation of a threat to Norway, and the construction of this obstacle at the head of a long, narrow fjord lavishly protected by minefields and coastal artillery, is one of the many proofs offered by the Norwegian coast-line that Hitler's intelligence was successfully deluded. It was called 'the English Channel' because the citizens felt that, if the Allies could get across the Atlantic, and across the North Sea, and all the way up the fjord, they would probably manage, somehow, to get across the big ditch in the High Street.

I was surprised, as well as touched, by the warmth of my welcome. I had, after all, been the harbinger of doom and disaster; I had aroused in stout hearts and bewildered minds hopes which were soon proved cruelly false; no single action of mine had done anybody in Namsos any good, indeed I cannot remember one which failed to inconvenience the population and endanger the town. 'It is 126 years', I had often, and sometimes querulously, been reminded in 1940, 'since Norway was involved in war.' Now people who had been children then, apprised by the local paper of my presence, stopped me in the street and said how glad they were that I had come back. I suppose the truth is that in a small place the past, however unpalatable, is converted quite quickly into legend; and legend, especially in a small place, is something to cherish in all its aspects.

Fanny, for a short spell the Force-Commander's elfin cook-house-keeper, now a handsome lady with five children, apologised for deserting our quarters and seemed not to blame us at all for deserting her country. Other old acquaintances took the same line: so did the man I had come to see, though he had suffered worse than any of the survivors of 1940.

Henrik Andersen was then harbourmaster of Namsos, and the Allies owed a great deal to him. It was he who, on the day I landed and while I was still under a cloud as a putative impersonator, persuaded the four pilots whom the Navy needed, to go out and guide the destroyers in. In the crucial following nights the small harbour was regularly overcrowded with ships, all anxious to get away before the quick dawn came. When the troops disembarked, they found none of the normal apparatus of a base – no Embarkation Staff Officers, no Military Police, no signs directing traffic, nothing – except Henrik Andersen, and Martin Lindsay, and me; and it was up to us, with such volunteer help as we could scrounge, to restore the status quo – to put the gangways and the coils of rope and all the other stage-properties back where they had been the day before, so that the Luftwaffe's first, early-morning emissary would take back to Trondheim the same *mise en scène* that his cameras had recorded yesterday.

It was mainly thanks to Andersen that this *trompe l'oeil* succeeded, for five nights, in its purpose, that we won the game of hide-and-seek. When we left I handed over to him what was left of the thick wad of Norwegian bank-notes with which, by courtesy of the Bank of England, my theoretically clandestine mission had been provided.

Carton de Wiart took a poor view of the senior naval officer in charge of the arrangements for our evacuation. 'I don't know much about butterflies, but I've heard of a Red Admiral. Never realised there was a yellow variety.' When the last destroyer to leave Namsos had embarked the rearguard and the stragglers, she was ordered to open fire on the assorted vehicles which, now massed on the quay, had made possible our withdrawal. 'I only hope', the Force-Commander wrote, sub-acidly, in his official dispatch, 'that no Norwegians were killed'.

I asked Andersen if any had been killed. 'No,' he said, 'but a shell came through the harbourmaster's office and I felt most lonely. You had all gone. Nothing was left of Namsos, nobody there. Only me. And now this shell in my office. Lonely, that was how I felt.'

We were talking in a sort of private reception-room in the new hospital; Andersen, now in his late seventies, has to go there for monthly blood-transfusions. In the long years after the Allies left he worked for the Resistance: was betrayed: and fell into the hands of Rinnan, a young sadist quisling working for the Gestapo who was executed, with six of his associates after the war. Andersen was atrociously tortured and condemned to be shot. An elderly German, who had nominally taken over his duties as harbourmaster, interceded for him. Andersen was reprieved; he would be transported to a concentration camp in Germany. But the ship which was to transport him was sunk by the RAF and Andersen survived the war.

From his son's letters I had expected to meet a ghost, a man wandering in his mind, inarticulate, moribund. Not a bit of it. Reprieved from a formal execution, he has because of what was done to him lived under the shadow of death for more than a quarter of a century; only constant blood transfusions kept him alive. Yet nobody could have been jollier, more perceptive, less self-pitying, more grateful for being made by King George VI a member of the order to which, at the time of writing, a majority of the Beatles still belong.

He remembered Carton de Wiart as 'a lovely man'. The Allied Force Commander was not given to hyperbole, but I think he might have returned the compliment, suitably modified.

An airman's letter

The Times, 18 June 1940

This letter was written by an English bomber pilot and left with his Commanding Officer, unsealed, with instructions that it be sent to his mother if he was killed. On 30 May 1940, his Wellington was shot down over Veurne, near Ostend, while on a night raid supporting the BEF's retreat to Dunkirk. There were no survivors. His CO read the letter (for security reasons) and was so impressed by its patriotic tone that he asked the pilot's mother if it could be published anonymously. After it appeared in *The Times* the paper received half a million requests for copies. In 1981 the pilot was identified as Flying Officer Vivian Rosewarne, from No. 38 Squadron based at Marham in Norfolk. He is buried in Veurne Communal Cemetery (Grave 1, Row B). His age is recorded as 'unknown'. His name is also recorded on the Roll of Honour of the British Union of Fascists.

Dearest Mother,

Though I feel no premonition at all, events are moving rapidly, and I have instructed that this letter be forwarded to you should I fail to return from one of the raids which we shall shortly be called upon to undertake. You must hope on for a month, but at the end of that time you must accept the fact that I have handed my task over to the extremely capable hands of my comrades of the Royal Air Forces, as so many splendid fellows have already done.

First, it will comfort you to know that my role in this war has been of the greatest importance. Our patrols far out over the North Sea have helped to keep the trade routes clear for our convoys and supply ships, and on one occasion our information was instrumental in saving the lives of the men in a crippled lighthouse relief ship. Though it will be difficult for you, you will disappoint me if you do not at least try to accept the facts dispassionately, for I shall have done my duty to the utmost of my ability. No man can do more, and no one calling himself a man could do less.

I have always admired your amazing courage in the face of continual setbacks; in a way you have given me as good an education and background as anyone in the country; and always kept up appearances without ever losing faith in the future. My death would not mean that your struggle has been in vain. Far from it. It means that your sacrifice is as great as mine. Those who serve England must expect nothing from her; we debase ourselves if we regard our country as merely a place in which to eat and sleep.

History resounds with illustrious names who have given all, yet their sacrifice has resulted in the British Empire, where there is a measure of peace, justice, and freedom for all, and where a higher standard of civilization has evolved, and is still evolving, than anywhere else. But this is not only concerning our own land. Today we are faced with the greatest organized challenge to Christianity and civilization that the world has ever seen, and I count myself lucky and honoured to be the right age and fully trained to throw my weight into the scale.

For this I have to thank you. Yet there is more work for you to do. The home front will still have to stand united for years after the war is won. For all that can be said against it, I still maintain that this war is a very good thing; every individual is having the chance to live and dare all for his principles like the martyrs of old. However long the time may be, one thing can never be altered – I shall have lived and died an Englishman. Nothing else matters one jot nor can anything ever change it.

You must not grieve for me, for if you really believe in religion and all that it entails that would be hypocrisy. I have no fear of death; only a queer elation... I would have it no other way. The universe is so vast and so ageless that the life of one man can only be justified by the measure of his sacrifice. We are sent to this world to acquire a personality and a character to take with us that can never be taken from us. Those who just eat and sleep, prosper and procreate, are no better than animals if all their lives they are at peace.

I firmly and absolutely believe that evil things are sent into the world to try us; they are sent deliberately by our Creator to test our mettle because He knows what is good for us. The Bible is full of cases where the easy way out has been discarded for moral principles.

I count myself fortunate in that I have seen the whole country and known men of every calling. But with the final test of war I consider my character fully developed. Thus at my early age my earthly mission is already fulfilled and I am prepared to die with just one regret, and one only – that I could not devote myself to making your declining years more happy by being with you; but you will live in peace and freedom and I shall have directly contributed to that, so here again my life will not have been in vain.

Your loving Son.

The Second Armistice at Compiègne, 21 June 1940

William L. Shirer [from *The Rise and Fall of The Third Reich*, New York and London, 1959]

William L. Shirer (1904–1993), the son of an American lawyer, toured Europe in 1925 and while in Paris found work with the *Chicago Tribune*. After learning French, German, Italian and Spanish he became a foreign correspondent. In 1933 he married a Viennese photographer. Ed Murrow recruited Shirer for CBS in 1937. As its Berlin representative, Shirer provided a regular commentary of the developments in Nazi Germany, mostly censored by the Nazis, who he loathed. The Nazis made it impossible for Shirer to report the truth, and so he left the country in December, 1940.

Shirer's first book, *Berlin Diary*, was published in 1941. *The Rise and Fall of The Third Reich* (1959) portrays the Nazi regime as tawdry and brutal, reflecting the observation by German-born philosopher Hannah Arendt about the 'banality of evil'. The 'great granite block' referred to by Shirer below, with its robust inscription, was blown up by the Germans. The railway carriage, Car No 2419D of the Wagons-Lits Co., was taken to Berlin shortly after the ceremony and put on public display. Accounts differ as to its fate – it was either deliberately burnt to prevent its humiliating re-use in 1945, or destroyed in a British air raid in 1944. An identical carriage from

222

the same 1913 series, Car No.2439 D, can be visited today at the clearing in Compiègne.

———◆◈◆———

I FOLLOWED THE GERMAN ARMY into Paris that June, always the loveliest of months in the majestic capital, which was now stricken, and on 19 June got wind of where Hitler was going to lay down his terms for the armistice which Petain had requested two days before. It was to be on the same spot where the German Empire had capitulated to France and her allies on 11 November 1918: in the little clearing in the woods at Compiègne. There the Nazi warlord would get his revenge, and the place itself would add to the sweetness of it for him. On 20 May, a bare ten days after the great offensive in the West had started and on the day the German tanks reached Abbeville, the idea had come to him. Jodl noted it in his diary that day: 'Fuehrer is working on the peace treaty... First negotiations in the Forest of Compiègne.' Late on the afternoon of 19 June I drove out there and found German Army engineers demolishing the wall of the museum where the old *wagon-lit* of Marshal Foch, in which the 1918 armistice was signed, had been preserved. By the time I left, the engineers, working with pneumatic drills, had torn the wall down and were pulling the car out to the tracks in the centre of the clearing on the exact spot, they said, where it had stood at 5 am on 11 November 1918, when at the dictation of Foch the German emissaries put their signatures to the armistice.

And so it was that on the afternoon of 21 June I stood by the edge of the forest at Compiègne to observe the latest and greatest of Hitler's triumphs, of which, in the course of my work, I had seen so many over the last turbulent years. It was one of the loveliest summer days I ever remember in France. A warm June sun beat down on the stately trees – elms, oaks, cypresses and pines – casting pleasant shadows on the wooded avenues leading to the little circular clearing. At 3:15 P.M. precisely, Hitler arrived in his big Mercedes, accompanied by Goering, Brauchitsch, Keitel, Raeder, Ribbentrop and Hess, all in their various uniforms, and Goering, the lone Field Marshal of the Reich, fiddling with his field marshal's baton. They alighted from their automobiles some two hundred yards away, in front of the Alsace-Lorraine statue, which was draped with German war flags so that the Fuehrer could not see (though I remembered from previous visits in happier days) the large sword, the sword of the victorious Allies of 1918, sticking through a limp eagle representing the German Empire of the Hohenzollerns. Hitler glanced at the monument and strode on.

I observed his face [I wrote in my diary]. It was grave, solemn, yet brimming with revenge. There was also in it, as in his springy step, a note of the triumphant conqueror, the defier of the world. There was something else... a sort of scornful, inner joy at being present at this great reversal of fate – a reversal he himself had wrought.

When he reached the little opening in the forest and his personal standard had been run up in the centre of it, his attention was attracted by a great granite block which stood some three feet above the ground.

Hitler, followed by the others, walks slowly over to it [I am quoting my diary], steps up, and reads the inscription engraved (in French) in great high letters:

'HERE ON THE ELEVENTH OF NOVEMBER 1918 SUCCUMBED THE CRIMINAL PRIDE OF THE GERMAN EMPIRE – VANQUISHED BY THE FREE PEOPLES WHICH IT TRIED TO ENSLAVE.'

Hitler reads it and Goering reads it. They all read it, standing there in the June sun and the silence. I look for the expression in Hitler's face. I am but fifty yards from him and see him through my glasses as though he were directly in front of me. I have seen that face many times at the great moments of his life. But today! It is afire with scorn, anger, hate, revenge, triumph.

He steps off the monument and contrives to make even this gesture a masterpiece of contempt. He glances back at it, contemptuous, angry – angry, you almost feel, because he cannot wipe out the awful, provoking lettering with one sweep of his high Prussian boot. He glances slowly around the clearing, and now, as his eyes meet ours, you grasp the depth of his hatred. But there is triumph there too – revengeful, triumphant hate. Suddenly, as though his face were not giving quite complete expression to his feelings, he throws his whole body into harmony with his mood. He swiftly snaps his hands on his hips, arches his shoulders, plants his feet wide apart. It is a magnificent gesture of defiance, of burning contempt for this place now and all that it has stood for in the twenty-two years since it witnessed the humbling of the German Empire.

Hitler and his party then entered the armistice railway car, the Fuehrer seating himself in the chair occupied by Foch in 1918. Five minutes later the French delegation arrived, headed by General Charles Huntziger, commander of the

Second Army at Sedan, and made up of an admiral, an Air Force general and one civilian, Lèon Noël, the former ambassador to Poland, who was now witnessing his second debacle wrought by German arms. They looked shattered, but retained a tragic dignity. They had not been told that they would be led to this proud French shrine to undergo such a humiliation, and the shock was no doubt just what Hitler had calculated. As Halder wrote in his diary that evening after being given an eyewitness account by Brauchitsch:

'The French had no warning that they would be handed the terms at the very site of the negotiations in 1918. They were apparently shaken by this arrangement and at first inclined to be sullen.'

Perhaps it was natural, even for a German so cultivated as Halder, or Brauchitsch, to mistake solemn dignity for sullenness. The French, one saw at once, were certainly dazed. Yet, contrary to the reports at the time, they tried, as we now know from the official German minutes of the meetings found among the captured Nazi secret papers, to soften the harsher portions of the Fuehrer's terms and to eliminate those which they thought were dishonourable. But they tried in vain.

'It was like everything German – overdone': Crete, 1941

Evelyn Waugh
[from *The Diaries of Evelyn Waugh*, London, 1976]

Evelyn Waugh (1903–66), author, diarist, and wartime commando became disillusioned with his fellow officers and the war itself as a direct result of his experience in Crete. It is fair to say that some of his fellow officers were disillusioned with him. He landed at Suda Bay on 26 May 1941 as Intelligence Officer with Bob Laycock's commandos to reinforce the garrison, commanded by General Freyberg. At this stage the battle was only six days old but the British and Commonwealth troops were already in retreat to the south of the island, following the successful German air-borne assault on the Maleme airfield. Waugh was evacuated by destroyer on 30 May. Much of the material in the diary was incorporated into *The Sword of Honour* trilogy [London, 1966].

Churchill himself was critical of Freyberg: 'The whole seems to have been of static defence of positions, instead of the rapid extirpation at all costs of the airborne landing parties.' If troops transported in Ju 52 aircraft had been prevented from landing at Maleme, the German General Student's parachute troops might have been defeated (as it was, two-thirds of the 10,000 German parachutists were killed or wounded while in the air or on landing). Freyberg received Ultra intelligence (decrypts from encoded messages sent via German Enigma machines that the Germans thought secure), before the invasion revealing the dropping and landing zones, but was convinced that a seaborne invasion would follow the airborne assault. Freyburg's son has loyally claimed that Maleme was lost because any major defence would have jeopardised the secret of Ultra.

The consensus among historians today is that Crete could have been held by General Freyberg. However, even if the invasion from the air had been defeated, the north of the island and the Navy would still have suffered heavy air attacks. The island could not have been used as a refuelling base for the Royal Navy without substantial air defence forces, and these were needed in North Africa. An analysis by the British Chief of Naval Operation in 1943 blamed 'lax discipline' which 'has permeated many units' but added that 'no Service gave due weight to the... overwhelming superiority of the German Air Force'. A War Office report distributed immediately after the battle to officers blamed 'tools [that] were totally inadequate' and also the 'pip squeak' guns that defended Maleme, 'Italian 75's with indifferent ammunition' which 'fragmented very poorly'. The report added for good measure a silly bit of prejudice straight out of *Dad's Army*: 'The German parachute troops exhibited in marked degree the well known characteristics of their race – an intense dislike of the bayonet.' The conclusion was, however, fair: 'The deciding factors were the lack of fighter cover and the determination of the German air attack in the face of heavy casualties.'

3,764 German soldiers were killed in the battle. After Crete, Hitler told Student: 'The parachute arm is one that relies entirely on surprise. That surprise factor is now exhausted... the day of the Paratroops is over.'

———◆◆◆◆◆———

We next went to Freyberg's headquarters; he was in a camouflaged tent off the Suda-Heraklion road, east of the junction with the Sphakia road. He was composed but obtuse.

Bob said he was worried about his left flank which was in the air.

'My dear boy, don't worry about that. The Boche never work off the roads.'

Bob asked if it was a defence to be held to the last man and last round.

'No, a rearguard. Withdraw when you are hard pressed.'

It was now light. We kept our truck and drove to the further side of the first rise of the south road where we found Graham and brigade HQ and D Battalion. All the road which we travelled was densely packed with motor transport and marching men. When we were going forward we had to plough slowly through them; coming back they climbed onto the truck presuming we were heading for Sphakia.

We picked up one man in colonel's uniform who spoke in the most affected voice I ever heard, saying, 'By Jove don't cher know old man.' He said he had been in charge of a transit camp at Canea. It was too dark to see his face but he seemed quite young. I wondered at the time and have continued to wonder since if he were a German. I had decided to make investigations when the truck got stuck temporarily and he disappeared into the dark and the mob saying, 'Thanks no end.' It occurs to me now he may have been a private soldier masquerading as an officer to get transport.

Our headquarters were off the road on the side of a hill, facing south, covered in rock and gorse.

Freddy made an attempt to arrange tactical groups of the sort he had heard about at the Staff College. The signallers were useless since their apparatus was all sunk in Suda Bay. Sergeant Lane had shown intelligence in getting hold of a few tinned stores. We each got a packet of biscuits and some bully beef. Most of us were already tired and thirsty but not hungry. Besides our usual headquarters we had attached a Presbyterian minister and a caddish fellow, sacked by Pedder, called Murdoch.

At 8 o'clock the German aeroplanes appeared and remained in the sky more or less continually all day. There were seldom less than half a dozen or more than a dozen overhead at a time. They were bombing the country to the west of us and in Suda Bay, but did not trouble us that morning. As soon as they appeared the rabble on the roads went to ground. When there was half an hour's pause they resumed their retreat.

Bob produced some written orders for a timed rearguard action lasting two days. A Battalion was to fall back through D and take up an intermediate position, etc. Bob sent me forward in the truck to give Hound his orders. I had rather vague memories of his position from the night before and drove about for some time in No Man's Land. There were plenty of aeroplanes about. When they came directly overhead we pulled into the shade and sheltered in the ditch.

At one point in our journey General Weston popped out of the hedge; he seemed to have lost his staff and his head.

'Who the hell are you and where are you going?'

I told him.

'Where's Laycock ?'

I showed him on my map.

'Don't you know better than to show a map? It's the best way of telling the enemy where headquarters are.'

It did not seem worth pointing out that we were not headquarters, just two lost officers meeting at the side of the road. He said he wanted a lift back to Laycock. I said I was going forward to find Hound. 'I used to command here once,' he said wistfully.

At length I came across a Layforce anti-tank rifleman concealed in the hedge about a mile east of Suda on the coast road. He said that headquarters were vaguely on his left. I put the truck under the best cover available, left my servant and the driver, and went forward on foot. There were vineyards and olive groves south of the road running up to the edge of the hills where the country became scrub and rock.

Quarter of a mile off the road was a domed church and some scattered farm buildings. The olive groves were full of trenches and weapon pits. I walked about for half an hour trying to find Hound. Some of the trenches had stray colonials or Royal Army Medical Corps details in them; some had Layforce. A Battalion kept no lookouts although they were not being directly bombed. They just crouched as low as possible and hid their heads. The bombing was all going on in the hills, three-quarters of a mile or more to the south; here the enemy were systematically working over the scrub with dive-bombing and machine-gunning. I knew there were no British there, except a few stragglers taking a short cut for home, and thought that a way was being cleared for an infantry advance. I reported this later but we had no troops to spare and nothing could be done. Late that evening the Germans worked through and cut off a company of D Battalion holding the road between Suda and the junction. I do not know if this company surrendered or fought it out.

After asking two officers who made excuses for not leaving their holes I found one who cheerfully consented to take me to Hound. He took me to the furthest of the farm buildings and went back to his company. I went into a tin-roofed shed and found two NCOs sitting at a table.

I said, 'I was told Colonel Hound was here.'

'He is,' they said.

I looked round, saw no one. Then they pointed under the table where I saw their commanding officer sitting hunched up like a disconsolate ape. I saluted and gave him his orders. He did not seem able to take them in at all.

He said, 'Where's Colonel Bob? I must see him.'

I said I was on my way back there now.

'Wait till the blitz is over. I'll come too.'

After a time the aeroplanes went home for refreshment and Hound emerged. He still looked a soldierly figure when he was on his feet. 'We had a burst of machine gun right through the roof,' he said half apologetically. I think this was a lie as the aeroplanes were concentrated on the hillside all that forenoon.

I took him to Bob. He showed no inclination to go back to his battalion but could still talk quite reasonably when there was no aeroplane overhead. Soon they came back and he lay rigid with his face in the gorse for about four hours. If anyone stretched a leg, he groaned as though he had broken all his limbs and was being jolted. 'For Christ's sake keep still.'

A squadron of dive-bombers now started work to the east of us; they came round and round regularly and monotonously like the horses at Captain Hance's. Just below us there was a very prominent circular cornfield in a hollow and they used this as their pivot so that they were always directly overhead flying quite low, then they climbed as they swung right, dived and let go their bombs about a mile away. I do not know what their target was; Freyberg's headquarters had been somewhere in that area. At first it was impressive, but after half an hour deadly monotonous. It was like everything German – overdone.

'A Date That Will Live In Infamy' – Pearl Harbor, 7 December 1941

President Franklin D. Roosevelt, Washington DC, 8 December 1941

At 7.53 a.m. on Sunday 7 December 1941, Japanese carrier-based aircraft attacked the U.S. naval base at Pearl Harbor, Hawaii. The US decision to embargo oil and other strategic materials to Japan unless she quit China and Indochina – which would have led to a humiliating loss of face – had prompted the 'unprovoked' attack.

The air raid caught the Americans by surprise, although it had famously been predicted by Army Brigadier General William Mitchell in 1924 – he predicted that Japan would attack and that it would begin at 7.30 a.m., only half an hour out. In 1937, Lieutenant Commander Logan C. Ramsay published an article in *US Naval Institute Proceedings* warning that neat ranks of battleships as at Pearl would be vulnerable to air attack and advised dispersal and constant air patrols – he too predicted that the enemy would be Japan but by then it was more obvious. When the Japanese attacked he was at Pearl Harbor and broadcast 'AIR RAID Pearl Harbor... This is no drill.'

The attack lasted until 9.45 a.m. Eight battleships were damaged, five sunk. In addition 188 planes were destroyed plus three cruisers and three destroyers. But the main targets – the U.S. Pacific Fleet aircraft carriers, *Lexington*, *Enterprise* and *Saratoga* – escaped damage because they were at sea. In all 2,335 American servicemen and 68 civilians were killed, including over one thousand on the battleship USS *Arizona* after a bomb exploded in the forward magazine.

The nation united behind President Franklin D. Roosevelt, ending the isolationist movement. On Monday 8 December he appeared before Congress and asked for a declaration of war against Japan. The vote for war would have been unanimous but for Representative Jeanette Rankin casting the only negative vote because she thought, 'The British are such clever propagandists, they might have cooked up the whole story.' Roosevelt had no Congressional sanction for war against Japan's allies, Germany and Italy, and while he was still debating how to obtain such a vote, Hitler and Mussolini both obliged by declaring war on the United States.

MR. VICE PRESIDENT, Mr. Speaker, members of the Senate and the House of Representatives:

Yesterday, December 7, 1941 – a date which will live in infamy – the United States of America was suddenly and deliberately attacked by naval and air forces of the Empire of Japan.

The United States was at peace with that nation, and, at the solicitation of Japan, was still in conversation with its government and its Emperor looking toward the maintenance of peace in the Pacific.

Indeed, one hour after Japanese air squadrons had commenced bombing in the American island of Oahu, the Japanese Ambassador to the United States and his colleague delivered to our Secretary of State a formal reply to a recent American message. And, while this reply stated that it seemed useless to continue the existing diplomatic negotiations, it contained no threat or hint of war or of armed attack.

It will be recorded that the distance of Hawaii from Japan makes it obvious that the attack was deliberately planned many days or even weeks ago. During the intervening time the Japanese Government has deliberately sought to deceive the United States by false statements and expressions of hope for continued peace.

The attack yesterday on the Hawaiian Islands has caused severe damage to American naval and military forces. I regret to tell you that very many American lives have been lost. In addition, American ships have been reported torpedoed on the high seas between San Francisco and Honolulu.

Yesterday the Japanese Government also launched an attack against Malaya.

Last night Japanese forces attacked Hong Kong.

Last night Japanese forces attacked Guam.

Last night Japanese forces attacked the Philippine Islands.

Last night the Japanese attacked Wake Island.

And this morning the Japanese attacked Midway Island.

Japan has therefore undertaken a surprise offensive extending throughout the Pacific area. The facts of yesterday and today speak for themselves. The people of the United States have already formed their opinions and well understand the implications to the very life and safety of our nation.

As Commander-in-Chief of the Army and Navy I have directed that all measures be taken for our defense, that always will our whole nation remember the character of the onslaught against us.

No matter how long it may take us to overcome this premeditated invasion, the American people, in their righteous might, will win through to absolute victory.

I believe that I interpret the will of the Congress and of the people when I assert that we will not only defend ourselves to the uttermost but will make it very certain that this form of treachery shall never again endanger us.

Hostilities exist. There is no blinking at the fact that our people, our territory and our interests are in grave danger.

With confidence in our armed forces, with the unbounding determination of our people, we will gain the inevitable triumph. So help us God.

I ask that the Congress declare that since the unprovoked and dastardly attack by Japan on Sunday, December 7, 1941, a state of war has existed between the United States and the Japanese Empire.

'We are going to finish with this chap Rommel once and for all'

General Montgomery, address to his officers,
El Alamein, 13 August 1942

General Bernard Montgomery (1887–1976) arrived in Cairo on 12 August 1942, and assumed command of the 8th Army the next day, when he made this address to his officers. He had not been Churchill's first choice, which had been General 'Strafer' Gott, but Gott had been shot down and killed as he flew to take command. The British were in North Africa to prevent Axis troops seizing the Suez Canal, a vital Allied artery. General Montgomery was not then the 'second most popular figure in England', as Harold Nicolson later described him. His popularity was achieved by winning battles but 'never has there been such a careful creation of a legend', as Nicolson remarked. Only MacArthur (and maybe Patton) exceeded Monty, as he became known, in the art of self-promotion.

Some desert veterans were demoralised and needed a boost; retreat is never good for morale. For these officers, convinced of German superiority in equipment, professionalism and tactics, Monty's swagger was what they looked for. They needed a general who had the confidence that he was the master of General Rommel, the Desert Fox, who seemed invincible. General Horrocks of 13

Corps, after listening to Monty's pep talk below, swooned, 'Isn't he *marvellous*?' But not all were won over. In the elite 7th Armoured Division, for instance, there were officers who were distinctly unimpressed with Monty's braggadocio:

> *'… we did not at all look upon ourselves as a demoralised army in need of a miracle… when Monty arrived to talk to us, we regarded him as a funny little man in an Australian hat with a nasal voice who spoke in excruciating clichés which embarrassed rather than uplifted us.'*
>
> [Letter to *The Times*, 27/9/01]

But Monty's speech below is army language at its best – simple, unpretentious and direct.

●➤●✕●◆●

I want first of all to introduce myself to you. You do not know me. I do not know you. But we have got to work together; therefore we must understand each other, and we must have confidence each in the other. I have only been here a few hours. But from what I have seen and heard since I arrived I am prepared to say, here and now, that I have confidence in you. We will then work together as a team; and together we will gain the confidence of this great Army and go forward to final victory in Africa.

I believe that one of the first duties of a commander is to create what I call 'atmosphere', and in that atmosphere his staff, subordinate commanders, and troops will live and work and fight.

I do not like the general atmosphere I find here. It is an atmosphere of doubt, of looking back to select the next place to which to withdraw, of loss of confidence in our ability to defeat Rommel, of desperate defence measures by reserves in preparing positions in Cairo and the Delta.

All that must cease.

Let us have a new atmosphere.

The defence of Egypt lies here at Alamein and on the Ruweisat Ridge. What is the use of digging trenches in the Delta? It is quite useless; if we lose this position we lose Egypt; all the fighting troops now in the Delta must come here at once, and will. *Here* we will stand and fight; there will be no further withdrawal. I have ordered that all plans and instructions dealing with further withdrawal are to be burnt, and at once. We will stand and fight *here*.

If we can't stay here alive, then let us stay here dead.

I want to impress on everyone that the bad times are over. Fresh Divisions from the UK are now arriving in Egypt, together with ample reinforcements for our present Divisions. We have 300 to 400 Sherman new tanks coming and these are actually being unloaded at Suez *now*. Our mandate from the Prime Minister is to destroy the Axis forces in North Africa; I have seen it, written on half a sheet of notepaper. And it will be done. If anyone here thinks it can't be done, let him go at once; I don't want any doubters in the party. It can be done, and it will be done: beyond any possibility of doubt.

Now I understand that Rommel is expected to attack at any moment. Excellent. Let him attack.

I would sooner it didn't come for a week, just to give me time to sort things out. If we have two weeks to prepare we will be sitting pretty; Rommel can attack as soon as he likes, after that, and I hope he does.

Meanwhile, we ourselves will start to plan a great offensive; it will be the beginning of a campaign which will hit Rommel and his Army for six right out of Africa.

But first we must create a reserve Corps, mobile and strong in armour, which we will train *out of the line*. Rommel has always had such a force in his Africa Corps, which is never used to hold the line but which is always in reserve, available for striking blows. Therein has been his great strength. We will create such a Corps ourselves, a British Panzer Corps; it will consist of two armoured Divisions and one motorized Division; I gave orders yesterday for it to begin to form, back in the Delta.

I have no intention of launching our great attack until we are completely ready; there will be pressure from many quarters to attack soon; *I will not attack until we are ready*, and you can rest assured on that point.

Meanwhile, if Rommel attacks while we are preparing, let him do so with pleasure; we will merely continue with our own preparations and *we* will attack when *we* are ready, and not before.

I want to tell you that I always work on the Chief of Staff system. I have nominated Brigadier de Guingand as Chief of Staff Eighth Army. I will issue orders through him. Whatever he says will be taken as coming from me and will be acted on *at once*. I understand there has been a great deal of 'bellyaching' out here.

By bellyaching I mean inventing poor reasons for *not* doing what one has been told to do.

All this is to stop at once.

I will tolerate no bellyaching.

If anyone objects to doing what he is told, then he can get out of it: and at once. I want that made very clear right down through the Eighth Army.

I have little more to say just at present. And some of you may think it is quite enough and may wonder if I am mad.

I assure you I am quite sane.

I understand there are people who often think I am slightly mad; so often that I now regard it as rather a compliment.

All I have to say is that if I am slightly mad, there are a large number of people I could name who are raving lunatics!!

What I have done is to get over to you the 'atmosphere' in which we will now work and fight; you must see that that atmosphere permeates right through the Eighth Army to the most junior private soldier. All the soldiers must know what is wanted; when they see it coming to pass there will be a surge of confidence throughout the Army.

I ask you to give me your confidence and to have faith that what I have said will come to pass.

There is much work to be done.

The orders I have given about no further withdrawal will mean a complete change in the layout of our dispositions; also, we must begin to prepare for our great offensive.

The first thing to do is to move our HQ to a decent place where we can live in reasonable comfort and where the Army Staff can all be together and side by side with the HQ of the Desert Air Force. This is a frightful place here, depressing, unhealthy and a rendezvous for every fly in Africa; we shall do no good work here. Let us get over there by the sea where it is fresh and healthy. If officers are to do good work they must have decent messes, and be comfortable. So off we go on the new line.

The Chief of Staff will be issuing orders on many points very shortly, and I am always available to be consulted by the senior officers of the staff. The great point to remember is that we are going to finish with this chap Rommel once and for all. It will be quite easy. There is no doubt about it.

He is definitely a nuisance. Therefore we will hit him a crack and finish with him.

Vergissmeinnicht ('Forget-me-not'): Elegy for an 88 Gunner

Keith Douglas

Born in Tunbridge Wells, Keith Douglas (1920–1944), studied English and poetry at Oxford under the celebrated rural poet Edmund Blunden. In 1940 he went to Sandhurst, and in February 1941 was commissioned into the 2nd Derbyshire Yeomanry. Later that year he went to North Africa, joining the cavalry regiment, the Sherwood Rangers Yeomanry, and began training for tank warfare. But he was assigned a role as a staff officer. The Sherwood Rangers were an old, somewhat snobbish Yeomanry regiment which had still been horsed when it moved to Palestine in 1940, where they swapped their horses for artillery, then tanks. Most of the officers were landed gentry; Douglas was not, and furthermore he had been to the 'wrong' school. Douglas resented their sneering superiority. He himself was described by a fellow officer as 'recklessly outspoken' in the mess and 'insufferably knowledgeable', not traits that endeared him to his more dull-witted colleagues. Douglas, in turn, wrote in the poem Aristocrats (1943) of their 'stupidity and chivalry', and lampoons them – with some affection: 'How can I live among this gentle / obsolescent breed of heroes, and not weep? / … It is not gunfire I hear, but a hunting horn.'

When the battle of El Alamein (23 October–4 November 1942) began – in which Montgomery overwhelmed Rommel's static defence, forcing his retreat to Tunis – Douglas left HQ, commandeered a lorry and joined his regiment in the desert.

His war poetry shows the influence of Isaac Rosenberg and Wilfred Owen, and uses vivid imagery without sentiment, death being its ever-present theme. His use of half-rhyme in *Vergissmeinnicht* is a conscious borrowing from, and homage to, Owen.

Three weeks gone and the combatants gone
returning over the nightmare ground
we found the place again, and found
the soldier sprawling in the sun.
The frowning barrel of his gun
overshadowing. As we came on
that day, he hit my tank with one
like the entry of a demon.
Look. Here in the gunpit spoil
the dishonoured picture of his girl
who has put: Steffi. *Vergissmeinnicht*
in a copybook gothic script.
We see him almost with content,
abased, and seeming to have paid
and mocked at by his own equipment
that's hard and good when he's decayed.
But she would weep to see today
how on his skin the swart flies move;
the dust upon the paper eye
and the burst stomach like a cave.
For here the lover and killer are mingled
who had one body and one heart.
And death who had the soldier singled
has done the lover mortal hurt.

Plunder and horror in the desert

Keith Douglas
[from *From Alamein to Zem Zem*, London, 1946]

On 15 January 1943, Douglas was wounded at Wadi Zem Zem.
While recuperating he wrote From Alamein to Zem Zem, a bleak
and honest narrative of his war. He rejoined his regiment and was
promoted to captain, but did no further fighting until D-Day. The
Rangers, equipped with DD Sherman amphibious tanks, landed
at Gold Beach on 6 June 1944 and spearheaded the liberation of
Bayeux. On 9 June Douglas and his squadron stopped outside the
small village of St Pierre, still held by Germans. Douglas left his tank
to reconnoitre. A mortar shell exploded above his head and he was
killed instantly, his premonition of death fulfilled. He was buried by
a hedge near where he fell; his body now lies in Tilly-sur-Seulles
CWGC cemetery.

This extract from Douglas' posthumously published memoir
of the desert war takes place after the breakthrough at Alamein,
with Rommel's forces beaten. Stragglers were mostly demoralised.
That the Germans used allied transport was not unusual; captured
guns and lorries of all description were used by both sides, which
explains in part why troops were shot up from the air by their
own side. Douglas' Crusader III tank (Cruiser Mark VI) had a crew
of five, one 6 pdr gun (an improvement from the Mk I/II's 2 pdr)

and a road speed of 28 mph. The Crusader had been designed and developed by hasty committee decisions, and it showed. Although fast, mobile and with a low silhouette, which made it difficult to hit when charging in the desert, it shed its caterpillar track too often and was prone to breaking down in the stress of battle. The armour was too thin to compete with German Panzers, or even the Italian 47mm gun. But in the grim circumstances of 1941 and 1942, it was the best that was available for British armoured units in Egypt, and remained in service until the arrival of Grants and Shermans relegated the Crusader to an auxiliary role. A total of 5,300 were built. The M13 referred to was the standard Italian medium tank with an adequate 47mm gun, but slow, with an unreliable engine and poorly armoured.

As we reached the top of the valley we could see a long stream of lorries, mostly Chevrolet 3-tonners and 15 cwts., moving nose to tail along beside the railway line below us. I thought they were probably the column which had been travelling to our right, and anyway, seeing no guns among them, I ignored Evan's protests and we slithered down the slope to meet them. What a haul it would have been if they had been Germans, I thought.

We came down beside one of the trucks and moved at the column's speed, about 10 miles an hour, our right track about a yard from the lorry's wing. I looked into the cab, the driver was a German. I saw him a second or two earlier than he saw me. My driver, of course, who was driving blind, by my directions, continued stolidly alongside the lorry. The German glanced casually sideways at us, and away again. Then a terrible thought struck him. All this was comically visible on his face. He looked sideways again, seemed to confirm his worst fears and swerved violently into the railway embankment, jumping out before the truck stopped moving. Men came piling out of the back in colossal confusion. We halted and waited for them to surrender. But our appearance had been too sudden. They were in a panic. The crew of the lorry behind them could not make out what they were doing. Their conversation translated roughly into 'What the hell are you doing?' 'A tank! A tank! English tank?' 'Where?' (unanswered). The other crew became infected. They all fled up the bank towards the sea. This was disconcerting; I felt very annoyed and shouted after them insults and invitations to return in a mixture of English and German. But they would not. I suppose we could have killed a good many of them as they ran, with my revolver and our tommy gun. But this seemed a futile thing to do. They were surrounded and had no rations, and like a few other fighting soldiers I lack the true ferocity of Battle School Instructors and armchair critics. Besides, the whole situation was too ridiculous to attempt to introduce a serious note. We backed the tank and threw a hand grenade or two at one of the lorries without much effect. Then we blazed off at it with the six-pounder at a range of about 20 yards, but appeared to have missed. When we went closer I saw there were three holes as clean as a whistle through the dashboard and engine. In the end we dismounted and tommy-gunned the engines of the three lorries which had halted. The rear vehicles of the column had turned and made off back down the line. Those in front had driven sedately on unaware of what was happening behind them. While they were doing this I had launched frantic wireless messages into the casual conversations still audible from the regiment, begging someone to come and help bag the rest of the lorries. But Edward was talking to his gunner or driver or otherwise distracted and never heard one of my four messages. At last Tom answered: 'Nuts three I heard you. But we can't do anything about it at the moment. We're going to be busy. Destroy what you can and rejoin. Over.' I acknowledged this as the last of the runners were gaining the far crest. After destroying the three vehicles I seized a couple of blankets, of which we were short, from one of the lorries and a kitbag from a pile of them in the back of another, and turned after the tail of the column. But at this moment the microphone went dead and, being still lost, with the consciousness that petrol was running low, I took no notice of two other German vehicles which passed me, and they ignored me; we drove past each other at a distance of about 50 yards. As we crossed the railway line a man who had been hiding the other side of the embankment sprang up and ran across it. Evan fired the tommy gun at him, which was a senseless thing to do. Anyway, he missed him.

As we topped the next rise we saw below us our own twenty-five- pounders and several other vehicles of our column dispersed straddling the railway line. The enemy vehicles must have run into some part of the column. There was a small station there – Galal Station, the name written on a tin plate – and there we halted while I called up Tom to find out where the squadron was. We sorted out the kitbag and an impressive first-aid set which Evan had found, full of bright scissors and instruments. I found clean underclothes, a dark khaki cotton shirt, and trousers of the same colour, apparently brand new, made of very rough cloth and quite well cut, with sloping pockets and a belt sewn in the waist. There was even a metal ring to hang a watch on, with a small pocket for the watch underneath it. I took these clothes and a khaki high-necked jersey, and gave Evan the rest to divide with the driver. They were more interested in badges, combs, razors, hair-cream, etc., which were all there.

We set off to find some petrol, and while we were filling up heard the battle begin on the air. Several tanks reporting targets, and the Artillery observation officers promising their fire. There seemed to be a great many enemy tanks. The twenty-five-pounders began to fire over the hill in front, and we heard the tanks reporting direct hits of their own guns. Suddenly the voice of some tank N.C.O. who had switched to the A set by mistake, and thought he was still on Internal Communication, broke into the messages, shouting, almost screaming. 'Bloody good shot! You've 'it 'im. You've 'it the bugger. Go on Lofty, give 'im another. Go on. 'It 'im again'… rising to a crescendo.

Obviously this was a new kind of action; the voices of the participants seemed like those of boys in a shooting gallery. We poured petrol in as fast as it would go, slopping it over the top of the big tin funnel in our excitement and spilling it down the sides of the tank. But long before we had finished filling up someone's voice in the earphones said: 'They're surrendering'. And we arrived to find the battle of Galal Station over. The regiment had accounted for twenty-seven tanks. A long row of derelict Italian M13s stood by the railway line, some blazing, others apparently undamaged. From one of these I took a small Biretta automatic and its ammunition, as I passed the derelicts to take up my position watching the sea, which I had not seen since leaving Alexandria.

During the afternoon I washed, shaved, and dressed in my new shirt and trousers and the high-necked jersey, tying a blue German handkerchief with a red stripe in it round my neck. Except for beret and boots, the enemy had clothed me completely—and on my belt hung my new Biretta and the Luger I had taken in my first action. When I had completed my toilet, feeling hugely pleased with myself in my brand-new clothes, I walked down to the railway line, leaving a look-out in the top of the tank, to see if I could get another Biretta for Raoul, who would by now be in hospital in Alex or Cairo.

I approached a brand-new-painted M13, with no sign of any damage, from which the crew had apparently fled at the sight of their comrades' discomfiture. There was a promising cask and a sack on the outside of the tank, which we opened. But the cask only contained water, and the sack nothing but little round tins with a smelly Italian kind of bully beef in them. So I climbed on to the turret – the small side doors which stood open on most of the other tanks were closed. I prepared to lower myself through the top. It was dark in the turret, and I leant over the manhole first, trying to accustom my eyes to the darkness and to see if there were any Birettas on the side shelves inside. A faint sweet smell came up to me which reminded me of the dead horse I once saw cut up for our instruction at the Equitation School.

Gradually the objects in the turret became visible: the crew of the tank – for, I believe, these tanks did not hold more than two – were, so to speak, distributed round the turret. At first it was difficult to work out how the limbs were arranged. They lay in a clumsy embrace, their white faces whiter, as those of dead men in the desert always were, for the light powdering of dust on them. One with a six-inch hole in his head, the whole skull smashed in behind the remains of an ear – the other covered with his own and his friend's blood, held up by the blue steel mechanism of a machine-gun, his legs twisting among the dully gleaming gear levers. About them clung that impenetrable silence I have mentioned before, by which I think the dead compel our reverence. I got a Biretta from another tank on the other side of the railway line.

In the evening we closed into night leaguer, facing westwards again. Tom was in high spirits; he and Ken Tinker had found an Italian hospital, and their tanks were loaded inside and out with crates of cherries, Macedonian cigarettes, cigars and wine; some straw-jacketed Italian Chianti issue, some champagne, and a bottle or two of brandy, even some Liebfraumilch. We shared out the plunder with the immemorial glee of conquerors, and beneath *the old star-eaten blanket of the sky* lay down to dream of victory.

The next day, of course, was an anticlimax. We turned west again and made for Fuka, on the last lap to Mersa, from which the appearance of the enemy tanks at Galal had distracted us. Everyone kept his eyes skinned more for loot than for prisoners, and in dismounting to examine the contents of a stranded lorry I lost my Luger, which fell out of my pocket unnoticed. Later in the morning I saw a crate full of Chianti bottles lying in an infantry weapon pit and was for telling my driver to stop and collecting them. But before I could speak he had run clean over them. There was an almighty explosion and the tank lumbered on.

Evan and the driver emerged and jumped to the ground, the driver shouting 'She won't steer'. He had left the clutch in and I jumped down with them, ran round the tank and saw that the track and skirting were blown off one side and she was rolling on the great wheels, from which the solid rubber tyres were blown to shreds, while the sprocket and the other track drove her. In spite of wild protestations from Evan and the driver, Skelton, who had quite lost their senses for the moment, and imagined that to enter the tank was to court death (though if they had been outside it they would have been already dead)—I got in again and switched off the engine. Some sort of light anti-tank gun began firing at us very inaccurately. The shot kicked up the dust short of us, and as I ran about looking at the damage and back to the big blackened hole where the inviting box of Chianti bottles had been, I was dimly aware of them getting on to us for line and making a huge correction for range with their next shot, which flew well over our heads. I called up Edward and explained what had happened. 'O.K.,' he said. 'Change on to another of your children; can you see what that is firing at you? Over.' 'Nuts three. No. It's solid shot of some kind. Off.' Another tank came up, we flung my kit on it and caught up with the others, who were still advancing.

The gun did not fire again, but we saw vehicles escaping along the top of a kind of sand cliff in front of us. We were switched on to a southerly course by the Brigadier, and climbed on to the plateau, after stalking carefully up on vehicle after vehicle, only to find them burnt-out derelicts. Fuka aerodrome had been evacuated, nothing of any use to us remained, and soon afterwards we crossed the coast road near another landing ground, where the wreckage of a Spitfire lay among that of several Italian and German fighters. There were one or two very well-dressed Italian officers waiting for us, who proved to be the vanguard of that long, straggling column of defeated Italians and Germans which found its own way down to the cage at Fuka. That evening it rained for the first time since the beginning of the battle.

Speech to 3rd Army

General George S. Patton Jr.,
5 June 1944, somewhere in England

General George Smith Patton (1885–1945), 'Old Blood and Guts', was a patrician American from the South, an Olympic horseman who was an early advocate of armoured warfare, having served in tanks during World War I at St.-Mihiel and the Argonne. A flamboyant and competitive showman and, like Montgomery, a prickly prima donna, he inspired II Corps in North Africa after their mauling at Kesserine Pass, drove 7th Army mercilessly through Sicily beating Monty to Messina, but came unstuck after slapping a shell-shocked soldier and was relieved of command by Eisenhower. Patton next 'commanded' a fictitious army group in South-East England prior to OVERLORD (the Normandy Invasion), as part of the FORTITUDE deception plan. The Germans fell for the bait; they could not believe that the Allies' finest field commander could be twiddling his thumbs.

But Eisenhower, the Allied Expeditionary Forces' Supreme Commander, needed him to lead US 3rd Army in the breakout from Normandy. With his new command, Patton charged through France without a care for his flanks, the speed of advance (and Monty tying down German armour to the east) preventing German organised resistance. His aggressive, robust approach to combat is evident in a comment he made after seeing a German soldier blow up a bridge, killing several GIs. 'He then put up his hands… The Americans took him prisoner, which I considered the height of folly.'

His profanity was tactical. He is quoted as telling his nephew:

'When I want my men to remember something important, to really make it stick, I give it to them double dirty. It may not sound nice to some bunch of little old ladies at an afternoon tea party, but it helps my soldiers to remember. You can't run an army without profanity; and it has to be eloquent profanity. An army without profanity couldn't fight its way out of a piss-soaked paper bag.'

Hardly a man of the people, the wealthy lover of classical history nevertheless knew how to rabble-rouse in finest barrack room language. He also knew the inspirational and mesmerising effect of image and charisma. He delivered the speech below, in a high-pitched voice like Monty's, standing with polished riding boots astride and pearl-handled revolvers shining.

Men, this stuff that some sources sling around about America wanting out of this war, not wanting to fight, is a crock of bullshit. Americans love to fight, traditionally. All real Americans love the sting and clash of battle… you are real men and all real men like to fight. When you, here, everyone of you, were kids, you all admired the champion marble player, the fastest runner, the toughest boxer, the big league ball players, and the All-American football players. Americans love a winner. Americans will not tolerate a loser. Americans despise cowards. Americans play to win all of the time. I wouldn't give a hoot in hell for a man who lost and laughed. That's why Americans have never lost nor will ever lose a war; for the very idea of losing is hateful to an American.

You are not all going to die. Only two percent of you right here today would die in a major battle. Death must not be feared. Death, in time, comes to all men. Yes, every man is scared in his first battle. If he says he's not, he's a liar... Americans pride themselves on being He Men and they ARE He Men. Remember that the enemy is just as frightened as you are, and probably more so. They are not supermen.

All through your Army careers, you men have bitched about what you call 'chicken shit drilling'. That, like everything else in this Army, has a definite purpose. That purpose is alertness... If you're not alert, sometime, a German son-of-a-bitch is going to sneak up behind you and beat you to death with a sockful of shit! There are four hundred neatly marked graves somewhere in Sicily. All because one man went to sleep on the job. But they are German graves, because we caught the bastard asleep before they did.

An Army is a team. It lives, sleeps, eats, and fights as a team. This individual heroic stuff is pure horse shit. The bilious bastards who write that kind of stuff for the *Saturday Evening Post* don't know any more about real fighting under fire than they know about fucking!

We have the finest food, the finest equipment, the best spirit, and the best men in the world. Why, by God, I actually pity those poor sons-of-bitches we're going up against. By God, I do.

My men don't surrender. I don't want to hear of any soldier under my command being captured unless he has been hit. Even if you are hit, you can still fight back. That's not just bullshit either. The kind of man that I want in my command is just like the lieutenant in Libya, who, with a Luger against his chest, jerked off his helmet, swept the gun aside with one hand, and busted the hell out of the Kraut with his helmet. Then he jumped on the gun and went out and killed another German before they knew what the hell was coming off. And, all of that time, this man had a bullet through a lung. There was a real man!

… Each man must not think only of himself, but also of his buddy fighting beside him. We don't want yellow cowards in this Army. They should be killed off like rats. If not, they will go home after this war and breed more cowards. The brave men will breed more brave men. Kill off the Goddamned cowards and we will have a nation of brave men…

Remember, men, you don't know I'm here. No mention of that is to be made in any letters. The world is supposed to be wondering what the hell has happened to me. I'm not supposed to be commanding this Army. I'm not supposed even to be in England. Let the first bastards to find out be the Goddamned Germans. Some day I want to see them raise up on their piss-soaked hind legs and howl, 'Ach! Jesus Christ! It's the Goddamned Third Army again and that son-of-a-f*cking-bitch Patton'.

We want to get the hell over there. The quicker we clean up this Goddamned mess, the quicker we can take a little jaunt against the purple pissing Japs and clean out their nest, too. Before the Goddamned Marines get all of the credit.

Sure, we want to go home. We want this war over with. The quickest way to get it over with is to go get the bastards who started it. The quicker they are whipped, the quicker we can go home. The shortest way home is through Berlin and Tokyo. And when we get to Berlin, I am personally going to shoot that paper hanging son-of-a-bitch Hitler. Just like I'd shoot a snake.

… War is a bloody, killing business. You've got to spill their blood, or they will spill yours. Rip them up the belly. Shoot them in the guts. When shells are hitting all around you and you wipe the dirt off your face and realize that instead of dirt it's the blood and guts of what once was your best friend beside you, you'll know what to do!

I don't want to get any messages saying, 'I am holding my position.' We are not holding a Goddamned thing. Let the Germans do that. We are advancing constantly and we are not interested in holding onto anything, except the enemy's balls. We are going to twist his balls and kick the living shit out of him all of the time… We are going to go through him like crap through a goose; like shit through a tin horn!

We become operational officially tomorrow, and doubtless from time to time there will be some complaints that we are pushing people too hard. I don't give a good goddamn about such complaints. I believe in the old and sound rule that an ounce of sweat will save a gallon of blood. The harder we push, the more Germans we'll kill, and the more Germans we kill, the fewer of our men will be killed…

There is one great thing that you men will all be able to say after this war is over and you are home once again. You may be thankful that twenty years from now when you are sitting by the fireplace with your grandson on your knee and he asks you what you did in the great World War II, you WON'T have to cough, shift him to the other knee and say, 'Well, your Granddaddy shovelled shit in Louisiana.' No, Sir, you can look him straight in the eye and say, 'Son, your Granddaddy rode with the Great Third Army and a Son-of-a-Goddamned-Bitch named George Patton!'

One man's D-Day

Iain Macleod [from *The Spectator*, 5 June 1964]

Iain Macleod (1913–1970) was a brilliant staff officer, who recognised – unlike some – that he was 'only a staff officer' and 'the day of course belonged, above all, to the fighting infantry. No praise can be too high for them.' But, as he writes with pride and modesty, he 'was there'. D-Day, 6 June 1944, the invasion of German-occupied Normandy, saw the largest amphibious operation ever mounted. Over 150,000 men landed by sea and air on that day, and 20,000 vehicles. Some 7,000 ships sailed from English ports. By nightfall on 6 June the Allies had suffered under 5,000 casualties, far less than the Supreme Commander, General Eisenhower, had feared.

From D-Day to the Liberation of Paris (25 August 1944), the 62 German divisions committed to the battle sustained enormous damage, comparable to that Germany suffered at Stalingrad. 12 SS Panzer Hitlerjugend Division, for example, suffered 95 per cent losses. Germany lost around 1,500 tanks, 3,500 guns and 20,000 vehicles; her casualties numbered 450,000 killed, wounded or captured. Allied casualties were about 200,000, with 40,000 killed. During the preparatory bombing, and during the campaign itself, some 28,000 Allied aircrew lost their lives.

A Conservative politician and bridge-player, Macleod died just days after being appointed Chancellor by Edward Heath. The famous description of him by Lord Salisbury as 'too clever by half' is invariably quoted misleadingly because Salisbury went on to say '… in his relationship to the white communities of Africa'. Nevertheless it indicates a subtle and skilful politician whose loss to the government was grievous.

I had graduated from the Staff College early in February 1944, and had had exactly one day out of my leave when the telegram arrived. I was to report with the rank of Major to an address in Ashley Gardens, near Victoria Station. There were no other details. When I arrived. I found myself an extra DAQMG (Deputy Assistant Quarter Master General) on the planning staff of the famous 50th (Northumbrian) Division. 50 Div., as everyone knew them, had been brought back from the Sicilian campaign to take part in the assault on France. The attack was now planned on a five-division front with 50 Div. in the centre. On our right two American Divisions of the American 1st Army; on our left the 3rd British and 3rd Canadian Divisions. 50 Div. was almost the size of a small Corps when it landed. A fourth infantry Brigade and an Armoured Brigade came under command. So did a crowd of artillery units, and a proportion of the 'comics' – special units often with Heath Robinson-type equipment designed for a special task. In all, there were about 40,000 men.

I did not in this planning stage expect to land with the Division. Probably when the planning was over I would either be given another appointment or, more likely, be held temporarily in Montgomery's pool of staff officers to wait for the inevitable vacancies that the assault would bring. But under the strain of the planning the AA and QMG fell ill. Tom Black, the divisional DAQMG, was promoted in his place and I took over Tom's job. I studied the landing sheets again. H plus forty, I saw, was 'my' time. In other words, I was due to land forty minutes after the first wave of assault troops went in. I did not know when D-Day was, but by an odd chance I learned where the invasion was to take place. Thumbing through a file in the Headquarters of 2nd Army I saw a receipt for a map marked 'TOP SECRET OVERLORD' (the invasion code name). To most people the receipt would have meant nothing, but I had just come from the Staff College at Camberley and recognised the map sheet number as the one, based on St Lô, which we had used in a staff exercise. I took the receipt away and burned it. So we were not to land in the Pas de Calais, but in Normandy.

Slowly order began to emerge from chaos. We met our Naval Force G at Weymouth and the staffs wove the plans together. We rehearsed endlessly at Studland Bay in Dorset. And in due course in the last two days of May a tide of men and machines began to roll towards Southampton. By 1 June we were afloat. No more telephones, and very little to do. If we hadn't thought of everything already, it was too late. We knew now when D-Day was to be – 5 June. We knew exactly where we were to land, exactly where the different headquarters were to be established and, above all, what the objectives were for the Division on D-Day. I spent most of the time (and nearly all D-Day itself) with Lieutenant-Colonel 'Bertie' Gibb, then ADOS in charge of Ordnance Supplies, and of many other things. Even by 50 Div. standards, Bertie was an exceptional staff officer. He is my only check on the accuracy of my memory, for I kept no written record of the landing. I have also confirmed the outline of the attack from Major Ewan Clay's book. But my account does not pretend to historical accuracy. It is, as I remember it, one man's D-Day. The day of course belonged, above all, to the fighting infantry. No praise can be too high for them. I was only a staff officer. But I was there.

D-Day itself was postponed for twenty-four hours until 6 June Even so, the weather was cold and the sea was rough. General Eisenhower took the greatest gamble in all military history when he launched his armada on such uncertain seas. He was proved right.

The Divisional HQ was split between two ships, and I found myself with men of the 1st Hampshires of 231 Brigade. For the Division this was the second seaborne assault. For 231 Brigade, the third. Moreover, the 50th Division, which had been the last Division to leave the beaches of Dunkirk, was now one of those chosen to be the first to land in Normandy. I had not been with them in 1940, but I had, in fact, been away from France for a few days less. It was about 10 June, long after Dunkirk, that I had left St Nazaire in a hospital ship. Four years later, and in the company of the finest fighting Division of the Army, I was going back.

Perhaps I was helped by my early voyages on the Minch, but I slept soundly enough through the rough night, and came on deck somewhere around first light. The waves were still choppy and the landing was going to be a hazardous and in part a haphazard affair. But the day was becoming warm. The coast of Normandy began to take shape through the haze. And then as full light began to come one saw the ships and the planes. It was a sight so paralysing that tears came to my eyes. It was as if every ship that had ever been launched was there, and even as if the sea had yielded up her wrecks. It was as if every plane that had ever been built was there, and, so it seemed in fantasy, as if the dead crews were there too. There had never been since time began such a rendezvous for fighting men: there never will be again. And I remember reciting, not in scorn, but out of sheer delight at being part of that great company in such a place, 'And gentlemen in England now abed...'

As the fire from the naval guns began to blot out the shore defences, and the endless drone of the planes and the whine of their bombs rose to a crescendo, so came H-hour.

50 Div. were to assault on a front of two brigades, the 69th on the left and the 231st on the right. The Hampshires were to land just east of Le Hamel and to take the village and then the other coastal villages, especially Arromanches which was earmarked as the site of the artificial port called Mulberry. It meant for them a day of heavy fighting and severe casualties. The commanding officer was wounded, and the second-in-command killed. But it was also a day of glory for the regiment that must rank high, perhaps first, among all the Hampshires' battle honours. Watching the LCAs (Landing Craft Assault) carrying the Hampshires pull away and switchback to the shore, and while waiting for our own sea taxi, I thought that as a martial gesture I would load my revolver. When I unbuttoned my ammunition pouch, I found that my batman, who knew more about war than I did, had filled it not with bullets but with boiled sweets. He was quite right. They proved much more useful.

Few things went exactly as planned, and the biggest disappointment was the failure of the secret waterproofed tanks to negotiate the heavy seas. They were supposed to paddle through the last few miles to the beach and provide covering fire for the assaulting companies. In view of the weather, it was then decided to take the craft to the beach, and disembark the tanks. The same dilemma came to the Americans assaulting the strongly-held Omaha beach to our right, but here a different and a tragic decision was taken. In spite of the seas, sixty-four tanks were launched and all were swamped. Nearly all the crews were drowned and, of course, cover fire was lost.

Presently Bertie and I climbed with elderly dignity down the scrambling nets that were slung over the ship's sides and dropped down into our LCA. We began to cruise in to the beach. Something now went wrong. Perhaps the naval officer in charge decided that too many craft were trying to get ashore at once, perhaps the underwater mines obstructed us. In any event, we began to circle a few hundred yards away from the beach. Quite a long time passed. The sun grew hotter, and I began to doze. Suddenly and equally for no reason that I could see, we stopped turning and ran straight for the beach. The landing ramp smacked down and one stepped or jumped according to taste into the thigh-deep water. Bertie and I stepped, and waded carefully ashore.

The beach was alive with the shambles and the order of war. There were dead men and wounded men and men brewing tea. There were men reorganising for a battle advance, and men doing absolutely nothing. There were even some German prisoners waiting patiently for heaven knows what. There was a whole graveyard of wrecked ships and craft and tanks of every size. It was like an absurdly magnificent film by Cecil B. de Mille: It was like war.

We wandered over the beaches and climbed the dunes behind them. Everything seemed oddly quiet. The minefields were most carefully marked ('Achtung Minen'!) and wired. The villages to left and right of us were still German-held, although we did not realise it at the time. We must have taken a sand track between them.

We met very few people on the way to the orchard at Meuvaines which was to be our D-Day headquarters. Only a motley collection of vehicles had arrived, but one of them was the intelligence truck and in it a staff officer was busy marking up the reports of the progress of the leading battalions. We were about a mile and a half inland.

The rest of the day is a patchwork of memories. There was a flurry of shots into the orchard from a small nest of Germans we had overlooked. There was a journey back to the beaches to see the build-up. There was a journey on the back of a policeman's motor-cycle to find the forward brigades, and establish contact with their staff captains. I can't remember when I ate, but I remember what I ate. We had been issued with twenty-four-hour packs of concentrated dried food. I expect they had a taste as evil as their appearance. But I don't think many people in 50 Div. tasted them. 50 Div. were used to looking after themselves. From somewhere my batman produced both the great delicacies of 1944 – tinned steak pudding and tinned Christmas pudding. These and whisky were my food.

Night began to fall. Nearly all our objectives had been taken. Patrols were moving into Bayeux, which was to fall next morning. The St Leger feature was in our grasp. The 47th Royal Marine Commando (under our command for the landings) had started its successful battle for Port-en-Bessin. Hideous close fighting in the Bocage lay ahead, but at least on the 50 Div. front the day had gone well.

My batman had secured a corner of the farmer's barn for me, and I was thinking of snatching some sleep when the door opened and Tom Black looked in:

'Is Iain here?' I followed him outside.

'What's up?'

'Nothing. I thought we'd have a drink.'

We stood under the trees, drinking from his flask and looking back towards the sea. A few fast German fighter planes were making a tip-and-run raid on the beach, and the red tracer bullets climbed lazily into the sky after them. I looked at my watch. It was exactly midnight. I had lived through D-Day. We had expected anything up to 40 per cent casualties in the landing, and somehow I had been convinced that I would be killed. Now, equally unreasonably, I became convinced that I would live through the war. I would see our second child, who was to be born in October. There would be a life after the war. D-Day was over.

Sudden death in Burma

George MacDonald Fraser, Burma, 1945
[from *Quartered Safe Out Here*, London, 1992]

George MacDonald Fraser (b. 1926) joined the Border Regiment aged 18 in 1943, a time when the regiment formed part of the 17th Indian ('Black Cat') Division of 14th Army. He later served in the Gordon Highlanders. He has been a newspaperman and successful writer of film scripts but his enduring literary legacy will be the *Flashman* series and *Quartered Safe Out Here*.

In 1942 Japan had seized Burma, cutting off the Chinese government's last land route to its allies by closing the Burma Road. Japan advanced towards India, and along the coast towards Singapore. The 17th Division was formed after Singapore fell in February 1942, with the loss of over 100,000 Allied troops (including 33,000 British and 17,000 Australian). The Division fought in nearly all the major actions of the Burma Campaign (the longest British campaign of the war): the retreat to Imphal, then the return across the Irrawaddy, down the Chindwin towards Rangoon. Fraser was a rarity, a man of high education and erudition who preferred to remain in the ranks. He made Lance Corporal several times but was always stripped of even this lowly rank for mislaying army equipment like tea urns. His descriptions of life – and death – in his section is marked by Cumbrian humour. One word perhaps sums up the experience – confusion.

But he reveres his grumbling, profane comrades and rightly so. At Meiktila, where this incident took place, General Slim – commanding 14th Army – won his greatest strategic victory with men such as these. Slim fooled the Japanese commander, General Katamura, by a feint towards Mandalay but secretly moved his strike force of the 17th Division and 255th Tank Brigade across the Irrawaddy, and then sped the armour towards Meiktila, Katamura's communications and supply centre, which fell to the 17th on 3 March 1945. Around 2,000 Japanese were killed: 'the enemy garrison [had] to be killed almost to a man', recorded the Regimental history. Counter-attacks were defeated, and the road to Rangoon was open. Slim called it 'a magnificent feat of arms'. Fraser records with pride the words Slim spoke, at a reunion, to the men who defeated the 'invincible' jungle fighters of Japan:

'And then recall that exhilarating dash that carried you across the Irrawaddy... And there you met the Japanese army in the open, and you tore it apart.'

———◆•※◆•———

The first time I smelt Jap was in a deep dry river bed in the dry Belt. Somewhere near Meiktila. I can no more describe the smell that I could describe a colour, but it was heavy and pungent and compounded of stale cooked rice and sweat and human waste and... Jap. Quite unlike the clean acrid woodsmoke of an Indian village, the rather exotic and faintly decayed odour of the bashas [Footnote reads: native houses, large huts] in which the Burmese lived – and certainly nothing like the cooking smells of the Baluch hillmen and Gurkhas of our brigade, or our own British aromas. It was outside my experience of Oriental stenches – so how did I know it was Jap? Because we were deep inside enemy-held territory, and who else would have dug the three bunkers facing me in the high bank, as I stood, feeling extremely lonely, with a gallon tin of fruit balanced precariously on one shoulder and my rifle at the trail in my other hand?

I had never seen a live Japanese at this time. Dead ones beyond counting, corpses sprawled by the roadside, among the huts and bashas of abandoned villages, in slit-trenches and fox-holes, all the way, it seemed, from Imphal south to the Irrawaddy...

It was then that I smelt Jap, rank and nasty. The question was, did it come from Jap *in situ,* or had he just left his stink behind him? Was he lurking within, wondering who was outside throwing tins of fruit about, or was he long gone to the south'ard? If he was present, was he as scared as I was? No, he couldn't be.

The lunatic thought crossed my mind that the best way of finding out was to heave one of my two grenades into the nearest doorway and hit the deck, finger on trigger, waiting to see what emerged. And bloody clever I'd look when the section came running to the scene and found me bombing empty bunkers – I was a very young soldier then, you understand, and sensitive; I had no wish to be looked at askance by veterans of Oyster Box and Kennedy Park (Three months later I'd have heaved in both grenades *and* the tin of fruit, and anything else handy; better to be laughed at than dead – and I wouldn't have been laughed at.)

Anyway, hesitation was pointless. I couldn't leave the bunkers uninvestigated; I couldn't tell young Gale, our platoon commander, that I'd been too terrified; I couldn't leave them unreported. It was that simple; anyway, they *looked* empty.

I lowered the fruit tin carefully to the ground, pushed the safety catch forward on my rifle, made sure my kukri was loose in its sheath, touched the hilt of the dirk in my small pack for luck, and moved delicately towards the nearest entrance, hugging the nullah side, I waited, listening, not a sound, just that hellish smell. I edged closer, and saw where most of it was coming form.

Just inside the doorway, where an unwary foot would tread on it, was a *punji*, which is a sharpened stake set in the ground point upwards, that point usually being smeared with something nice and rotten, guaranteed to purify the victim's bloodstream. Some *punjis* are elaborate cantilevered affairs set to swing out of a darkened bunker and impale you; I had even heard of a crossbow variety, triggered by touching a taut cord. This was a conventional one, decorated with excrement by the look of it. But how old was it? (The things one does for a living; trying to determine the age of Jap crap, for eighteen rupees a week.)

Old or new, it didn't suggest anyone in residence. I took a huge breath and slipped inside, dropping to one knee – and there wasn't a thing to be seen but dim earth walls and a couple of Jap mess-tins, still half full of rice. I crouched there, wet with fear and relief, keeping my finger well away from the trigger. I'd willingly have stayed there permanently, recovering, but it would be dark soon, so, carefully avoiding the *punji* (modern war is a pretty Stone Age business, when you think about it), I stepped outside again.

The second bunker looked more promising. The earth on one side of the doorway had fallen in, and the dead fire in its entrance was days old. There seemed to be rubbish poled within, and the whole thing had an ancient, neglected look, so I passed it by and cautiously approached Number 3. Its doorway was so wide that I could see in to the back of the little cavern. I tossed a stone in, listening, and then nipped inside – empty, bare walls, and nothing but a crumpled Kooa [Footnote reads: 'A brand of Chinese cigarettes, presumably looted by the Japanese. We smoked captured supplies of them; they weren't bad.'] packed in one corner.

I came out of that bunker feeling pretty heroic, and was retrieving my fruit tin when it occurred to me that I *ought* to go into the second one, too, just to make a job of it. And I was moving towards it when I heard a faint, distant whistle from over the top of the bank – little Nixon, for certain, wondering where his wandering boy had got to. I ran up the nullah, and found a crack in its side only about twenty yards farther on. I scrambled, heaving the tin ahead of me, clawing my way over the lip to find Nick standing about ten yards off, and Sergeant Hutton hastening towards me with blood in his eye.

'Where the hell 'ave you been?' he blared. 'Wanderin' aboot like a bloody lost soul, what d'ye think yer on?'

'There were bunkers,' I began, but before I could get out another word Nick has shouted 'Doon, Jock!' and whipped up his rifle.

How I managed it I have no idea, but I know my feet left the ground and I hit the deck facing back the way I had come. Whatever Nick had seen was in that direction, and I wanted to get a good look at it – I suppose it was instinct and training combined, for I was scrabbling my rifle forward as I fell and turned together. And I can see him now, and he doesn't improve with age.

Five yards away, not far from where the bunkers must have been, a Jap was looking towards us. Half his naked torso was visible over the lip of the bank – how the hell he had climbed up there, God knows – and he was in the act of raising a large dark object, about a foot across, holding it above his head. I had a glimpse of a contorted yellow face before Nick's rifle cracked behind me, three quick shorts, and I'd got off one of my own when there was a deafening explosion and I was blinded by an enormous flash as the edge of the nullah dissolved in a cloud of dust and smoke. I rolled way, deafened, and then debris came raining down – earth and stones and bit of Jap, and when I could see again there was a great yawning bit out of the lip of the nullah, and the smoke and dust was clearing above it.

'Git doon!' snapped Hutton, as I started to rise. Suddenly, as if by magic, the section were there behind me, on the deck or kneeling, every rifle covering the lip, and Hutton walked forward and looked into the nullah.

'Fook me,' he said. 'Land mine. Fook me. Y'awreet, Jock?' I said I was.

'Wheer th'ell did'e coom frae? The booger!'

I told him, no doubt incoherently, about the bunkers: that I'd checked two and been on the way to the third when Nick had whistled. 'It looked empty,' I said.

'Well it bloody well wasn't, was it?' he shouted, and I realised he was not only angry, but shaken. 'Duke, giddoon theer an' 'ev a dekko! Rest o'you, git back in extended line – move!'

Nick was recharging his magazine. I realised that I was trembling. 'Land mine?' I said. 'Did you hit it?'

'Nivver,' said he. 'Ah hit him, though. Naw, he would have it wired. Suicide squad, waiting' to blaw oop anyone that cam' near 'im.' He grinned at me. 'Might ha' bin thee, Jock boy. Ye shoulda give us a shout man.'

I explained why I hadn't, and he shook his head. 'Nivver ga in on yer own, son. That's 'ow ye finish up dyin' Tojo's way. Ye wanna die yer own fookin' way.'

A Foxhole at night on a Pacific island

Norman Mailer

[from *The Naked and the Dead*, New York, 1948]

Norman Mailer was born in New Jersey in 1923 to a South African Jewish father and an adoring mother. The family moved to run-down Brooklyn, where Mailer learnt street-fighting; his pugilism stayed with him.

The fiercely driven young Mailer beat the competition at his state school and aged 17 enrolled at Harvard to study aeronautical engineering, although he really wanted to 'become a major writer' and write a great American novel. Harvard fuelled his sense of being an outsider. After graduating, Mailer joined the army in March 1944, landing on Luzon at the tail end of the Philippines campaign. He was briefly a rifleman with a reconnaissance platoon but a fellow soldier remembered that Private Mailer 'had more combat with his supervisors than he did with the enemy.'

Nevertheless this was the experience he needed for his epic novel. Shortly after his discharge he began writing *The Naked and the Dead*. The book was a huge critical and commercial success. Mailer was famous at 25. Only Mary McCarthy, who thought it reeked of 'ambition', and Gore Vidal who thought it a crib of *Dos Passos* and a 'fake', dissented. Truman Capote once dismissed Mailer as 'just a rewrite man'. Mailer's literary invention was the nonfictional novel; sex, politics, drugs and conspiracy were his themes, and protest and fisticuffs his habit – with wives, with Capote and Vidal (he didn't like homosexuals), even with bespectacled McGeorge Bundy, President Johnson's mild foreign policy advisor. But there is no denying the book's power and ability to shock. The intensity is evidence that Mailer did indeed, however briefly, taste the fear of battle at the sharp end.

———◆◆✕◆◆———

Roth felt terribly alone after Minetta left him. He gazed into the jungle, and got into the hole behind the machine-gun as silently as he could. Something like this was beyond him, he told himself; he didn't have the nerves for it. This took a younger man, a kid like Minetta or Polack, or one of the veterans.

He was sitting on two cartridge boxes, and the handles cut into his bony rump. He kept shifting his weight, and moving his feet about. The hole was very muddy from the evening storm, and everything about him felt damp. His clothes had been wet for hours, and he had had to spread his blanket on the wet ground. What a way to live! He would have a cold by the morning, he was certain. He'd be lucky if it wasn't pneumonia.

Everything was very quiet. The jungle was hushed, ominous, with a commanding silence that stilled his breath. He waited, and abruptly the utter vacuum was broken and he was conscious of all the sounds of the night woods – the crickets and frogs and lizards thrumming in the brush, the soughing of the trees. And then the sounds seemed to vanish, or rather his ear could hear only the silence; for several minutes there was a continual alternation between the sounds and the quiet, as if they were distinct and yet related like a drawing of some cubes which perpetually turn inside-out and back again. Roth began to think; there was some heavy thunder and lightning in the distance, but he did not worry about the threat of rain. For a long time he listened to the artillery, which sounded like a great muffled bell in the heavy moist night air. He shivered and crossed his arms. He was remembering what a training sergeant had said abut dirty fighting and how the Japs would sneak up behind a sentry in the jungle and knife the man. 'He'd never know at all,' the sergeant had said, 'except maybe for one little second when it was too late.'

Roth felt a gnawing, guttish fear, and turned around to look at the ground behind him. He shuddered, brooding over such a death. What an awful thing to happen. His nerves were taut. As he tried to see the jungle beyond the little clearing past the barbed wire, he had the kind of anxiety and panic a child has when the monster creeps up behind the hero in a horror movie. Something clattered in the brush, and Roth ducked in his hole, and then slowly peeked above it, trying to discern a man or at least some recognizable object in the deep shapes and shadows of the jungle. The noise stopped, and then after ten seconds began again. It was a scratching urgent sound, and Roth sat numbly in the hole, feeling nothing but the beat of his pulse throughout his entire body. His ears had become giant amplifiers and he was detecting a whole gamut of sounds, of sliding and scraping, of twigs cracking, of shrubs being rustled, which he had not noticed before. He bent over the machine-gun, and then realized that he didn't know whether Minetta had cocked it completely or left it half-loaded. It meant that he would have to pull back the bolt and release it in order to be certain, and he was terrified of the noise it would make. He took up his rifle, and tried to loose the safety lever quietly, but it clicked into place quite audibly. Roth flinched at the noise, and then gazed into the jungle, trying to locate the particular place from which the sounds were coming. But they seemed to originate everywhere, and he had no idea of their distance and what caused them. He heard something rustle, and he turned his rifle clumsily in that direction, and waited, the sweat breaking out on his back. For an instant he was tempted to shoot, blindly and furiously, but he remembered that that was very dangerous. 'Maybe they don't see me either,' he thought, but he did not believe it. The reason he did not fire was for fear of what Sergeant Brown would say. 'If you fire without seeing anything to aim at, you just give away the position of your hole, and they'll throw a grenade in on you,' Brown had told him. Roth trembled. He was beginning to feel resentful; for some time he had been convinced that the Japs were watching him. Why don't you come on? he wondered desperately. By now his nerves were so taut that he would have welcomed an attack.

He pressed his feet into the thick mud of the hole, and, still looking onto the jungle, picked some mud off his boots with one hand and began to knead it like a piece of clay. He was unconscious of doing this. His neck had begun to pain him from the tension with which he held himself. It seemed to him that the hole was terribly open and that there was not enough protection. He felt bitter that a man should have to stand guard in an open hole with only a machine-gun before him.

There was a frantic scuffling behind the first wall of jungle and Roth ground his jaws together to keep from uttering a sound. The noises were coming closer like men creeping up, moving a few feet and then halting, before approaching another few feet. He fumbled around the tripod of the machine-gun to find a grenade, and then held it in his hand wondering where to throw it. The grenade seemed extremely heavy, and he felt so weak that he doubted if he could hurl it more than ten yards. In training he had been told the effective range of a grenade was thirty-five yards, and he was afraid now that he would be killed by his own grenade. He replaced it beneath the machine-gun, and just sat there.

'The world of a nightmare':
Bergen-Belsen Concentration Camp

Richard Dimbleby, 19 April 1945
[BBC broadcast, Bergen-Belsen]

The BBC's first war correspondent, Richard Dimbleby (1913–65) covered the Spanish Civil War, including the bombardment of Barcelona, and subsequently the allied campaigns of World War Two. He was the first correspondent to fly with Bomber Command.

Initially the BBC refused to broadcast Richard Dimbleby's first, harrowing impressions. He had broken down five times when attempting to record it. The BBC wavered because they wanted confirmation from other sources and agencies that his story was true – there was a reluctance to believe stories of German 'frightfulness' because so many of the 'atrocities' reported in the previous war turned out to be fiction and rumour. But this one was horribly, visibly true. Dimbleby persisted, rang Broadcasting House and told the BBC's management snug in Portland Place that he would never broadcast again if they suppressed his report. Dimbleby was too important and influential a journalist to snub or ignore. The broadcast went out and appalled a nation.

Belsen was not an extermination camp, but that was little consolation to the 40,000 inmates who lay in hideous filth within the camp, starving, 10,000 of whom were to die after liberation. A further 10,000 were lying dead in heaps around the camp when the British arrived. Typhus had broken out. The Germans surrendered the camp to the advancing British Second Army because they wanted the typhus contained and they no longer had the means to do so. The SS camp commander Josef Kramer welcomed the British as though he were an honourable soldier doing his duty. He had 'served' in Auschwitz, Dachau, Mauthausen and had been commander of Birkenau, where he had supervised the murder of hundreds of thousands of Hungarian Jews in just a few months. Kramer was a brute, by turns sadistic to prisoners and servile to superiors. He made not the slightest attempt to improve conditions in the camp – he did not bother, for example, to divert fresh water from a nearby stream. When the horror of the camp was revealed, he was arrested, placed in a room below ground where fish had been stored, and his belt and shoelaces removed in case he killed himself. His nerve went. When the door opened he cringed, expecting to be hanged. The day after his arrest, the senior British officer, Lieutenant-Colonel Richard Taylor of VIII Corps, forced Kramer to lead a thorough inspection of the camp. Taylor was enraged by what he saw. He turned to the interpreter. 'Tell him that when he hangs I hope he hangs slowly.'

At his trial before a British Military Court, Kramer attempted a defence of 'superior orders'. It failed, as it did for others at Nuremberg. Kramer was hanged with 11 other Belsen officials on Friday 13 December 1945 at Hemeln jail. Mr Albert Pierrepoint, the British official executioner, was flown in to carry out the mass hanging.

I PASSED THROUGH the barrier and found myself in the world of a nightmare. The living lay with their heads against the corpses and around them moved the awful ghostly procession of emaciated, aimless people with nothing to do and no hope of life. This day at Belsen was the most horrible of my life...

I picked my way over corpse after corpse in the gloom, until I heard one voice raised above the gentle undulating moaning. I found a girl, she was a living skeleton, impossible to gauge her age for she had practically no hair left, and her face was only a yellow parchment sheet with two holes in it for eyes. She was stretching out her stick of an arm and gasping something, it was 'English, English, medicine, medicine', and she was trying to cry but she hadn't enough strength. And beyond her down the passage and in the hut there were the convulsive movements of dying people too weak to raise themselves from the floor.

In the shade of some trees lay a great collection of bodies. I walked about them trying to count, there were perhaps 150 of them flung down on each other, all naked, all so thin that their yellow skin glistened like stretched rubber on their bones. Some of the poor starved creatures whose bodies were there looked so utterly unreal and inhuman that I could have imagined that they had never lived at all. They were like polished skeletons, the skeletons that medical students like to play practical jokes with.

At one end of the pile a cluster of men and women were gathered round a fire; they were using rags and old shoes taken from the bodies to keep it alight, and they were heating soup over it. And close by was the enclosure where 500 children between the ages of five and twelve had been kept. They were not so hungry as the rest, for the women had sacrificed themselves to keep them alive. Babies were born at Belsen, some of them shrunken, wizened little things that could not live, because their mothers could not feed them.

One woman, distraught to the point of madness, flung herself at a British soldier who was on guard at the camp on the night that it was reached by the 11th Armoured Division; she begged him to give her some milk for the tiny baby she held in her arms. She laid the mite on the ground and threw herself at the sentry's feet and kissed his boots. And when, in his distress, he asked her to get up, she put the baby in his arms and ran off crying that she would find milk for it because there was no milk in her breast. And when the soldier opened the bundle of rags to look at the child, he found that it had been dead for days.

There was no privacy of any kind. Women stood naked at the side of the track, washing in cupfuls of water taken from British Army trucks. Others squatted while they searched themselves for lice, and examined each other's hair. Sufferers from dysentery leaned against the huts, straining helplessly, and all around and about them was this awful drifting tide of exhausted people, neither caring nor watching. Just a few held out their withered hands to us as we passed by, and blessed the doctor, whom they knew had become the camp commander in place of the brutal Kramer.

Okinawa, Motobu Peninsula, 1945

William Manchester
[from *Goodbye, Darkness*, Boston, 1980]

The island of Okinawa was a vital forward air base for the invasion of mainland Japan, which was only 340 miles away. In all, 1,213 allied warships took part (including the British Pacific Fleet) and half a million men, comparable to D-Day. The Japanese commander, Ushijima, planned to inflict maximum losses on the invader, but not to risk losing his front-line troops in a vain attempt to stop the enemy on the beaches; the landings were thus unopposed. He planned a drawn-out battle using dug-out and foxhole and cave. And snipers. 'It's going to be really tough… I see no way to get them out except by blasting them out yard by yard,' predicted Major General John R. Hodge (24th Corps). He was right. For the Americans it was a battle above all of flamethrowers and grenades, the excavated tunnels and caves being impervious to air and sea bombardment. One division assaulted a single position about eleven times, losing twice the number of men (including reinforcements) originally in their company. Marine leaders suffered. Of the 18 infantry battalion commanders who landed with the 1st and 6th Marine Divs. four were killed and nine badly wounded. Okinawa's rain and mud added to the misery.

The fighting descended into vicious stalemate, but a shore-to-shore amphibious assault (4 June) caught the Japanese by surprise, and led to their defeat. Some 180,000 US combat and 115,000 support troops were landed during the campaign (1 April–2 July 1945). The price paid for Okinawa was fearful. The final toll of American battle casualties was the highest in any campaign against the Japanese, the total killed numbering 12,520, which included the American commander. A total of 763 planes were destroyed and 36 ships were sunk, mostly by Kamikaze.

97,000 Japanese defenders were killed and perhaps 25,000 civilians. Ushijima took his sword and committed *harakiri*. Of ordinary Japanese soldiers the US Official History notes: 'When cornered or injured, many of them would hold grenades against their stomachs and blow themselves to pieces – a kind of poor man's *harakiri*.' At the end, rape was commonplace – many young Japanese who expected to die wanted an experience of sex, however brutal. One novelty was that 7,400 Japanese actually surrendered, hitherto a rarity. Many more Japanese may have tried to surrender. Front-line US troops were wary of a Japanese soldier with hands raised, as the clenched fist might contain a grenade. The US Official History records a staggering 7,800 planes (including 1,900 Kamikaze, four out of five sent up) lost by the Japanese. Their navy lost 16 major ships sunk, including the largest battleship in the world, *Yamato*, sailing on a one-way mission with limited fuel and no air-cover.

William Manchester (1922–2004) was a journalist and author, son of a veteran of the Great War. His most famous work was *Death of a President* (1967), a lengthy, detailed and reverential account of the assassination of President Kennedy, whom he had met and befriended when both were recuperating from wounds in World War II. He had earlier written an 'adoring' profile of JFK in 1962. Mrs Kennedy therefore commissioned him to write the authorised history. But they fell out when Jackie thought Manchester too keen on money and indiscreet concerning her loathing of Lyndon Johnson, her husband's Vice President and successor. Manchester was a bookish New England Brahmin. To join the Marines he built himself up on bananas. He was an unlikely hero, this history student from the University of Massachusetts, but he fought grittily, was wounded twice and given up for dead, winning the Navy Cross and Silver Star. *Goodbye, Darkness* captures the sticky horror of battle in the Pacific.

This extract begins just after a shot has been fired at Manchester's squad from a shack in the jungle, revealing the presence of a Japanese sniper.

———◆⬩✕⬩◆———

My choices were limited. Moving inland was inconvenient; the enemy was there, too. I was on the extreme left of our perimeter, and somehow I couldn't quite see myself turning my back on the shack and fleeing through the rest of the battalion screaming, like Chicken Little, 'A Jap's after me! A Jap's after me!' Of course, I could order one of my people to take out the sniper; but I played the role of the NCO in Kipling's poem who always looks after the black sheep, and if I ducked this one, they would never let me forget it. Also, I couldn't be certain that the order would be obeyed. I was a gangling, long-boned youth, wholly lacking in what the Marine Corps called 'command presence' – charisma – and I led nineteen highly insubordinate men. I couldn't even be sure that Barney would budge. It is war, not politics, that makes strange bedfellows. The fact that I outranked Barney was in itself odd. He was a great blond buffalo of a youth, with stubby hair, a scraggly moustache, and a powerful build. Before the war he had swum breaststroke for Brown, and had left me far behind in two intercollegiate meets. I valued his respect for me, which cowardice would have wiped out. So I asked him if he had any grenades. He didn't; nobody in the section did. The grenade shortage was chronic. That sterile exchange bought a little time, but every moment

282

lengthened my odds against the Nip sharpshooter. Finally, sweating with the greatest fear I had known till then, I took a deep breath, told Barney, 'Cover me,' and took off for the hut at Mach 2 speed in little bounds, zigzagging and dropping every dozen steps, remembering to roll as I dropped. I was nearly there, arrowing in, when I realized that I wasn't wearing my steel helmet. The only cover on my head was my cloth Raider cap. That was a violation of orders. I was out of uniform. I remember hoping, idiotically, that nobody would report me.

Utterly terrified, I jolted to a stop on the threshold of the shack. I could feel a twitching in my jaw, coming and going like a winky light signalling some disorder. Various valves were opening and closing in my stomach. My mouth was dry, my legs quaking, and my eyes out of focus. Then my vision cleared. I unlocked the safety of my Colt, kicked the door with my right foot, and leapt inside.

My horror returned. I was in an empty room. There was another door opposite the one I had unhinged, which meant another room, which meant the sniper was in there – and had been warned by the crash of the outer door. But I had committed myself. Flight was impossible now. So I smashed into the other room and saw him as a blur to my right. I wheeled that way, crouched, gripped the pistol butt in both hands, and fired.

Not only was he the first Japanese soldier I had ever shot at; he was the only one I had seen at close quarters. He was a robin-fat, moon-faced, roly-poly little man with his thick, stubby, trunk like legs sheathed in faded khaki puttees and the rest of him squeezed into a uniform that was much too tight. Unlike me, he was wearing a tin hat, dressed to kill. But I was quite safe from him. His Arisaka rifle was strapped on in a sniper's harness, and though he had heard me, and was trying to turn toward me, the harness sling had him trapped. He couldn't disentangle himself from it. His eyes were rolling in panic. Realizing that he couldn't extricate his arms and defend himself, he was backing toward a corner with a curious, crablike motion.

My first shot had missed him, embedding itself in the straw wall, but the second caught him dead-on in the femoral artery. His left thigh blossomed, swiftly turning to mush. A wave of blood gushed from the wound; then another boiled out, sheeting across his legs, pooling on the earthen floor. Mutely he looked down at it. He dipped a hand in it and listlessly smeared his cheek red. His shoulders gave a little spasmodic jerk, as though someone had whacked him on the back; then he emitted a tremendous, raspy fart, slumped down, and died. I kept firing, wasting government property.

Already I thought I detected the dark brown effluvium of the freshly slain, a sour, pervasive emanation which is different from anything else you have known. Yet seeing death at that range, like smelling it, requires no previous experience. You instantly recognize the spastic convulsion and the rattle, which in his case was not loud, but deprecating and conciliatory, like the manners of civilian Japanese. He continued to sink until he reached the earthen floor.

His eyes glazed over. Almost immediately a fly landed on his left eyeball. It was joined by another. I don't know how long I stood there staring. I knew from previous combat what lay ahead for the corpse. It would swell, then bloat, bursting out of the uniform. Then the face would turn from yellow to red, to purple, to green, to black. My father's account of the Argonne had omitted certain vital facts. A feeling of disgust and self-hatred clotted darkly in my throat, gagging me.

Jerking my head to shake off the stupor, I slipped a new, fully loaded magazine into the butt of my .45. Then

I began to tremble, and next to shake, all over. I sobbed, in a voice still grainy with fear: 'I'm sorry.' Then I threw up all over myself. I recognized the half-digested C-ration beans dribbling down my front, smelled the vomit above the cordite. At the same time I noticed another odour; I had urinated in my skivvies. I pondered fleetingly why our excretions become so loathsome the instant they leave the body. Then Barney burst in on me, his carbine at the ready, his face grey, as though he, not I, had just become a partner in the firm of death. He ran over to the Nip's body, grabbed its stacking swivel – its neck – and let go, satisfied that it was a cadaver. I marvelled at his courage; I couldn't have taken a step toward that corner. He approached me and then backed away, in revulsion, from my foul stench. He said: 'Slim, you stink.' I said nothing. I knew I had become a thing of tears and twitchings and dirtied pants. I remember wondering dumbly: *Is this what they mean by 'conspicuous gallantry'?*

Ambush in Korea

P. J. Kavanagh

[from *The Perfect Stranger*, London, 1966]

The Korean War (1950–53) began when Communist North Korea crossed the 38th Parallel and invaded South Korea on 25 June 1950. The 38th Parallel divided Korea more or less in half.

Russia had declared war on Japan on 9 August 1945, the day the US plutonium bomb 'Fat Man' was dropped on Nagasaki, and quickly surged through Manchuria with little Japanese resistance. It was clear the Soviets would soon overrun the Japanese armies in Korea. Threatened with Soviet domination of the Korean peninsula, the US, on 10 August, reversed their previous view of Korea as strategically unimportant and proposed that the 38th Parallel should be the limit of the Russian advance. Surprisingly, for there was nothing to stop them grabbing the whole country, the Soviets agreed.

Under the banner of the UN, the United States and their South Korean allies, with significant British and Commonwealth forces (and smaller contributions from many other nations) stemmed the tide of invasion and ultimately restored South Korean independence, despite Chinese intervention (1 November 1950). It was notable for MacArthur's last great battle, the Inchon landing, and for being the one conflict before the Cuban missile crisis (1962) where the US seriously considered using nuclear weapons. UN troops suffered

142,000 casualaties. The US lost 36,576 dead. British casualties were three times those she would lose in the Falklands in 1982.

The Korean War was not unlike Vietnam, both politically and militarily, although the outcome was wholly different. The 'domino theory' prompted the US to defend a less than truly democratic state in the face of Communist aggression, in case its fall triggered a collapse of nearby non-Communist regimes. US casualties were roughly similar to those they would later suffer in Vietnam. And the performance of their troops was also much the same, with elites like the Marines fighting well, others very poorly. It was fought in often atrocious conditions, in extremes of heat and cold, and atrocities were committed on both sides. One combat historian called it 'the century's nastiest little war.'

The poet, actor and writer P. J. Kavanagh was born in England in 1931. Lieutenant Patrick Kavanagh fought with the Ulsters in Korea and was wounded. His memoir *The Perfect Stranger* won the Richard Hillary Prize in 1966, and has been described as 'a brilliant self-portrait by a born writer' and 'a fine memorial to youth and love'. He had volunteered to fight in Korea, having found National Service duty in the depot at home dreary. The incident below occurred during the Battle of the Imjin River (22–25 April 1951) when three Chinese divisions launched a surprise attack. The Imjin River runs vertically up the centre of South and North Korea, and through the 38th parallel. Determined British battalions of the Gloucesters (the 'Glorious Gloucesters'), Ulsters and Northumberland Fusiliers, and one formidable Belgian battalion, broke this arm of the spring Communist offensive, fighting against odds with inadequate artillery and negligible air support, inflicting 10,000 casualties while suffering 1,000 themselves.

On the enemy side of the ford approaching a large open space, a gap in the cliffs, they slow down, halt. The senior [British] officer confers with the junior in the offhand shorthand that passes for communication between them.

'Looks a bit fishy.'

'Yes.'

'Better push on a bit, though.'

'Right.'

He screwed his eyes up so tight he saw stars, private semi-voluntary comment on fatuousness. Slowly they move off again, pressing into the tautening membrane of the night. Grind, whirr, whine go the tracks, the engines, a defined envelope of noise in the white moon-silence.

Penetration! The membrane snaps. Flames, rockets, yells, a thousand Cup Final rattles, Guy Fawkes, one of the carriers in front goes up, whoosh! Christ! Fifty of us have run into a bloody army! Weapons, helmets, wireless sets, all go flying in the mad scramble to get out, back into the womb of the dark away from the red bee-swarms of the tracers.

'Come back,' he shouted. Not quite sure why, except that he didn't particularly fancy being left sitting there alone. Anyway it annoyed his schoolboy sense of order to see them running off into nowhere. Run home by all means, I'll come with you except the river's in the way, but not into the meaningless no-direction dark.

'Stop!'

Some do uncertainly. A few run on, never to be seen again, ever. He dismounts gingerly from his lonely chariot.

'Lie down, face your front and return the fire.'

Good notion that, keep us occupied for a bit. Irregular spiritless bangs begin around him.

'Get that Bren gun going.'

'There's something wrong with it, Sorr.'

'Mend it.'

Splendid stuff this. And will the First Cavalry, just in the nick, pennants a-flutter come riding riding... No. He wished he wasn't there.

'I can find nothing wrong with this Bren, Sorr, known to God or to man.'

Oh, the Irish, the irresistible cadence, unresisted. Probably too scared to put the thing together properly...

Stage-lit by the moon and the blazing carrier, the other carrier drivers, crouched invisible and blind behind their raised visors of armour, begin to yaw and swerve through the bullets on their way back home. Thinking, presumably, they can be of little use here. One goes over a prone soldier's pelvis.

His scream is a white wall of cold fear; the bullets falter and fall against it.

Morphia. Have little needled ampoules in trousers. Officers only for the control of. Might give Other Ranks other dreams. Stick it in his arm. Can't. 'You do it, Medical Orderly.' That delay an eternity of agony for the dying man. You coward. Couldn't stick a needle in a man's arm. No, couldn't. All right, coward. What to do with him? He can't be carried, must be left, alive, dying of pain.

He only joined us yesterday.

'They've got behind us, sir.'

Irregular shots from the dark back of them. Have an idea it's other officer comrade and remaining rest. Better go look. No point in crawling, take too long, better walk. Up! There! Look they love me they're emitting death rays, love rays. My public! The stinging lines of tracers, slow at first, accelerating and swish! past him... at least I'm not alone, there seem to be plenty of us death wishers about tonight. Smiling self-consciously he crossed the bullet-sighing dark.

'Take care of yourself, sir.'

Who was that? Hoarse concern. Love. Well, any leader was better than none; mutual need. Curious that warmed so much. Wonder who it was? Figures loom out of the black. Livingstone I presume?... I'm a dead duck if not...

'Brian?'

'Ah!'

Sheepish at having retreated further than his junior, Brian began to give terse textbook orders, obviously at sea, as well he might be.

'Get your men on their feet. We'll retire to a defensive position in that clump of trees over there.'

'But Brian, don't you think that...'

'Come on. Hurry!'

'Right.'

Defensive position my Aunt Fanny! Where does he think he is, Salisbury Plain? What's left of fifty of us taking on the whole bloody Chinese army. What we should be doing is getting out of here fast. On either side men drop as they move across the open field to the trees. There all is confusion. It seems for a moment as if there are enemy soldiers there too, only the curses sound reassuring.

'Sir, Leary's got hurt on the way across. Can I go and get him. Sir?'

'No.'

'But he's my mukker, Sir!'

Blank consternation. Greater love than this... Another face, contorted, is thrust into his –

'Sir, there's one of 'em moving about just down there. Shall I kill him, sir? shall I kill him? I'll throw this at him.' Brandishing a grenade, hopping up and down. You'd have his head in your knapsack too, wouldn't you, you blood-crazy little bastard. Takes people different ways apparently.

'Shall I kill-kill-kill um, Sir?'

'No.'

From the shadows in front of them the figure got up, seemed to fall down. If one of theirs surely wounded. Just possibly one of ours, Leary too hurt to cry out.

'No.' Here's Brian.

'I'll stay here with Corporal, three others and non-walking wounded. You take the rest back across the river. We'll give you covering fire and join you when you're across.'

Of all the fatuous plans! He's condemning himself and the others to death. Chances are we won't get through anyway and if he stays he certainly won't. Try to explain. All together. Can't leave you.

'That's an order.'

'Right.'

Move into chaste silver field, brilliant after the infested dark of the trees, holding out arms at an angle as though to draw the frightened men with him.

'Arrow head formation. Follow me.'

Close on me, Scouts! No one moves. Can hardly blame them. Neither would I. Better the evils that we know. They want to see what is going to happen to me. What is going to happen to me? The river looks a long way away.

Brrp.

Find face deep in earth. Instinctive fall. Raise head a little. Brrp. It's that lurching fellow the dancing maniac wanted to do in. Suicide pilot out to get the ociffer. Gingerly raise Sten, can just get him in sights – only about twenty yards away. Suddenly the empty field surrounding our privacy seems enormous. We are alone, face to face, belly-flat. Can't pull trigger. Can't. Don't like the sound of the silence that would follow. What a soldier! Brrp. That's it. It's a burp gun, fast firing from a large magazine makes a noise like a belch. He's firing in little bursts, taking his time, determined to get me, knows he's had it anyway. Much good it will do him.

Farewell Speech

General Douglas MacArthur [West Point, 12 May 1962]

General Douglas MacArthur (1880–1964) retired from the army in 1937 after a distinguished if controversial career. He was recalled by President Roosevelt to active duty, with the rank of Major General, when negotiations with the Japanese government broke down in June 1941. Already an advisor to the Philippine military (on a lavish salary), he was ordered to mobilize the Philippine Army (which was inducted into the US Army), and was sent one hundred B17 Flying Fortress bombers to bolster his force of 227 assorted fighter planes. But he did not believe the Japanese would attack, and did little, even after he heard of the assault on Pearl Harbor (7 December 1941). Half his air force was destroyed on the ground. US and Philippine troops were beaten and on 11 March 1942 MacArthur fled by torpedo boat to Australia, having been ordered to leave by the President. 'I came through and I shall return,' he pledged.

MacArthur was, despite this reverse, appointed Supreme Commander of the Southwest Pacific Area. He developed island-hopping tactics, amphibious landings on vulnerable islands, bypassing Japanese troop concentrations on fortified ones. This was the theory. In practice lesser numbers of defenders, well camouflaged and fanatical, were a formidable foe. But his strategy worked and he returned to the Philippines in October 1944, strutting ashore with his signature dark glasses and corncob pipe, twice, for the cameras.

292

He had fulfilled his pledge. After the war he administered occupied Japan, with liberal understanding of their concerns and customs. Appointed to command UN forces in the Korean War (1950–53), his early success was followed by culpable disregard for likely Chinese intervention, and then wilful insubordination when he tried to undermine his President's negotiations for a compromise peace. He was sacked. On 19 April 1951 he gave a farewell address to Congress that reeked of both his virtues and vices – by turns self-righteous, dishonest, melodramatic and mesmerising. He ended:

'I am closing my 52 years of military service. When I joined the Army, even before the turn of the century, it was the fulfilment of all of my boyish hopes and dreams. The world has turned over many times since I took the oath at West Point, and the hopes and dreams have all since vanished, but I still remember the refrain of one of the most popular barracks ballads of that day which proclaimed most proudly that old soldiers never die; they just fade away. And like the old soldier of that ballad, I now close my military career and just fade away, an old soldier who tried to do his duty as God gave him the light to see that duty. Good Bye.'

But it was not farewell. On 12 May 1962, the 82 year-old MacArthur accepted the Thayer Award from his alma mater, West Point Military Academy, where he had graduated in 1903, first out of a class of 93. The award was created in 1958 in memory of Colonel Sylvanus Thayer, the Academy's fifth superintendent, known as the 'Father of the Military Academy', to honour 'an outstanding citizen whose service and accomplishments in the national interest exemplify the Military Academy motto, Duty, Honor, Country.' Recipients have included distinguished soldiers like Eisenhower and Colin Powell, as well as Neil Armstrong, Reagan and Kissinger – and Bob Hope and Billy Graham. MacArthur rose to the occasion in his final farewell.

'Duty,' 'Honour,' 'Country' – those three hallowed words reverently dictate what you want to be, what you can be, what you will be. They are your rallying point to build courage when courage seems to fail, to regain faith when there seems to be little cause for faith, to create hope when hope becomes forlorn... They teach you in this way to be an officer and a gentleman.

And what sort of soldiers are those you are to lead? Are they reliable? Are they brave? Are they capable of victory?

Their story is known to all of you. It is the story of the American man at arms. My estimate of him was formed on the battlefields many, many years ago, and has never changed. I regarded him then, as I regard him now, as one of the world's noblest figures; not only as one of the finest military characters, but also as one of the most stainless...

In twenty campaigns, on a hundred battlefields, around a thousand campfires, I have witnessed that enduring fortitude... that invincible determination which have carved his statue in the hearts of his people.

... in memory's eye I see those staggering columns of the First World War, bending under soggy packs on many a weary march, from dripping dusk to drizzling dawn, slogging ankle deep through mire of shell-pocked roads; to form grimly for the attack, blue-lipped, covered with sludge and mud, chilled by the wind and rain, driving home to their objective, and for many, to the judgment seat of God.

I do not know the dignity of their birth, but I do know the glory of their death. They died unquestioning, uncomplaining, with faith in their hearts, and on their lips the hope that we would go on to victory. Always for them:

Duty, Honour, Country. Always their blood, and sweat, and tears, as they saw the way and the light.

And twenty years after, on the other side of the globe, against the filth of dirty foxholes, the stench of ghostly trenches, the slime of dripping dugouts, those boiling suns of the relentless heat, those torrential rains of devastating storms, the loneliness and utter desolation of jungle trails, the bitterness of long separation of those they loved and cherished, the deadly pestilence of tropic disease, the horror of stricken areas of war.

Their resolute and determined defence, their swift and sure attack, their indomitable purpose, their complete and decisive victory – always victory, always through the bloody haze of their last reverberating shot, the vision of gaunt, ghostly men, reverently following your password of Duty, Honour, Country.

... your mission remains fixed, determined, inviolable. It is to win our wars... Yours is the profession of arms, the will to win, the sure knowledge that in war there is no substitute for victory, that if you lose, the Nation will be destroyed, that the very obsession of your public service must be Duty, Honour, Country...

The long grey line has never failed us. Were you to do so, a million ghosts in olive drab, in brown khaki, in blue and grey, would rise from their white crosses, thundering those magic words: Duty, Honour, Country.

This does not mean that you are warmongers. On the contrary, the soldier above all other people prays for peace, for he must suffer and bear the deepest wounds and scars of war. But always in our ears ring the ominous words of Plato, that wisest of all philosophers: 'Only the dead have seen the end of war.'

The shadows are lengthening for me. The twilight is here. My days of old have vanished – tone and tints. They have gone glimmering through the dreams of things that were. Their memory is one of wondrous beauty, watered by tears and coaxed and caressed by the smiles of yesterday. I listen then, but with thirsty ear, for the witching melody of faint bugles blowing reveille, of far drums beating the long roll.

In my dreams I hear again the crash of guns, the rattle of musketry, the strange, mournful mutter of the battlefield. But in the evening of my memory I come back to West Point. Always there echoes and re-echoes: Duty, Honour, Country.

Today marks my final roll call with you. But I want you to know that when I cross the river, my last conscious thoughts will be of the Corps, and the Corps, and the Corps. I bid you farewell.

Shot, again

Tim O'Brien [from *The Things They Carried*, London, 1990]

The Vietnam War, fought between the Communist North and the non-Communist South and their respective allies, began for the US in 1959 when American combat troops were involved and ceased with their withdrawal in 1973, but it ended properly with the capitulation of South Vietnam to Northern troops on 30 April 1975. Several US administrations became embroiled, from Eisenhower through Johnson to Nixon, the latter extricating the US by bombing the North to the conference table and accepting a face-saving peace formula. Kennedy defined their motives: 'We have a problem in making our power credible [to the Russians] and Vietnam looks like the place.'

Tim O'Brien (b. 1947) was drafted into the US Army after graduating from Macalester College in Minnesota and went to Vietnam as an extremely reluctant soldier at the end of 1968, after the Viet Cong (South Vietnamese Communist guerrillas) and Northern regulars launched their Tet Offensive (Tet is the lunar new year). Although it burnt itself out, and the Viet Cong, or VC, were destroyed, it proved that official reports of an imminent US victory were exaggerated, with devastating repercussions on domestic morale. As the enemy was now the North Vietnamese regular army there was no clear strategy for victory, as invading North Vietnam might provoke Chinese intervention. So the war staggered on, eventually claiming over 50,000 American lives.

I was shot twice. The first time, out by Tri Binh, it knocked me against the pagoda wall, and I bounced and spun around and ended up on Rat Kiley's lap. A lucky thing, because Rat was the medic. He tied on a compress and told me to ease back, then he ran off toward the fighting. For a long time I lay there all alone, listening to the battle, thinking *I've been shot, I've been shot* – all those Gene Autry movies I'd seen as a kid. In fact, I almost smiled, except then I started to think I might die. It was the fear, mostly, but I felt wobbly, and then I had a sinking sensation, ears all plugged up, as if I'd gone deep under water. Thank God for Rat Kiley. Every so often, maybe four times altogether, he trotted back to check me out. Which took courage. It was a wild fight, guys running and laying down fire and regrouping and running again, lots of noise, but Rat Kiley took the risks. 'Easy does it,' he told me, 'just a side wound, no problem unless you're pregnant.' He ripped off the compress, applied a fresh one, and told me to clamp it in place with my fingers. 'Press hard,' he said. 'Don't worry about the baby.' Then he took off. It was almost dark when the fighting ended and the chopper came to take me and two dead guys away. 'Happy trails,' Rat said. He helped me into the helicopter and stood there for a moment. Then he did an odd thing. He leaned in and put his head against my shoulder and almost hugged me. Coming from Rat Kiley, that was something new.

On the ride into Chu Lai, I kept waiting for the pain to hit, but in fact I didn't feel much. A throb, that's all. Even in the hospital it wasn't bad.

When I got back to Alpha Company twenty-six days later, in mid-December, Rat Kiley had been wounded and shipped off to Japan, and a new medic named Bobby Jorgenson had replaced him. Jorgenson was no Rat Kiley. He was green and incompetent and scared. So when I got shot the second time, in the butt, along the Song Tra Bong, it took the son of a bitch almost ten minutes to work up the nerve to crawl over to me. By then I was gone with the pain. Later I found out I'd almost died of shock. Bobby Jorgenson didn't know about shock, or if he did, the fear made him forget. To make it worse, he bungled the patch job, and a couple of weeks later my ass started to rot away. You could actually peel off chunks of skin with your fingernail.

It was borderline gangrene. I spent a month flat on my stomach; I couldn't walk or sit; I couldn't sleep. I kept seeing Bobby Jorgenson's scared-white face. Those buggy eyes and the way his lips twitched and that silly excuse he had for a moustache. After the rot cleared up, once I could think straight, I devoted a lot of time to figuring ways to get back at him.

Getting shot should be an experience from which you can draw some small pride. I don't mean the macho stuff. All I mean is that you should be able to *talk* about it: the stiff thump of the bullet, like a fist, the way it knocks the air out of you and makes you cough, how the sound of the gunshot arrives about ten years later, and the dizzy feeling, the smell of yourself, the things you think about and say and do right afterward, the way your eyes focus on a tiny white pebble or a blade of grass and how you start thinking, Oh man, that's the last thing I'll ever see, *that* pebble, *that* blade of grass, which makes you want to cry.

Pride isn't the right word. I don't know the right word. All I know is, you shouldn't feel embarrassed. Humiliation shouldn't be part of it.

Diaper rash, the nurses called it. An in-joke, I suppose. But it made me hate Bobby Jorgenson the way some guys hated the VC, gut hate, the kind of hate that stays with you even in your dreams.

'We go to liberate and not to conquer'

Lieutenant-Colonel Tim Collins, battlefield speech,
Kuwaiti desert, 19 March 2003

This anthology began with Elizabeth I's great Armada speech. It is fitting that although we have otherwise included no pieces after Vietnam – literary value needs to pass a certain test of time – we end the chronological anthology with Tim Collins' speech in the Kuwaiti desert in 2003. Collins' exhortation is of a piece with the Tilbury speech – both 'stiffen the sinews, summon up the blood'. But there is a difference. Unlike Elizabeth, Collins does not resort to patriotism. Four centuries ago Elizabeth could appeal to a new sense of nationhood. Queen and Country, those distant abstractions, were not what Collins' men were fighting for and he knew it. They fought as a 'band of brothers', their loyalty was to each other, and what Collins needed to do was stir up 'hard-favoured rage', and the courage to kill their enemy. And being an honourable man he cautioned against needless cruelty. Respect for the foe was not a hallmark of Elizabeth.

Lieutenant-Colonel Collins (b. 1960), the 42-year-old Belfast-born commander of the 1st Battalion, Royal Irish Regiment, gave the address to his troops just hours before they went into battle. Collins later recalled: 'Our soldiers require their leaders to explain to them why they are going into conflict, and that's simply what I

301

was doing.' Collins' speech, delivered without a note, was made to around 800 men of his battlegroup (part of the 16 Air Assault Brigade) in the Kuwaiti desert about 20 miles from the Iraqi border. Collins was known as 'Nails', as in 'hard as'.

In a letter to Collins, Prince Charles called the speech 'stirring, civilised and humane'. President George W. Bush was said to have a copy pinned up on the wall of the Oval Office. Collins was awarded the OBE in October 2003. He left the army in January 2004, because he felt it had become 'a glorified Home Guard' due to under-funding and bureaucracy. 'If training is reduced, then we will… leave our young men and women open and liable to death and destruction on the battlefield…'

———◆◆✕◆●———

We go to liberate and not to conquer. We will not fly our flags in their country. We are entering Iraq to free a people, and the only flag that will be flown in that ancient land is their own. Don't treat them as refugees, for they are in their own country.

The enemy should be in no doubt that we are his Nemesis and that we are bringing about his rightful destruction. There are many regional commanders who have stains on their souls and they are stoking the fires of Hell for Saddam. As they die they will know their deeds have brought them to this place. Show them no pity. But those who do not wish to go on that journey, we will not send. As for the others, I expect you to rock their world.

I know men who have taken life needlessly in other conflicts. They live with the mark of Cain upon them. If someone surrenders to you, then remember they have that right in international law, and ensure that one day they go home to their family. The ones who wish to fight, well, we aim to please. If there are casualties of war, then remember, when they woke up and got dressed in the morning they did not plan to die this day. Allow them dignity in death. Bury them properly, and mark their graves.

You will be shunned unless your conduct is of the highest, for your deeds will follow you down history. Iraq is steeped in history. It is the site of the Garden of Eden, of the Great Flood, and the birth of Abraham. Tread lightly there. You will have to go a long way to find a more decent, generous and upright people than the Iraqis. You will be embarrassed by their hospitality, even though they have nothing...

There may be people among us who will not see the end of this campaign. We will put them in their sleeping bags and send them back. There will be no time for sorrow. Let's leave Iraq a better place for us having been there. Our business now, is north.

Afterword

The Next War

Osbert Sitwell (1892–1969)

The long war had ended.
Its miseries had grown faded.
Deaf men became difficult to talk to,
Heroes became bores.
Those alchemists
Who had converted blood into gold
Had grown elderly.
But they held a meeting,
Saying,
'We think perhaps we ought
To put up tombs
Or erect altars
To those brave lads
Who were so willingly burnt,
Or blinded,
Or maimed.
Who lost all likeness to a living thing,
Or were blown to bleeding patches of flesh
For our sakes.
It would look well.
Or we might even educate the children.'
But the richest of these wizards
Coughed gently;
And he said:
'I have always been to the front

– In private enterprise –,
I yield in public spirit
To no man.
I think yours is a very good idea
– A capital idea –
And not too costly…
But it seems to me
That the cause for which we fought
Is again endangered.
What more fitting memorial for the fallen
Than that their children
Should fall for the same cause?'
Rushing eagerly into the street,
The kindly old gentlemen cried
To the young:
'Will you sacrifice
Through your lethargy
What your fathers died to gain?
The world must be made safe for the young!'

And the children
Went…

Acknowledgements

Major General Patrick Cordingley, DSO, FRGS, commanded 7th Armoured Brigade during the first Gulf War. He is joint author (with Sue Limb) of *Captain Oates: Soldier & Explorer* (London, 1984) and author of *In the Eye of the Storm* (London, 1996), his personal history of Operation Desert Storm, in which he fought with such distinction. We are grateful for the Foreword he so kindly contributed.

We are also grateful to Maria Carnegie, David Cowell, The Thurrock Local History Society and Dr. Sanders Marble for help and advice; and to Dodie Buchanan, who was responsible for obtaining permission for copyright material to be reprinted in this anthology, and who has offered invaluable support. We have been encouraged throughout by our publishers, particularly Jennifer Barclay. We would also like to thank the copyright holders listed below for their kind permission to reprint the poems and prose herein. Despite our best endeavours we could not trace the copyright position of certain poems and extracts we have reproduced; we apologise for any unwitting infringement. If brought to our attention, the copyright position will be acknowledged in future editions.

We are indebted to the following for permission to reproduce copyright material, whether extracts from prose works or poems, in their possession (for details of original publication see individual titles in text): the extract from *My Bit* by George Ashurst has been reproduced by kind permission of the heirs and estate of George Ashurst; we are indebted to Michael Schmidt and Carcanet Press for *Goodbye To All That* (Jonathan Cape, 1929) by Robert Graves; Michael Leventhal and Greenhill Books (with especial thanks to the Rogerson family) for *Twelve Days* by Sidney Rogerson (1937 edition), reprinted 2006 by Greenhill Books as *Twelve Days on the Somme: A*

ACKNOWLEDGEMENTS

Memoir of the Trenches, 1916 by Sidney Rogerson, with an introduction by Malcolm Brown (ISBN: 1-85367-680-2 / 978-1-85367-
680-2); Barbara Levy Literary Agency and Viking Penguin for 'Attack'
and 'Counter-Attack' (© Siegfried Sassoon) by Siegfried Sassoon,
reprinted with the kind permission of the late George Sassoon;
'Pill Box' by Edmund Blunden is reproduced by permission of PFD
(www.pfd.co.uk) on behalf of the Estate of Mrs Claire Blunden; *The
Perfect Stranger* by P. J. Kavanagh is reprinted by permission of PFD
(www.pfd.co.uk) on behalf of: P. J. Kavanagh ©: as printed in the
original volume; we are indebted to A.M. Heath & Co. for *Homage
to Catalonia* by George Orwell; the family of the late Noel Monks
for *Eyewitness* by Noel Monks; *The Spectator* magazine for *Return
to Namsos: A Memoir of the Norwegian Campaign* by Peter Fleming;
Random House and John Hawkins and Associates for *The Rise and
Fall of the Third Reich* by William L. Shirer; The Orion Publishing
Group and Little, Brown & Co. for *The Diaries of Evelyn Waugh*;
Faber and Faber Ltd. and Faber Inc. for *'Vergissmeinnicht:* Elegy for
an 88 Gunner' and *Alamein to Zem Zem* by Keith Douglas; *The
Spectator* magazine for *One Man's D-Day* by Iain Macleod; Abner
Stein for *Goodbye Darkness* by William Manchester; HarperCollins
for *Quartered Safe Out Here* by George Macdonald Fraser; Lady
Jack Baer for *10 May, Germany invades the Lowlands*, an article
by Mollie Panter Downes which first appeared in the *New Yorker*
in May 1940, and has been extracted from *London War Notes
1939–1945* by Mollie Panter Downes, published by Longman,
1972; Lieutenant-Colonel Tim Collins for his battlefield speech
in the Kuwaiti desert, 2003; Andre Deutsch Ltd. for *The Naked
and the Dead* by Norman Mailer (extracted from the London ed.,
1949); Library of Congress for the speech by General MacArthur;
Curtis Brown representing the Estate of Winston S. Churchill
for permission to reprint the extract from *My Early Life* and for
permission to reprint edited extracts from the two wartime
parliamentary speeches contained herein.

Glossary of Abbreviations

ADC	Aide-de-Camp
C-in-C	Commander-in-Chief
CO	Commanding officer
CWGC	Commonwealth War Graves Commission
DSO	Distinguished Service Order
MC	Military Cross
NCO	Non-commissioned officer
VC	Victoria Cross

OTHER TITLES FROM SUMMERSDALE

The AGE of SCURVY

How a Surgeon, a Mariner and a
Gentleman helped Britain win the
Battle of Trafalgar

STEPHEN R. BOWN

The Age of Scurvy
How a Surgeon, a Mariner and a Gentleman helped Britain win the Battle of Trafalgar

Stephen R. Bown

£7.99 Paperback

ISBN: 1 84024 402 X
ISBN 13: 978 1 84024 402 X

During the Age of Sail, scurvy was responsible for more deaths at sea than war, piracy, storms and shipwreck combined. For centuries the scourge of the seas was treated with ineffective remedies like oil of vitriol, bloodletting, seawater and wort of malt, and countless mariners suffered an agonising death. It wasn't until the nineteenth century that citrus fruits became a mandatory part of the British navy's diet, turning its fortunes around. This is the compelling account of how three men solved the greatest mystery of the seafaring age, and so played a key role in Britain's successful blockade of the French and defeat of Napoleon. Although the cure for scurvy ranks among the greatest of human accomplishments, its impact on history has been largely ignored. Set during the era of wooden ships and press gangs, Captain Cook's voyages and the Battle of Trafalgar, *The Age of Scurvy* is both an important book and a classic adventure story.

- 'It sheds light on the life and times of the seamen of yore and is an absorbing read'

  **Polly Larner,
  The National Maritime Museun**

- 'The author tells this remarkable story with the skill of a master mariner'

  Globe and Mail

- 'Bown is a meticulous researcher and a gripping storyteller'
  Canadian Geographic

SPECTATOR
IN HELL

*A British soldier's
story of imprisonment
in Auschwitz*

Colin Rushton

SUMMERSDALE

Spectator in Hell

A British soldier's story of imprisonment in Auschwitz

Colin Rushton

£7.99 Paperback

ISBN: 1 84024 143 8
ISBN 13: 978 1 84024 143 8

North Africa, 1942. Arthur Dodd is taken prisoner by the German Army and transported to Oswiecim in Polish Upper Silesia. At the time he found no resonance in the German name for the place. They called it Auschwitz: a name now synonymous with man's darkest hour.

Auschwitz-Birkenau, the most infamous German death camp of the Second World War, functioned for the incarceration and extermination of those that the third Reich deemed 'undesirables': Jews, homosexuals, Communists. What is less known is that it was the fate of hundreds of British POWs to find it their prison, and to behold the atrocities meted out by Hitler's SS. This is the true story of one of those witnesses. Forced to do hard labour, starved and savagely beaten, Arthur though his life would end in Auschwitz. Determined to go down fighting, he sabotaged Nazi industrial work, did all he could to help alleviate the suffering of the Jewish prisoners, and aided a partisan group planning a mass break-out. A prisoner, an escapee, a survivor; Arthur Dodd – a Spectator in Hell.

- 'A human witness to inhumanity: Arthur Dodd's account is another important piece of evidence'
  ### *Legion, The Royal British Legion Magazine*

- 'A unique tale . . . history will be grateful that Arthur Dodd's story was told'
  ### *Scottish Legion News*

- 'The book is a harrowing addition to public knowledge of the Holocaust'
  ### *Soldier Magazine*

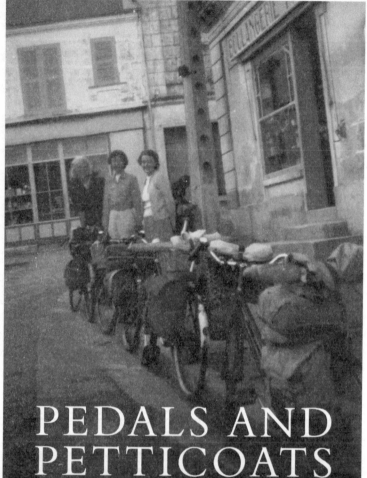

PEDALS AND PETTICOATS

On the road in post-war Europe

Mary Elsy

Pedals and Petticoats
On the road in post-war Europe

Mary Elsy

£7.99 Paperback

ISBN: 1 84024 439 9
ISBN 13: 978 1 84024 439 9

Five years after D-Day, Britain was still recovering from the aftermath of war when four British girls – Mary Elsy, her sister Barbara and their friends Agnes and Esme – hatched a daring plan to give up their jobs and cycle through Europe. They would camp together in one tent on a shoestring budget, and ride 3,000 miles through battle-scarred Germany, France, Austria, Italy, Spain, Belgium and Luxembourg. Although the Second World War was now firmly in the past, the ruined cities they found were a sobering reminder. At a time when few were travelling for recreation, Mary Elsy's party created a stir everywhere they went. With its fascinating cast of characters, *Pedals and Petticoats* is a charming eye-witness account of life in war-devastated Europe.

Mary Elsy is a travel writer and journalist, and the author of six books. She lives in London.

'I would find myself engrossed in his book, he was one
of my greatest inspirations and motivations to
get involved in the world of solo sailing'
Ellen McArthur

THE LONELY SEA
AND THE SKY

SIR FRANCIS CHICHESTER

The Lonely Sea and the Sky

Sir Francis Chichester

£9.99 Paperback

ISBN: 1 84024 207 8
ISBN 13: 978 1 84024 207 8

At the age of eighteen and with a taste for adventure, Francis Chichester emigrated to New Zealand with only ten pounds in his pocket. With the impetuousness of youth, he tried his hand at myriad jobs, including boxer, shepherd, lumberjack, gold prospector and door-to-door salesman. It was then that his real story began. Aviation became the first means for Chichester to satisfy his passion for travel, and in 1929 he embarked on his most famous flight: a solo enterprise in the *Gypsy Moth* from England to Australia. Shortly afterward, he would survive a near-death catastrophe in an attempt to fly solo around the world. A great sailor as well as aviator, further journeys came hot on the heels of Chichester's achievements in the air, including winning a trans-Atlantic race in the yacht *Gipsy Moth III*, despite having been diagnosed with cancer only two years previously. Chichester said he saw the race as part of his recovery plan. In 1967 he was knighted for his record-breaking conquests.

- 'Thank goodness this splendid white-knuckle ride is back in print'

    Cruising Magazine

- 'Cannot fail to inspire the reader'

    This England

www.summersdale.com